BEN 10™ CLASSICS

1 BEN HERE BEFORE

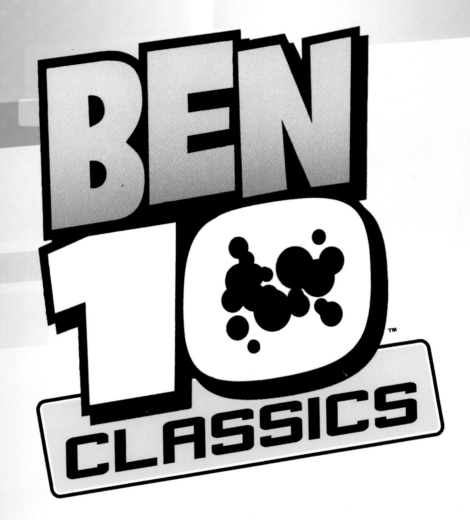

BEN 10 CLASSICS

VOLUME 1: BEN HERE BEFORE

Cover by Ethen Beavers

Collection Edits by Justin Eisinger and Alonzo Simon

Collection Design by Chris Mowry

Ben 10 created by Man of Action

Special Thanks to Laurie Halal-Ono and Marisa Marionakis of Cartoon Network.

IDW founded by Ted Adams, Alex Garner, Kris Oprisko, and Robbie Robbins

ISBN: 978-1-61377-734-3

16 15 14 13   1 2 3 4

Ted Adams, CEO & Publisher
Greg Goldstein, President & COO
Robbie Robbins, EVP/Sr. Graphic Artist
Chris Ryall, Chief Creative Officer/Editor-in-Chief
Matthew Ruzicka, CPA, Chief Financial Officer
Alan Payne, VP of Sales
Dirk Wood, VP of Marketing
Lorelei Bunjes, VP of Digital Services

Become our fan on Facebook **facebook.com/idwpublishing**
Follow us on Twitter **@idwpublishing**
Check us out on YouTube **youtube.com/idwpublishing**
www.IDWPUBLISHING.com

Originally published by DC Comics as CARTOON NETWORK ACTION PACK issues #2, 4, 6, 7, 9, and 11–18.

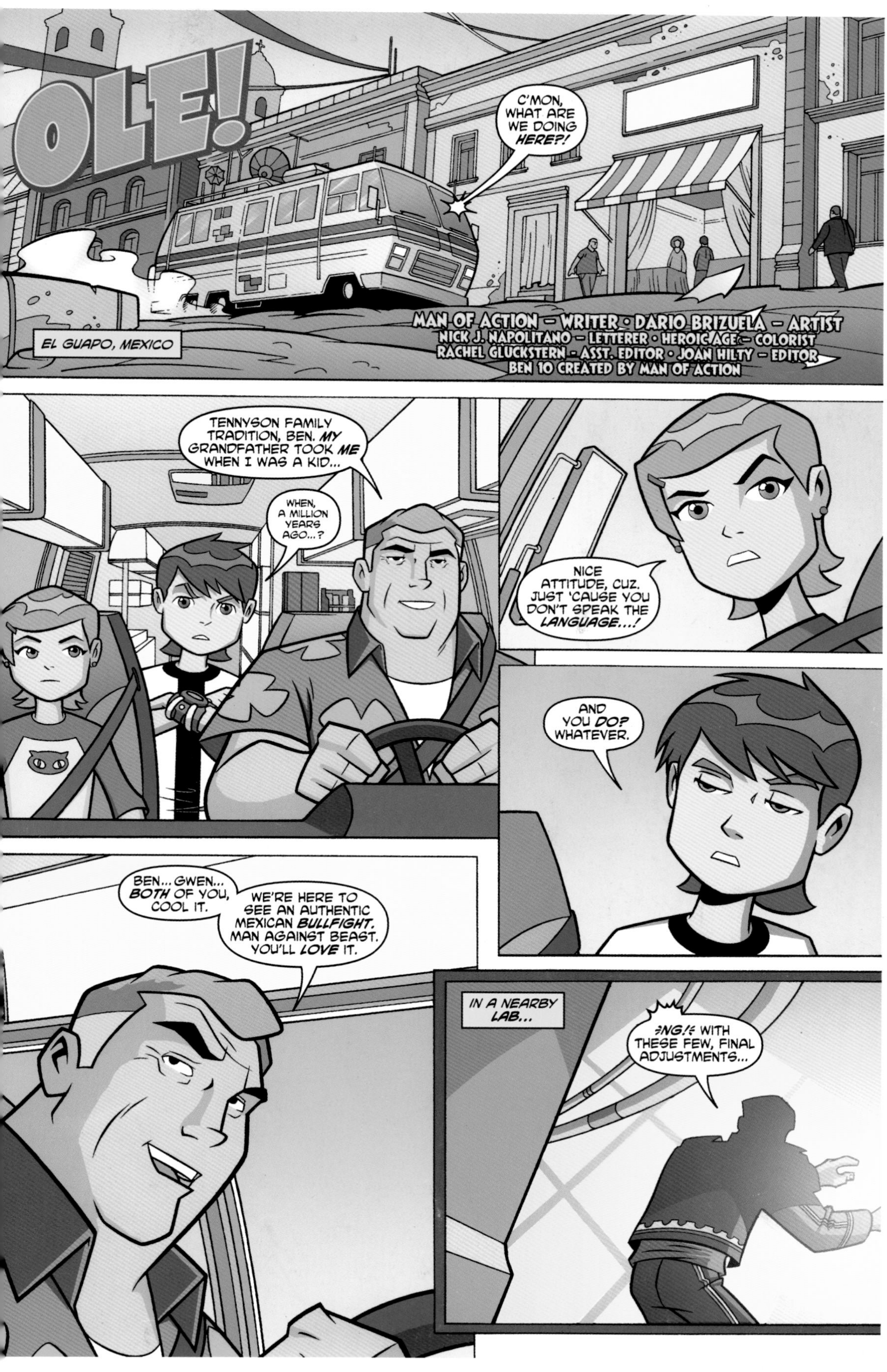
OLE!
C'MON, WHAT ARE WE DOING *HERE?!*
EL GUAPO, MEXICO
MAN OF ACTION – WRITER • DARIO BRIZUELA – ARTIST
NICK J. NAPOLITANO – LETTERER • HEROIC AGE – COLORIST
RACHEL GLUCKSTERN – ASST. EDITOR • JOAN HILTY – EDITOR
BEN 10 CREATED BY MAN OF ACTION
TENNYSON FAMILY TRADITION, BEN. *MY* GRANDFATHER TOOK *ME* WHEN I WAS A KID...
WHEN, A MILLION YEARS AGO...?
NICE ATTITUDE, CUZ. JUST 'CAUSE YOU DON'T SPEAK THE *LANGUAGE...!*
AND YOU *DO?* WHATEVER.
BEN... GWEN... *BOTH* OF YOU, COOL IT.
WE'RE HERE TO SEE AN AUTHENTIC MEXICAN *BULLFIGHT.* MAN AGAINST BEAST. YOU'LL *LOVE* IT.
IN A NEARBY *LAB...*
NG! WITH THESE FEW, FINAL ADJUSTMENTS...

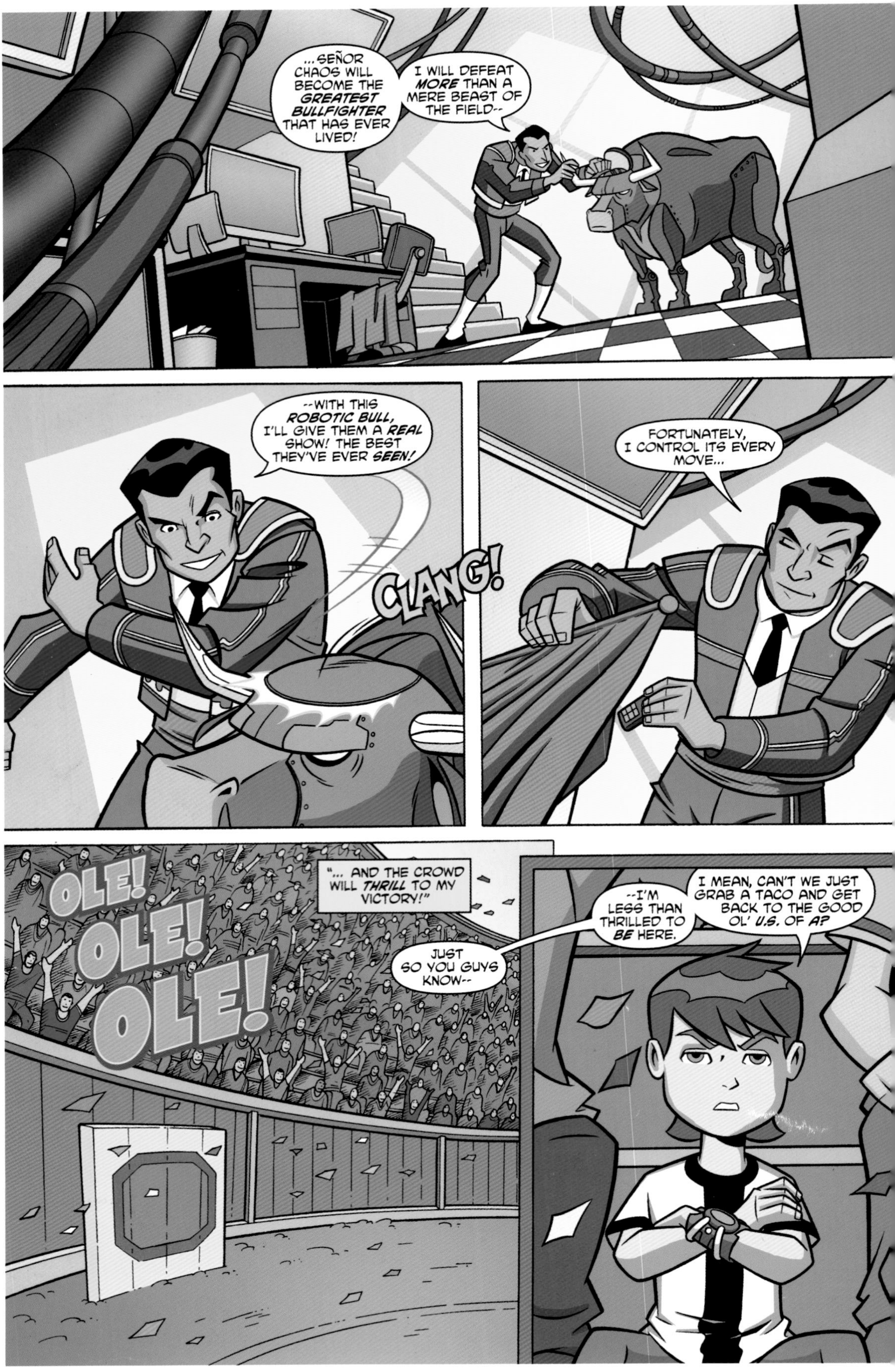

...SEÑOR CHAOS WILL BECOME THE GREATEST BULLFIGHTER THAT HAS EVER LIVED!
I WILL DEFEAT MORE THAN A MERE BEAST OF THE FIELD--
--WITH THIS ROBOTIC BULL, I'LL GIVE THEM A REAL SHOW! THE BEST THEY'VE EVER SEEN!
CLANG!
FORTUNATELY, I CONTROL ITS EVERY MOVE...
OLE! OLE! OLE!
"... AND THE CROWD WILL THRILL TO MY VICTORY!"
JUST SO YOU GUYS KNOW--
--I'M LESS THAN THRILLED TO BE HERE.
I MEAN, CAN'T WE JUST GRAB A TACO AND GET BACK TO THE GOOD OL' U.S. OF A?

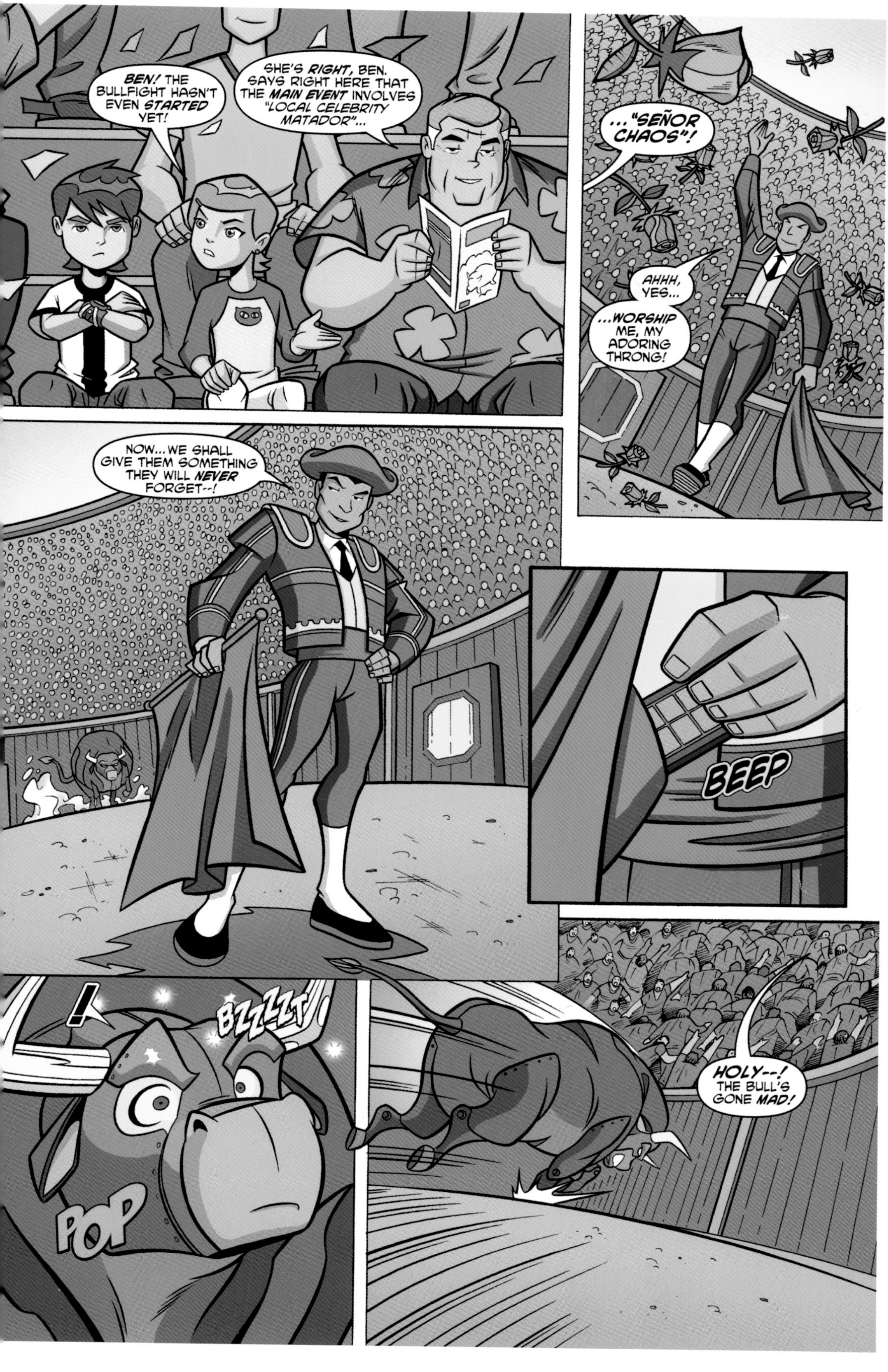
BEN! THE BULLFIGHT HASN'T EVEN STARTED YET!
SHE'S RIGHT, BEN. SAYS RIGHT HERE THAT THE MAIN EVENT INVOLVES "LOCAL CELEBRITY MATADOR"...
..."SEÑOR CHAOS"!
AHHH, YES...
...WORSHIP ME, MY ADORING THRONG!
NOW...WE SHALL GIVE THEM SOMETHING THEY WILL NEVER FORGET--!
BEEP
!
BZZZZT
POP
HOLY--! THE BULL'S GONE MAD!

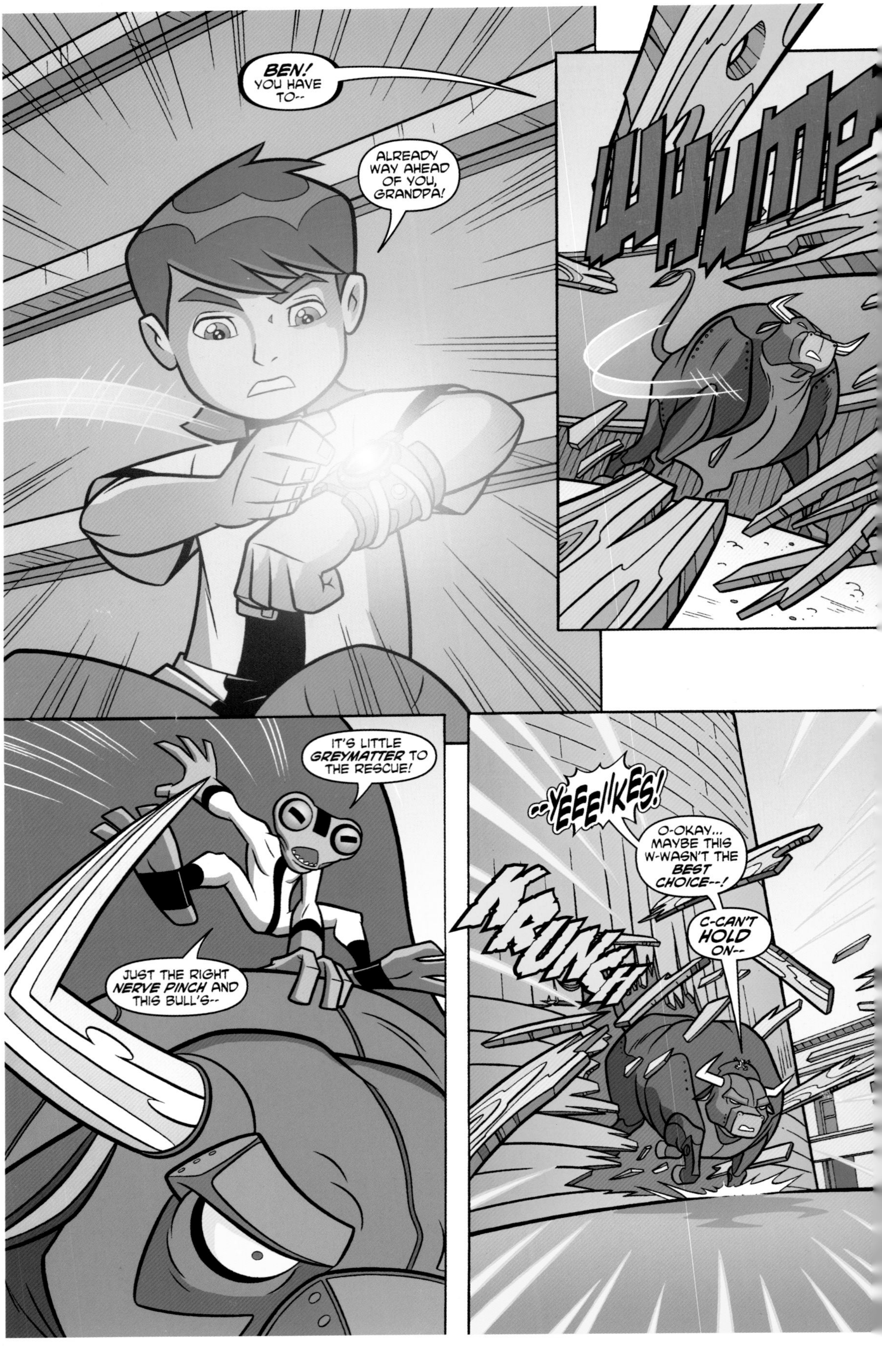
BEN! YOU HAVE TO--
ALREADY WAY AHEAD OF YOU, GRANDPA!
WHUMP
IT'S LITTLE GREYMATTER TO THE RESCUE!
JUST THE RIGHT NERVE PINCH AND THIS BULL'S--
--YEEEIIKES!
O-OKAY... MAYBE THIS W-WASN'T THE BEST CHOICE--!
KRUNCH
C-CAN'T HOLD ON--

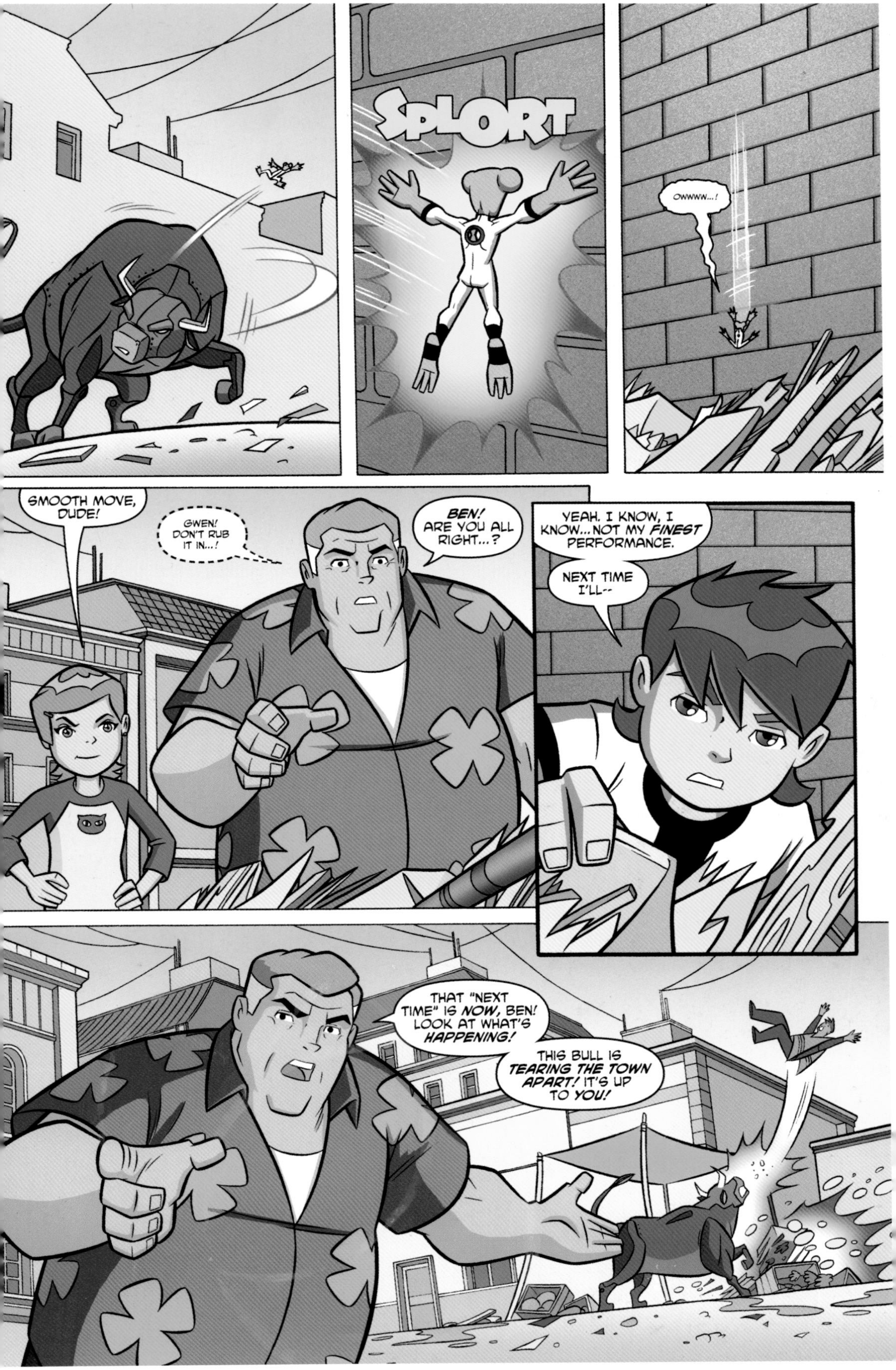
SPLORT
OWWWW...!
SMOOTH MOVE, DUDE!
GWEN! DON'T RUB IT IN...!
BEN! ARE YOU ALL RIGHT...?
YEAH. I KNOW, I KNOW... NOT MY FINEST PERFORMANCE.
NEXT TIME I'LL--
THAT "NEXT TIME" IS NOW, BEN! LOOK AT WHAT'S HAPPENING!
THIS BULL IS TEARING THE TOWN APART! IT'S UP TO YOU!

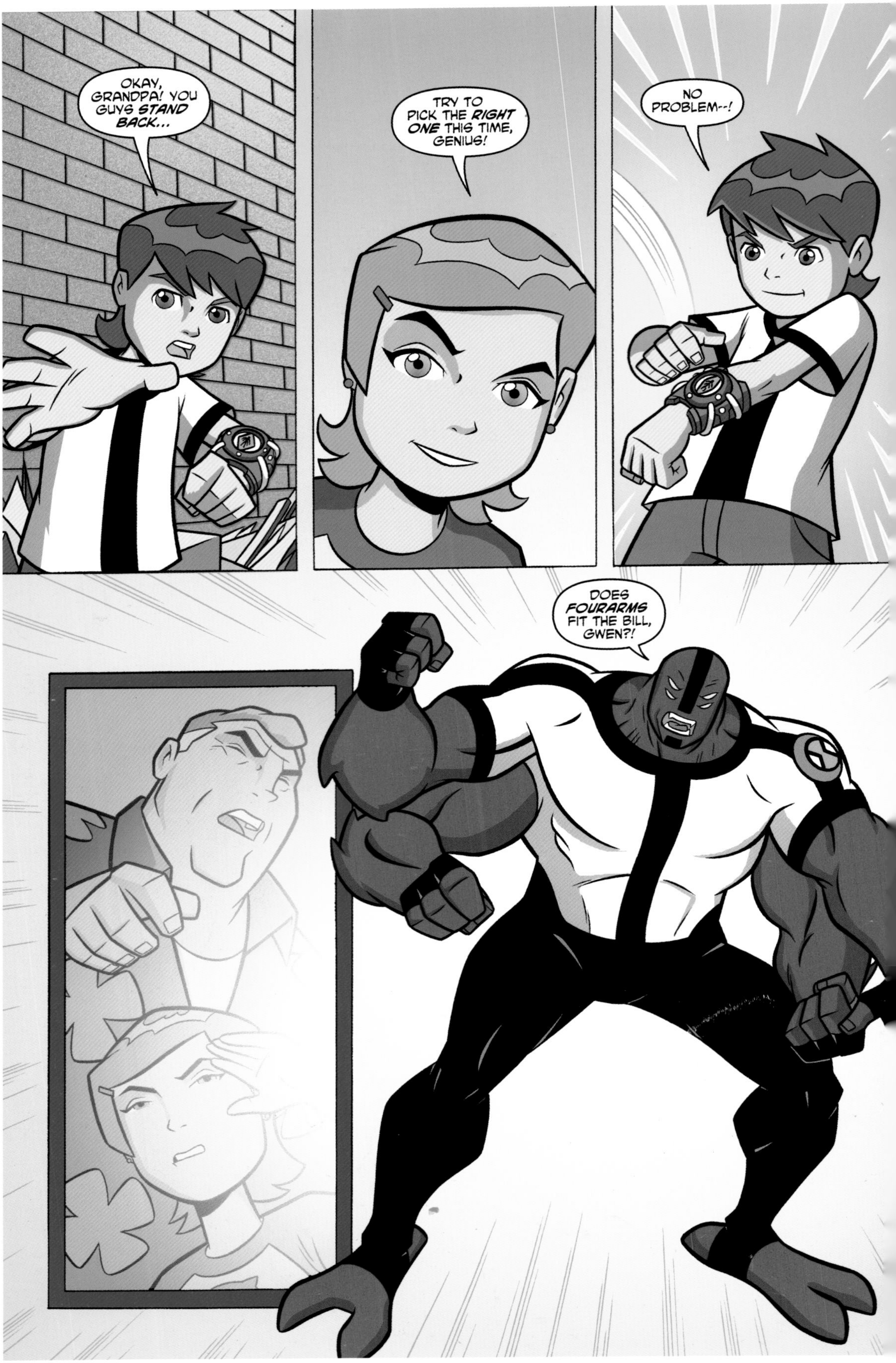
OKAY, GRANDPA! YOU GUYS STAND BACK...
TRY TO PICK THE RIGHT ONE THIS TIME, GENIUS!
NO PROBLEM--!
DOES FOURARMS FIT THE BILL, GWEN?!

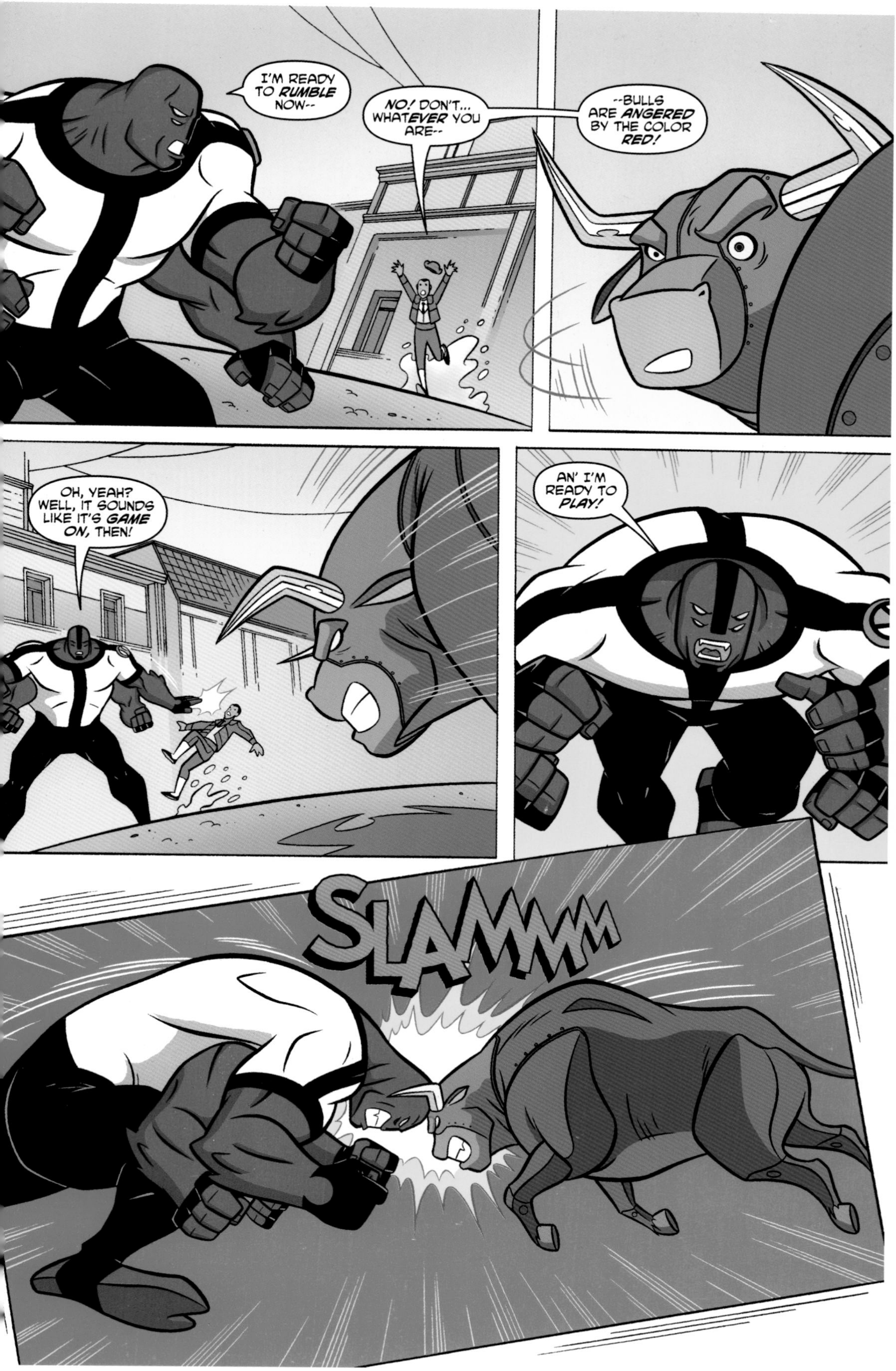
I'M READY TO RUMBLE NOW--
NO! DON'T... WHATEVER YOU ARE--
--BULLS ARE ANGERED BY THE COLOR RED!
OH, YEAH? WELL, IT SOUNDS LIKE IT'S GAME ON, THEN!
AN' I'M READY TO PLAY!
SLAMMM

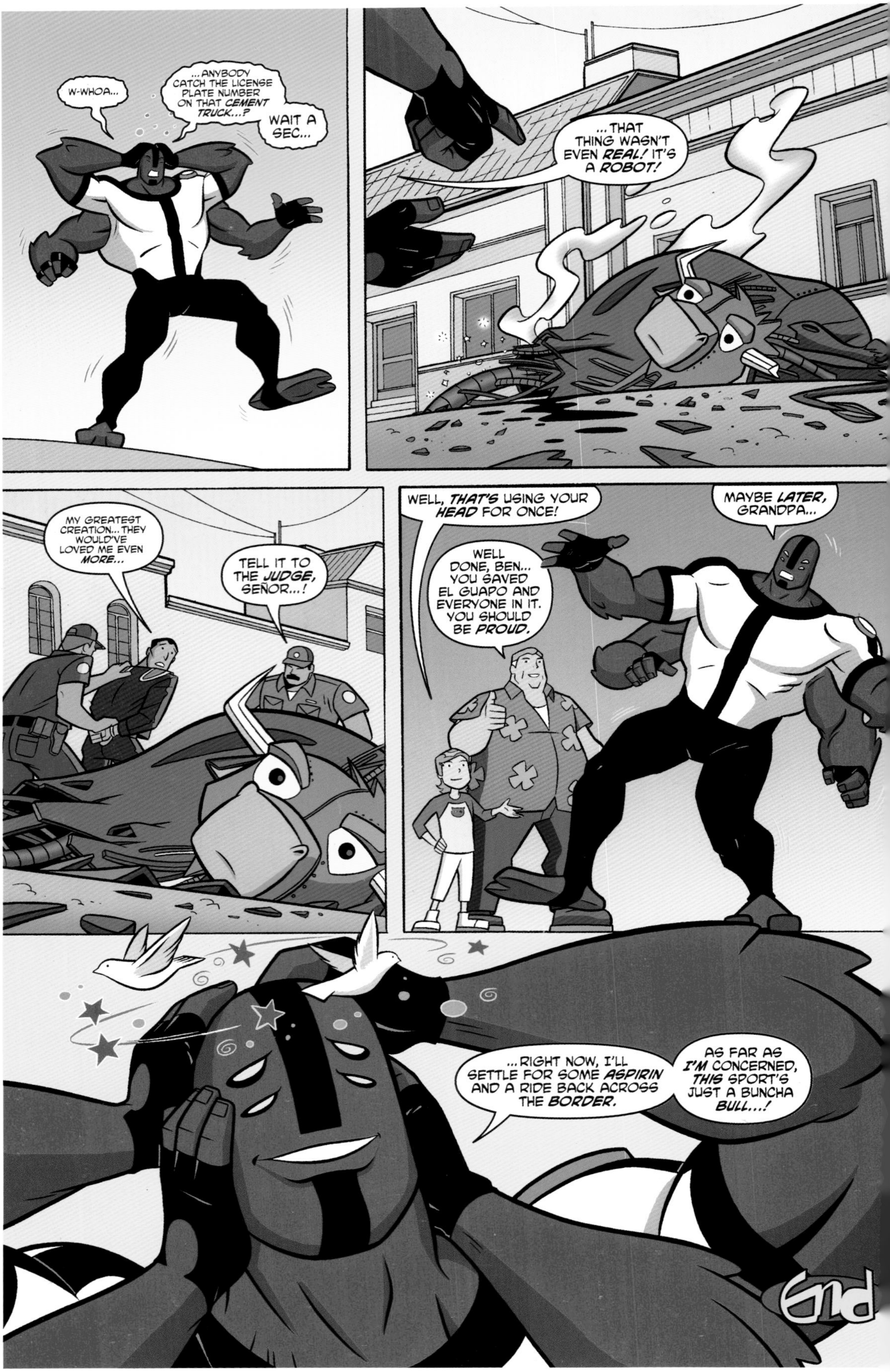
W-WHOA...
...ANYBODY CATCH THE LICENSE PLATE NUMBER ON THAT CEMENT TRUCK...?
WAIT A SEC...
...THAT THING WASN'T EVEN REAL! IT'S A ROBOT!
MY GREATEST CREATION... THEY WOULD'VE LOVED ME EVEN MORE...
TELL IT TO THE JUDGE, SEÑOR...!
WELL, THAT'S USING YOUR HEAD FOR ONCE!
WELL DONE, BEN... YOU SAVED EL GUAPO AND EVERYONE IN IT. YOU SHOULD BE PROUD.
MAYBE LATER, GRANDPA...
...RIGHT NOW, I'LL SETTLE FOR SOME ASPIRIN AND A RIDE BACK ACROSS THE BORDER.
AS FAR AS I'M CONCERNED, THIS SPORT'S JUST A BUNCHA BULL...!
End

BEN 10 FAST LANE

MAN OF ACTION WRITER DARIO BRIZUELA ARTIST STUDIO 1137 LETTERER HEROIC AGE COLORIST RACHEL GLUCKSTERN ASST. EDITOR JOAN HILTY EDITOR BEN 10 CREATED BY MAN OF ACTION

THEY'RE *AMAZING*, GRADY! HOW FAST ARE THEY GOING?

UP TO TWO HUNDRED AND TEN MILES AN HOUR, GWEN!

MY OLD FRIEND *GRADY* WAS NICE ENOUGH TO INVITE US.

I THOUGHT YOU MIGHT APPRECIATE A LITTLE FUEL-INJECTED FUN AFTER MONDAY'S DEBACLE AT THE LOUISIANAN *ANT FARM*.

WHAT DO *YOU* THINK, BEN?

...I THINK MY EARS ARE BLEEDING.

DON'T TELL ME YOU'RE *BORED*, BEN? LOOK AT THOSE FEATS OF HUMAN ENGINEERING! IT TAKES A LOT OF *SKILL* TO BE A RACECAR DRIVER!

SKILL? ALL THEY DO IS DRIVE AROUND IN A CIRCLE!

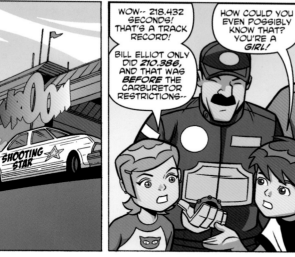

WOW-- 218.432 SECONDS! THAT'S A TRACK RECORD!

BILL ELLIOT ONLY DID *210.386*, AND THAT WAS *BEFORE* THE CARBURETOR RESTRICTIONS--

HOW COULD YOU EVEN POSSIBLY KNOW THAT? YOU'RE A *GIRL!*

SHOOTING STAR

SHE'S RIGHT, BEN! AND ON ANY OTHER DAY THAT WOULD BE A TRACK RECORD, BUT TODAY, WE'RE JUST LUCKY

HUH? YOU'VE GOT THE FINEST CAR OUT HERE. WHAT ELSE COULD POSSIBLY GO UP AGAINST HER?

--UH, WHAT IS *THAT!*

SPEAK OF THE DEVIL... AND HE SHOWS HIS TAILPIPE.

RUUMMMBLE

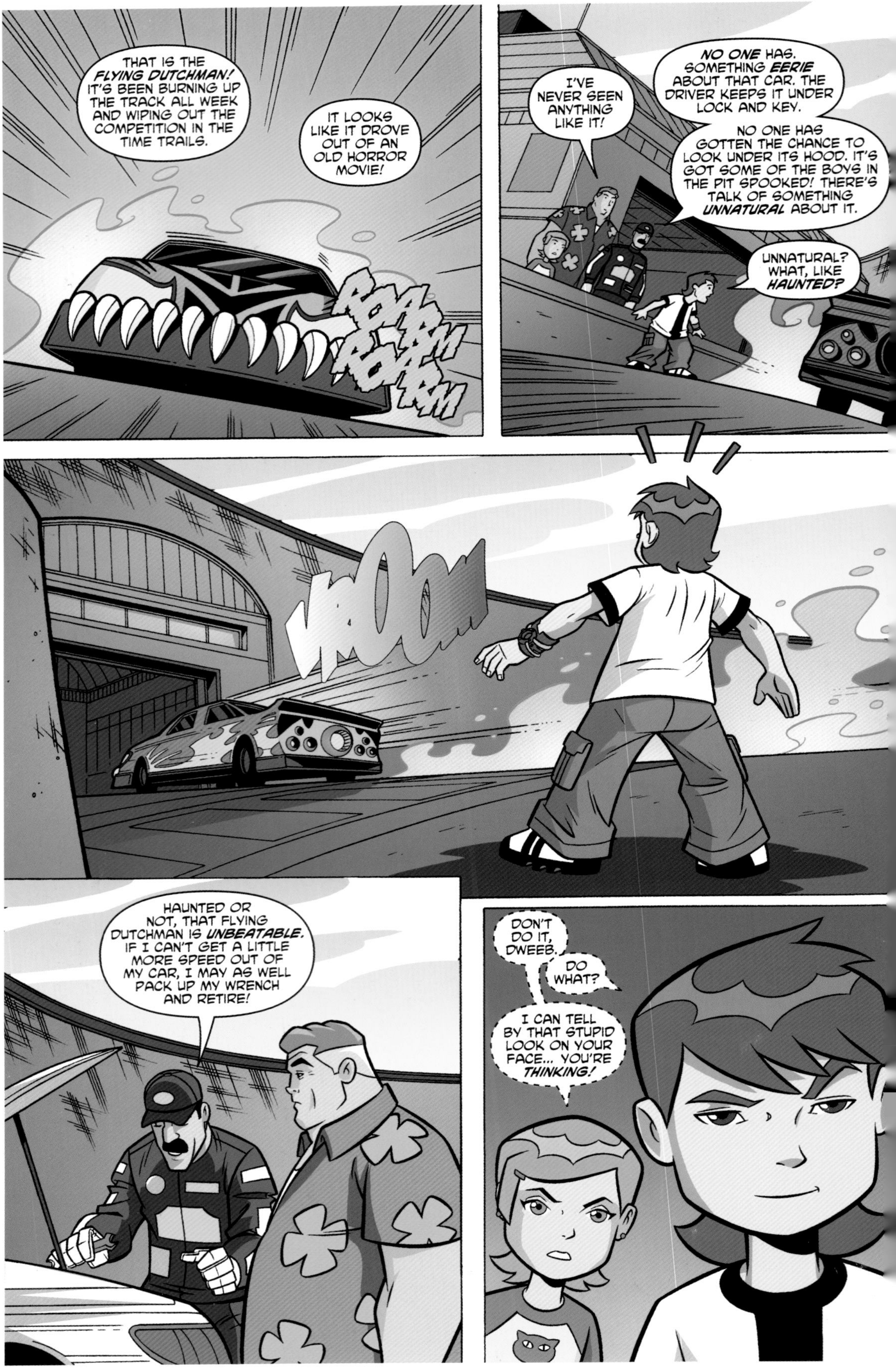
THAT IS THE FLYING DUTCHMAN! IT'S BEEN BURNING UP THE TRACK ALL WEEK AND WIPING OUT THE COMPETITION IN THE TIME TRAILS.
IT LOOKS LIKE IT DROVE OUT OF AN OLD HORROR MOVIE!
I'VE NEVER SEEN ANYTHING LIKE IT!
NO ONE HAS. SOMETHING EERIE ABOUT THAT CAR. THE DRIVER KEEPS IT UNDER LOCK AND KEY.
NO ONE HAS GOTTEN THE CHANCE TO LOOK UNDER ITS HOOD. IT'S GOT SOME OF THE BOYS IN THE PIT SPOOKED! THERE'S TALK OF SOMETHING UNNATURAL ABOUT IT.
UNNATURAL? WHAT, LIKE HAUNTED?
HAUNTED OR NOT, THAT FLYING DUTCHMAN IS UNBEATABLE. IF I CAN'T GET A LITTLE MORE SPEED OUT OF MY CAR, I MAY AS WELL PACK UP MY WRENCH AND RETIRE!
DON'T DO IT, DWEEB.
DO WHAT?
I CAN TELL BY THAT STUPID LOOK ON YOUR FACE... YOU'RE THINKING!

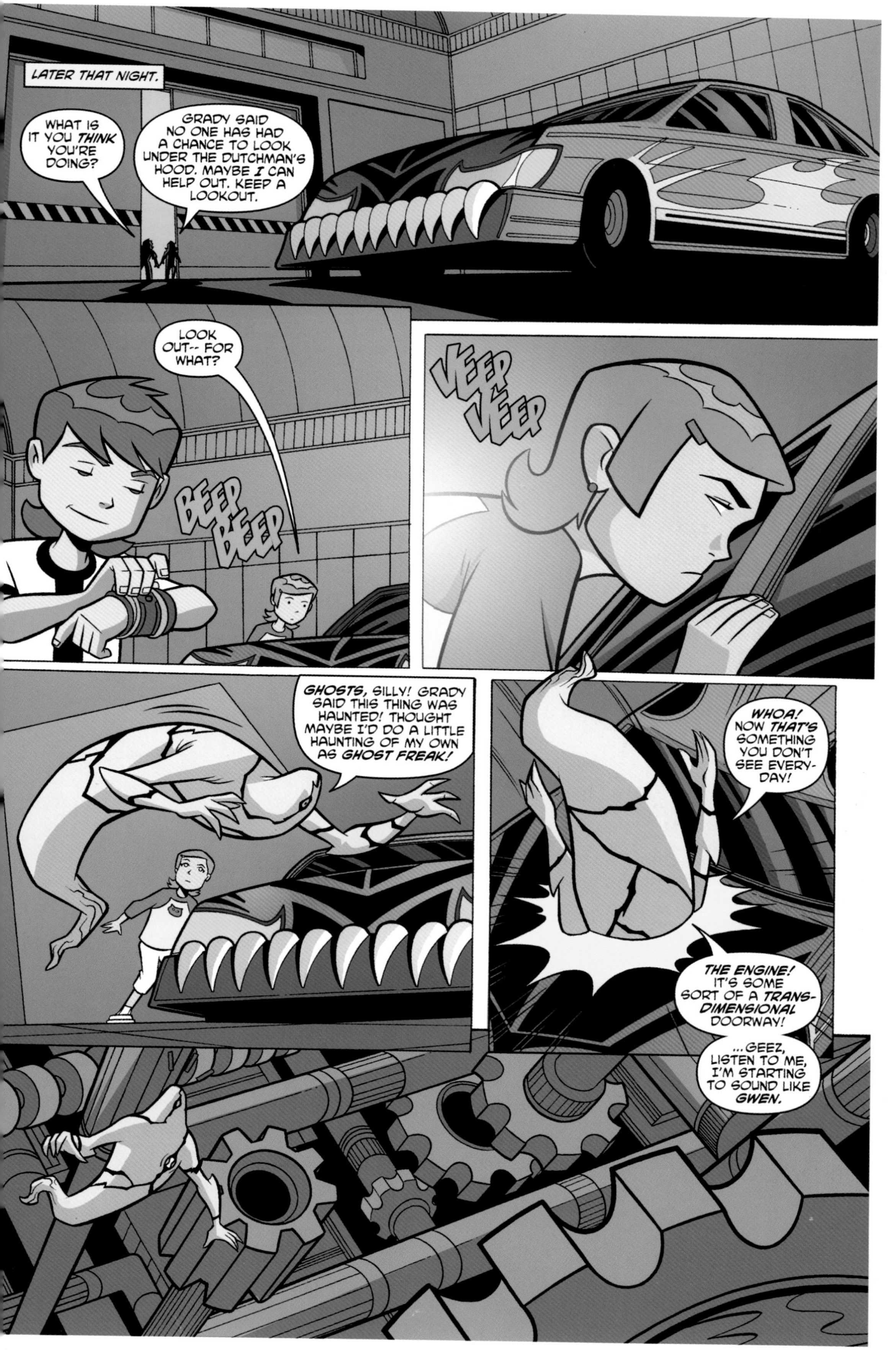
LATER THAT NIGHT.
WHAT IS IT YOU *THINK* YOU'RE DOING?
GRADY SAID NO ONE HAS HAD A CHANCE TO LOOK UNDER THE DUTCHMAN'S HOOD. MAYBE *I* CAN HELP OUT. KEEP A LOOKOUT.
LOOK OUT-- FOR WHAT?
BEEP BEEP
VEEP VEEP
GHOSTS, SILLY! GRADY SAID THIS THING WAS HAUNTED! THOUGHT MAYBE I'D DO A LITTLE HAUNTING OF MY OWN AS *GHOST FREAK!*
WHOA! NOW *THAT'S* SOMETHING YOU DON'T SEE EVERY-DAY!
THE ENGINE! IT'S SOME SORT OF A *TRANS-DIMENSIONAL* DOORWAY!
...GEEZ, LISTEN TO ME, I'M STARTING TO SOUND LIKE *GWEN.*

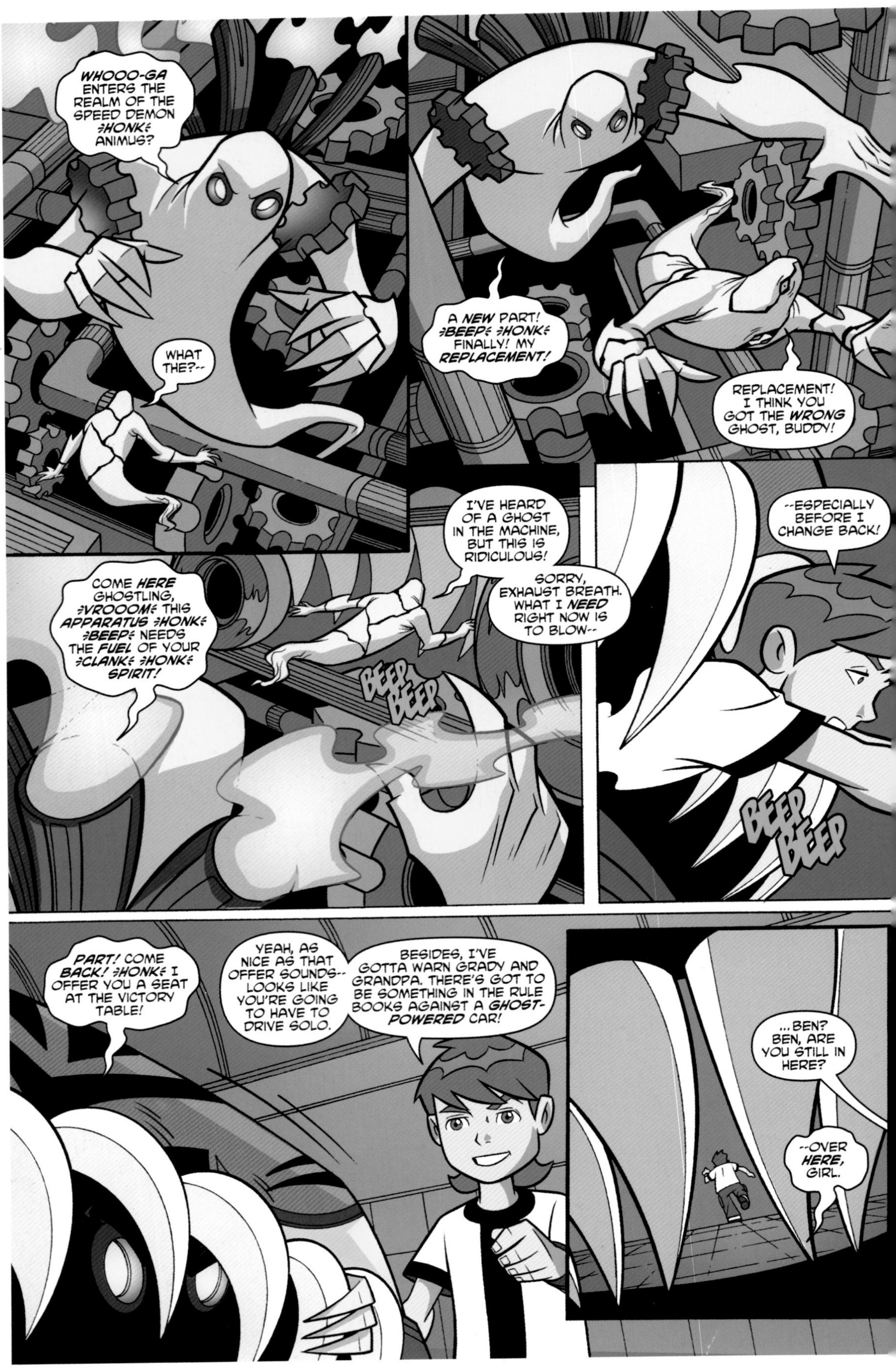
WHOOO-GA ENTERS THE REALM OF THE SPEED DEMON ⋟HONK⋞ ANIMUS?
WHAT THE?--
A NEW PART! ⋟BEEP⋞ ⋟HONK⋞ FINALLY! MY REPLACEMENT!
REPLACEMENT! I THINK YOU GOT THE WRONG GHOST, BUDDY!
COME HERE GHOSTLING, ⋟VROOOM⋞ THIS APPARATUS ⋟HONK⋞ ⋟BEEP⋞ NEEDS THE FUEL OF YOUR ⋟CLANK⋞ ⋟HONK⋞ SPIRIT!
I'VE HEARD OF A GHOST IN THE MACHINE, BUT THIS IS RIDICULOUS!
SORRY, EXHAUST BREATH. WHAT I NEED RIGHT NOW IS TO BLOW--
BEEP BEEP
--ESPECIALLY BEFORE I CHANGE BACK!
BEEP BEEP
PART! COME BACK! ⋟HONK⋞ I OFFER YOU A SEAT AT THE VICTORY TABLE!
YEAH, AS NICE AS THAT OFFER SOUNDS-- LOOKS LIKE YOU'RE GOING TO HAVE TO DRIVE SOLO.
BESIDES, I'VE GOTTA WARN GRADY AND GRANDPA. THERE'S GOT TO BE SOMETHING IN THE RULE BOOKS AGAINST A GHOST-POWERED CAR!
...BEN? BEN, ARE YOU STILL IN HERE?
--OVER HERE, GIRL.

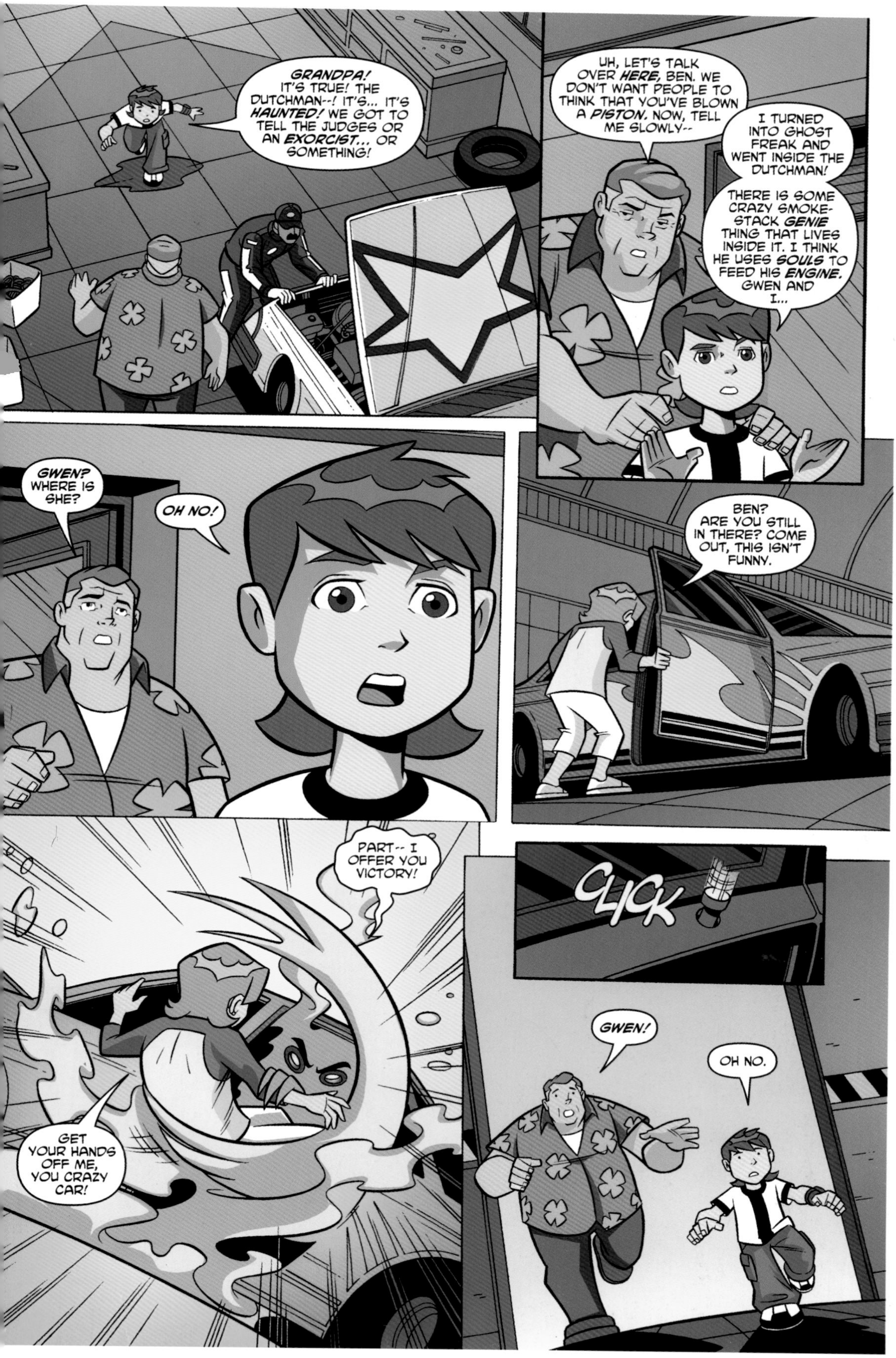
GRANDPA! IT'S TRUE! THE DUTCHMAN--! IT'S... IT'S HAUNTED! WE GOT TO TELL THE JUDGES OR AN EXORCIST... OR SOMETHING!
UH, LET'S TALK OVER HERE, BEN. WE DON'T WANT PEOPLE TO THINK THAT YOU'VE BLOWN A PISTON. NOW, TELL ME SLOWLY--
I TURNED INTO GHOST FREAK AND WENT INSIDE THE DUTCHMAN!
THERE IS SOME CRAZY SMOKE-STACK GENIE THING THAT LIVES INSIDE IT. I THINK HE USES SOULS TO FEED HIS ENGINE. GWEN AND I...
GWEN? WHERE IS SHE?
OH NO!
BEN? ARE YOU STILL IN THERE? COME OUT, THIS ISN'T FUNNY.
PART-- I OFFER YOU VICTORY!
GET YOUR HANDS OFF ME, YOU CRAZY CAR!
CLICK
GWEN!
OH NO.

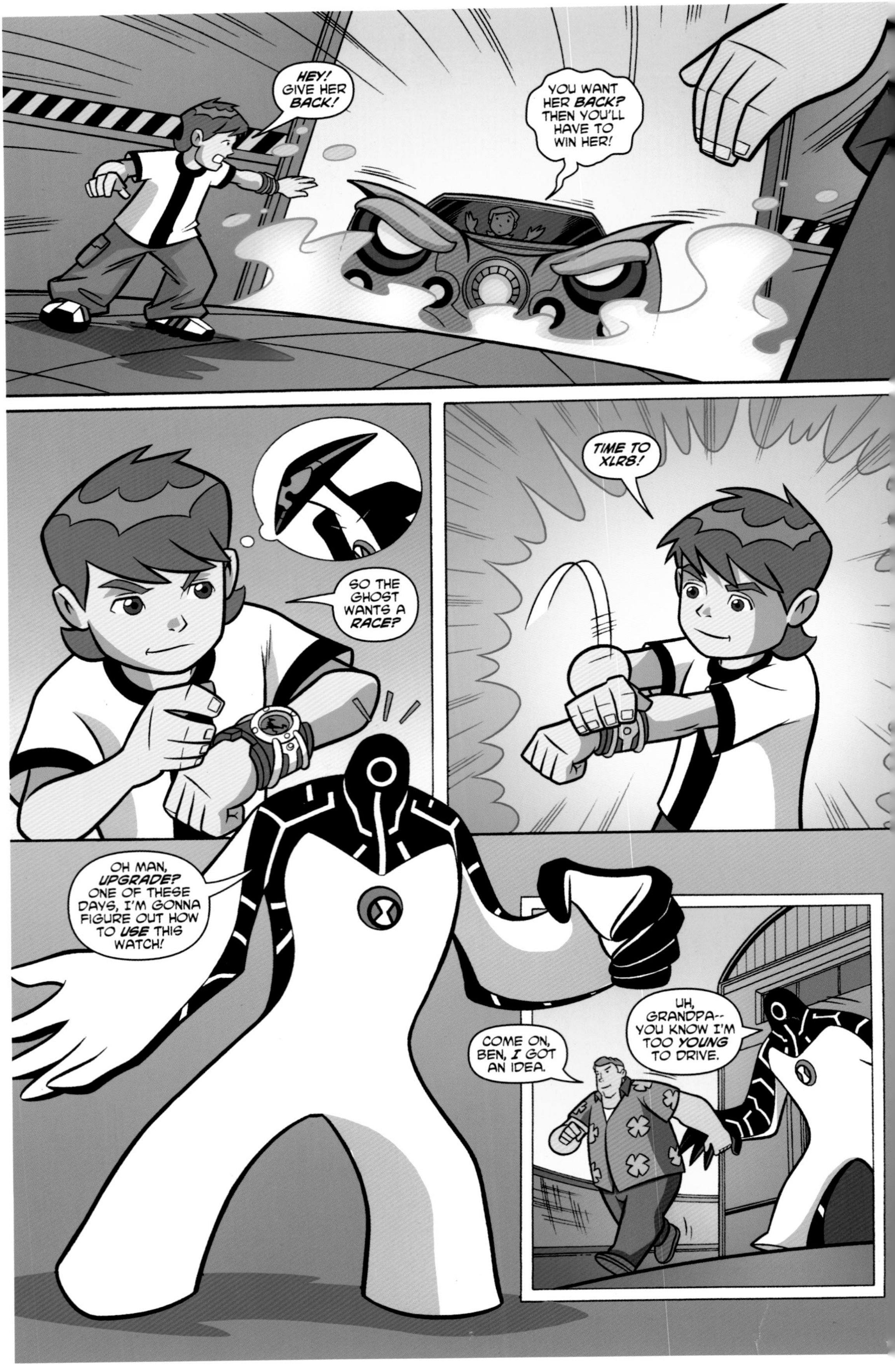
HEY! GIVE HER BACK!
YOU WANT HER BACK? THEN YOU'LL HAVE TO WIN HER!
SO THE GHOST WANTS A RACE?
TIME TO XLR8!
OH MAN, UPGRADE? ONE OF THESE DAYS, I'M GONNA FIGURE OUT HOW TO USE THIS WATCH!
UH, GRANDPA-- YOU KNOW I'M TOO YOUNG TO DRIVE.
COME ON, BEN, I GOT AN IDEA.

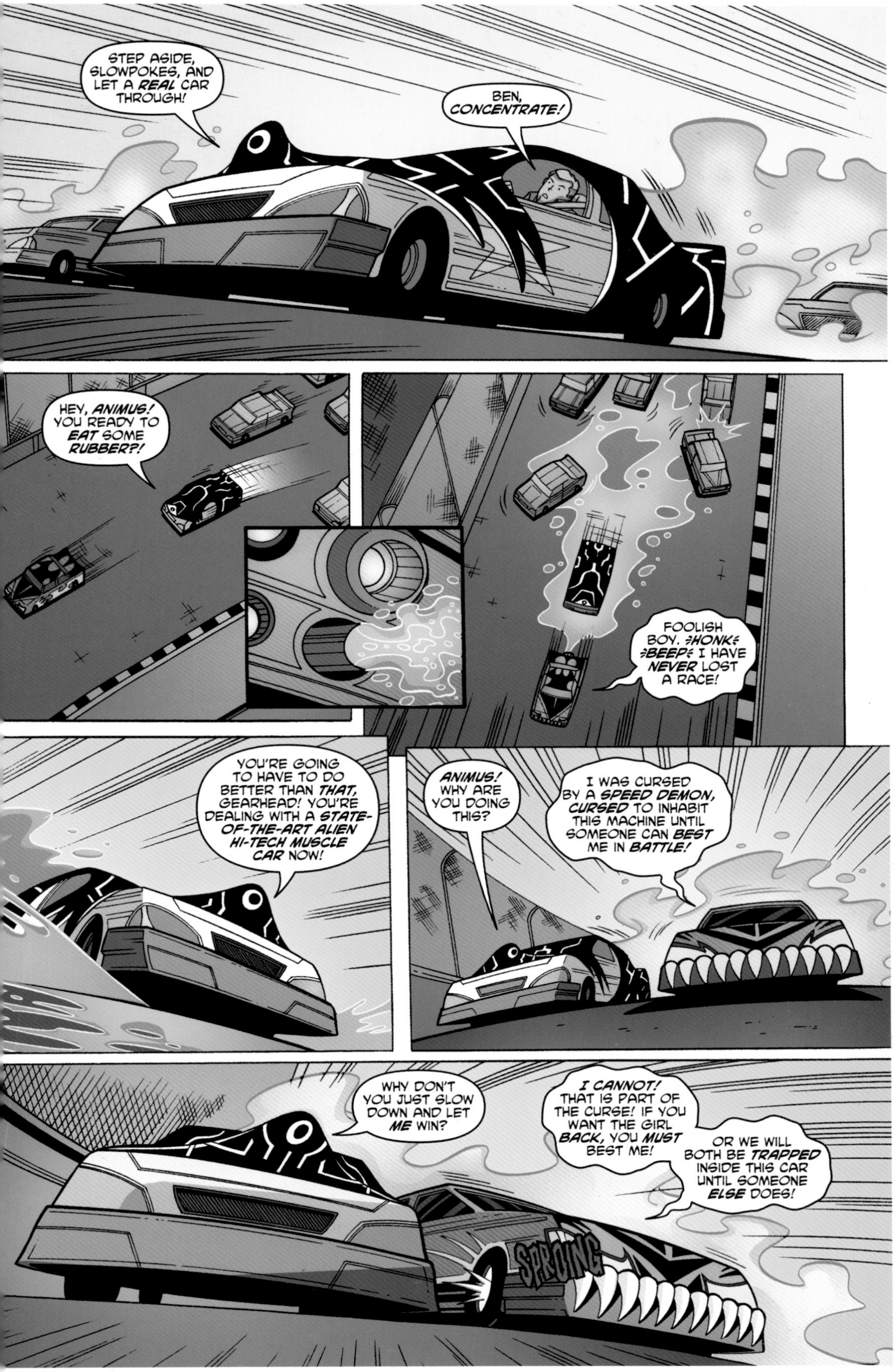
STEP ASIDE, SLOWPOKES, AND LET A REAL CAR THROUGH!
BEN, CONCENTRATE!
HEY, ANIMUS! YOU READY TO EAT SOME RUBBER?!
FOOLISH BOY. ≠HONK≠ ≠BEEP≠ I HAVE NEVER LOST A RACE!
YOU'RE GOING TO HAVE TO DO BETTER THAN THAT, GEARHEAD! YOU'RE DEALING WITH A STATE-OF-THE-ART ALIEN HI-TECH MUSCLE CAR NOW!
ANIMUS! WHY ARE YOU DOING THIS?
I WAS CURSED BY A SPEED DEMON, CURSED TO INHABIT THIS MACHINE UNTIL SOMEONE CAN BEST ME IN BATTLE!
WHY DON'T YOU JUST SLOW DOWN AND LET ME WIN?
I CANNOT! THAT IS PART OF THE CURSE! IF YOU WANT THE GIRL BACK, YOU MUST BEST ME!
OR WE WILL BOTH BE TRAPPED INSIDE THIS CAR UNTIL SOMEONE ELSE DOES!
SPROING

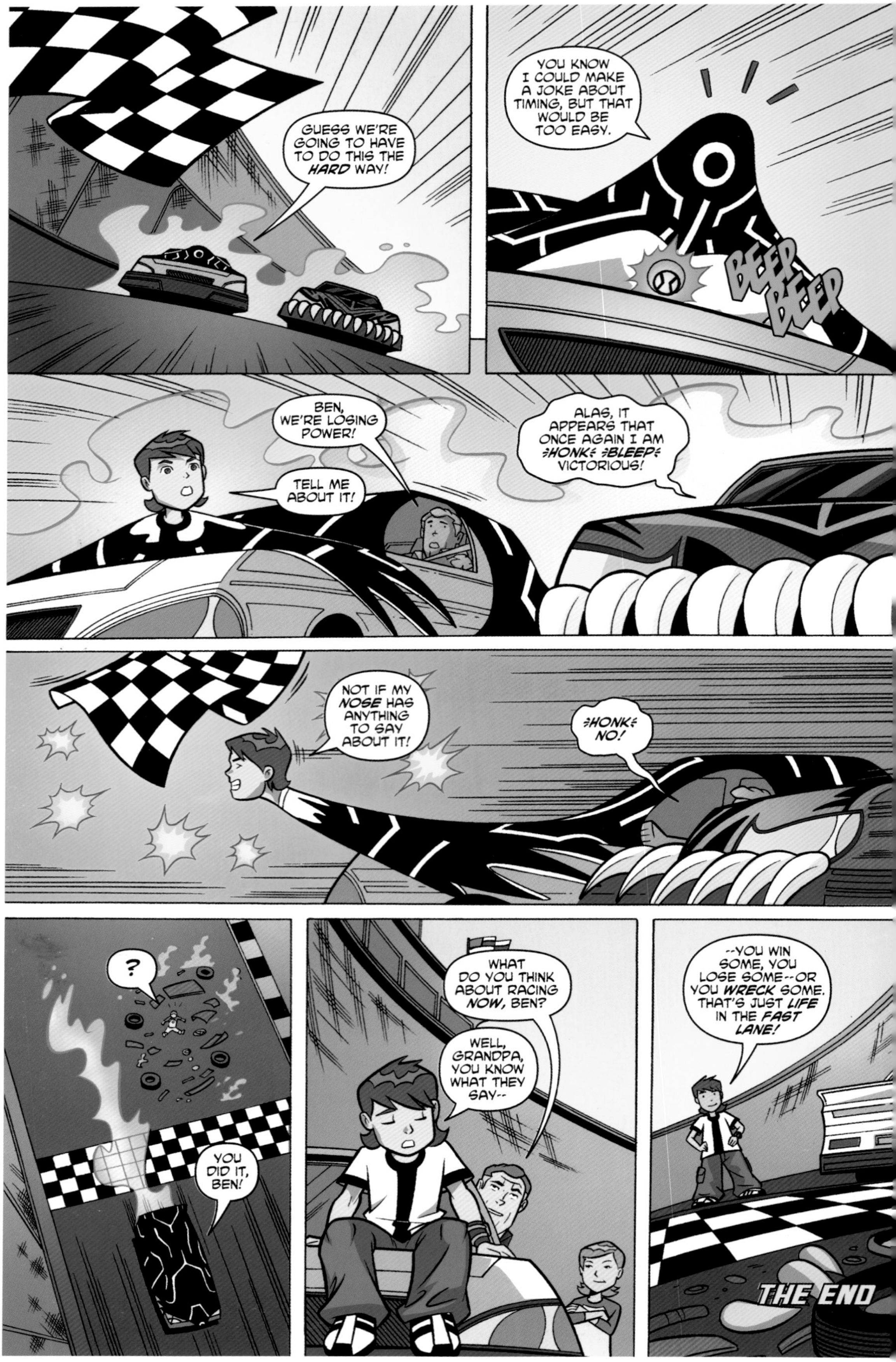
GUESS WE'RE GOING TO HAVE TO DO THIS THE HARD WAY!
YOU KNOW I COULD MAKE A JOKE ABOUT TIMING, BUT THAT WOULD BE TOO EASY.
BEEP BEEP
BEN, WE'RE LOSING POWER!
TELL ME ABOUT IT!
ALAS, IT APPEARS THAT ONCE AGAIN I AM *HONK* *BLEEP* VICTORIOUS!
NOT IF MY NOSE HAS ANYTHING TO SAY ABOUT IT!
HONK NO!
?
YOU DID IT, BEN!
WHAT DO YOU THINK ABOUT RACING NOW, BEN?
WELL, GRANDPA, YOU KNOW WHAT THEY SAY--
--YOU WIN SOME, YOU LOSE SOME--OR YOU WRECK SOME. THAT'S JUST LIFE IN THE FAST LANE!
THE END

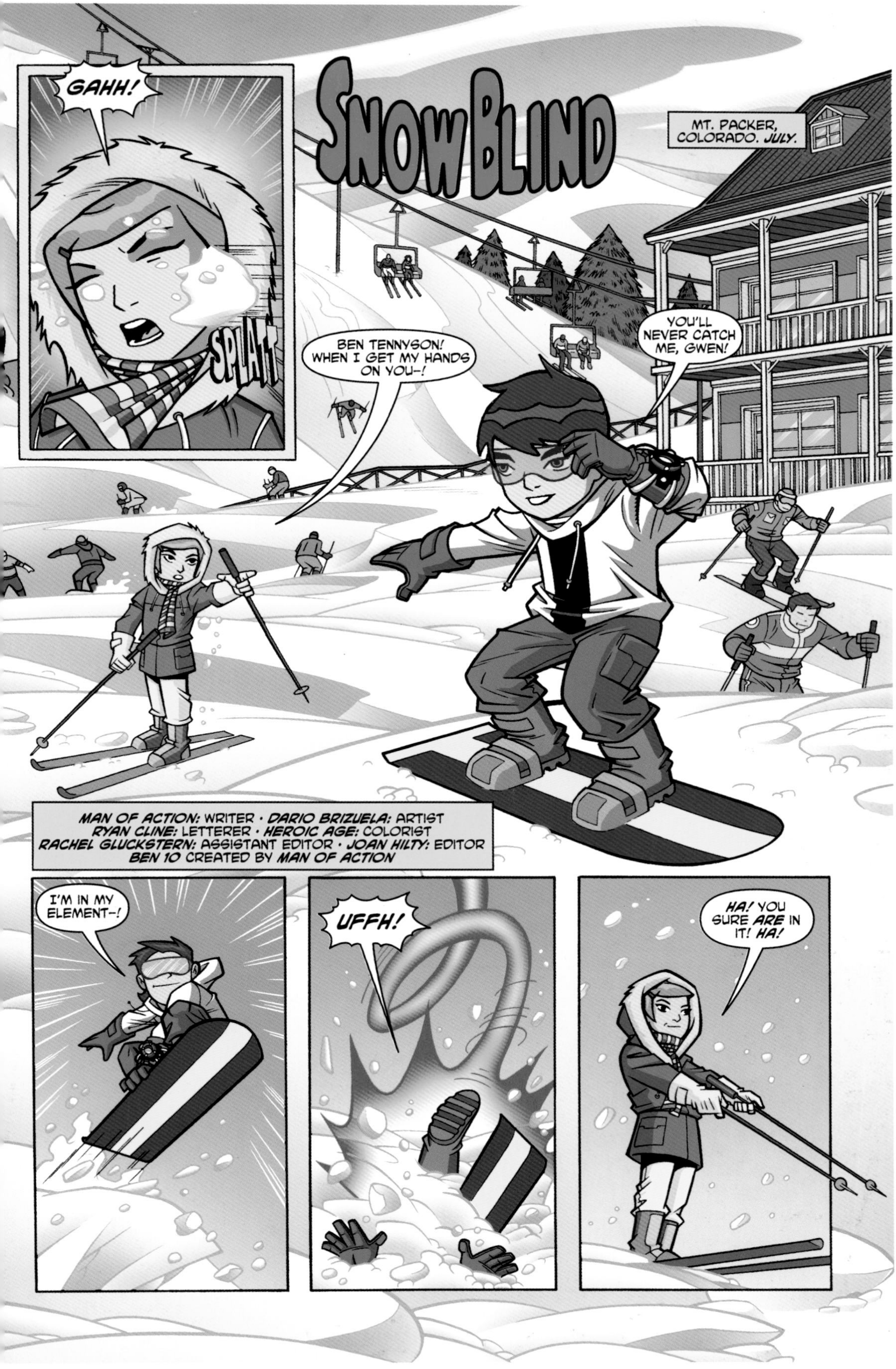
SNOWBLIND
GAHH!
SPLATT
MT. PACKER, COLORADO. JULY.
BEN TENNYSON! WHEN I GET MY HANDS ON YOU--!
YOU'LL NEVER CATCH ME, GWEN!
MAN OF ACTION: WRITER · DARIO BRIZUELA: ARTIST
RYAN CLINE: LETTERER · HEROIC AGE: COLORIST
RACHEL GLUCKSTERN: ASSISTANT EDITOR · JOAN HILTY: EDITOR
BEN 10 CREATED BY MAN OF ACTION
I'M IN MY ELEMENT--!
UFFH!
HA! YOU SURE ARE IN IT! HA!

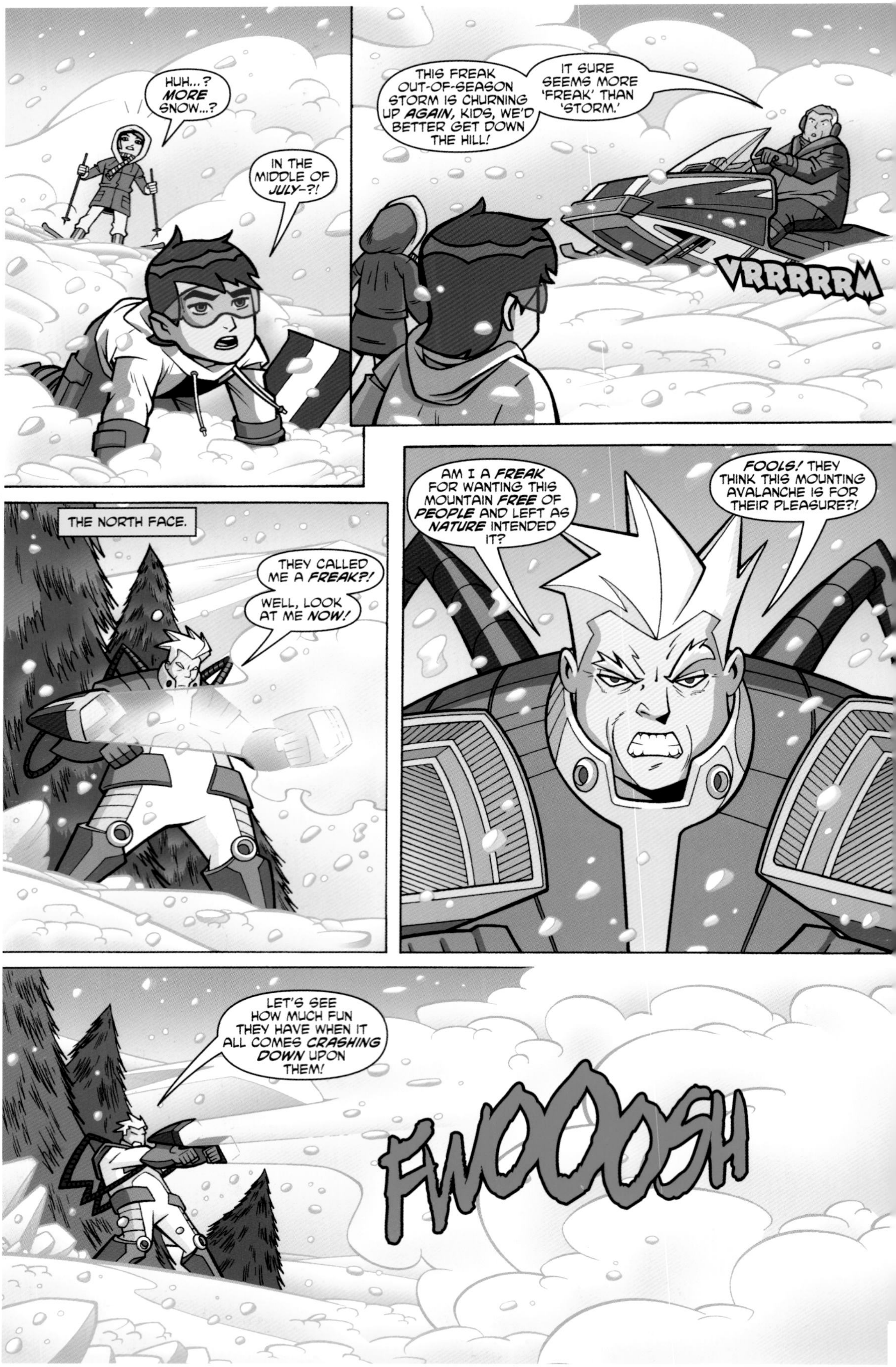
HUH...? MORE SNOW...?
IN THE MIDDLE OF JULY--?!
THIS FREAK OUT-OF-SEASON STORM IS CHURNING UP AGAIN, KIDS, WE'D BETTER GET DOWN THE HILL!
IT SURE SEEMS MORE 'FREAK' THAN 'STORM.'
VRRRRRRM
THE NORTH FACE.
THEY CALLED ME A FREAK?!
WELL, LOOK AT ME NOW!
AM I A FREAK FOR WANTING THIS MOUNTAIN FREE OF PEOPLE AND LEFT AS NATURE INTENDED IT?
FOOLS! THEY THINK THIS MOUNTING AVALANCHE IS FOR THEIR PLEASURE?!
LET'S SEE HOW MUCH FUN THEY HAVE WHEN IT ALL COMES CRASHING DOWN UPON THEM!
FWOOOSH

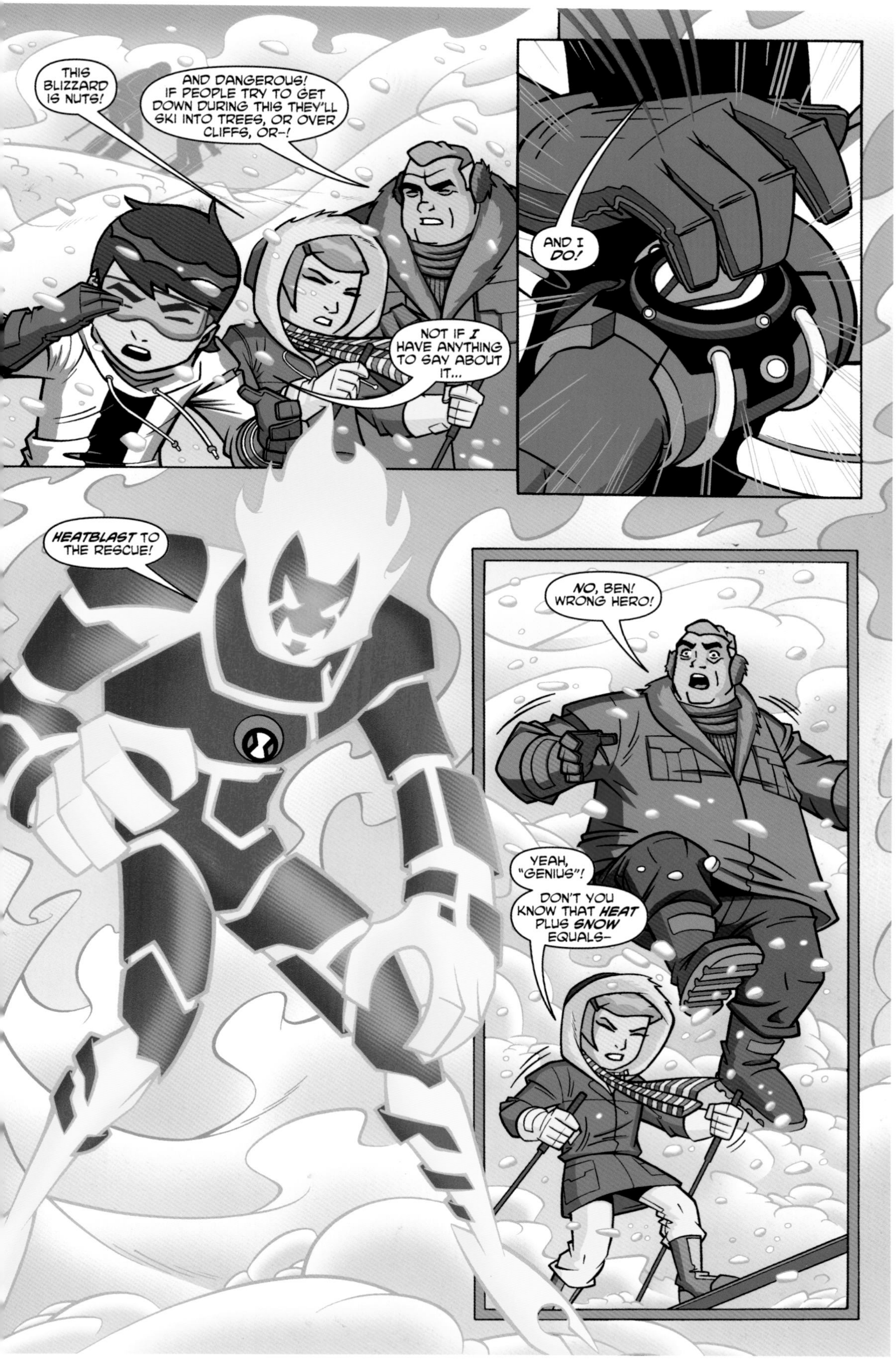

THIS BLIZZARD IS NUTS!
AND DANGEROUS! IF PEOPLE TRY TO GET DOWN DURING THIS THEY'LL SKI INTO TREES, OR OVER CLIFFS, OR--!
NOT IF I HAVE ANYTHING TO SAY ABOUT IT...
AND I DO!
HEATBLAST TO THE RESCUE!
NO, BEN! WRONG HERO!
YEAH, "GENIUS"!
DON'T YOU KNOW THAT HEAT PLUS SNOW EQUALS--

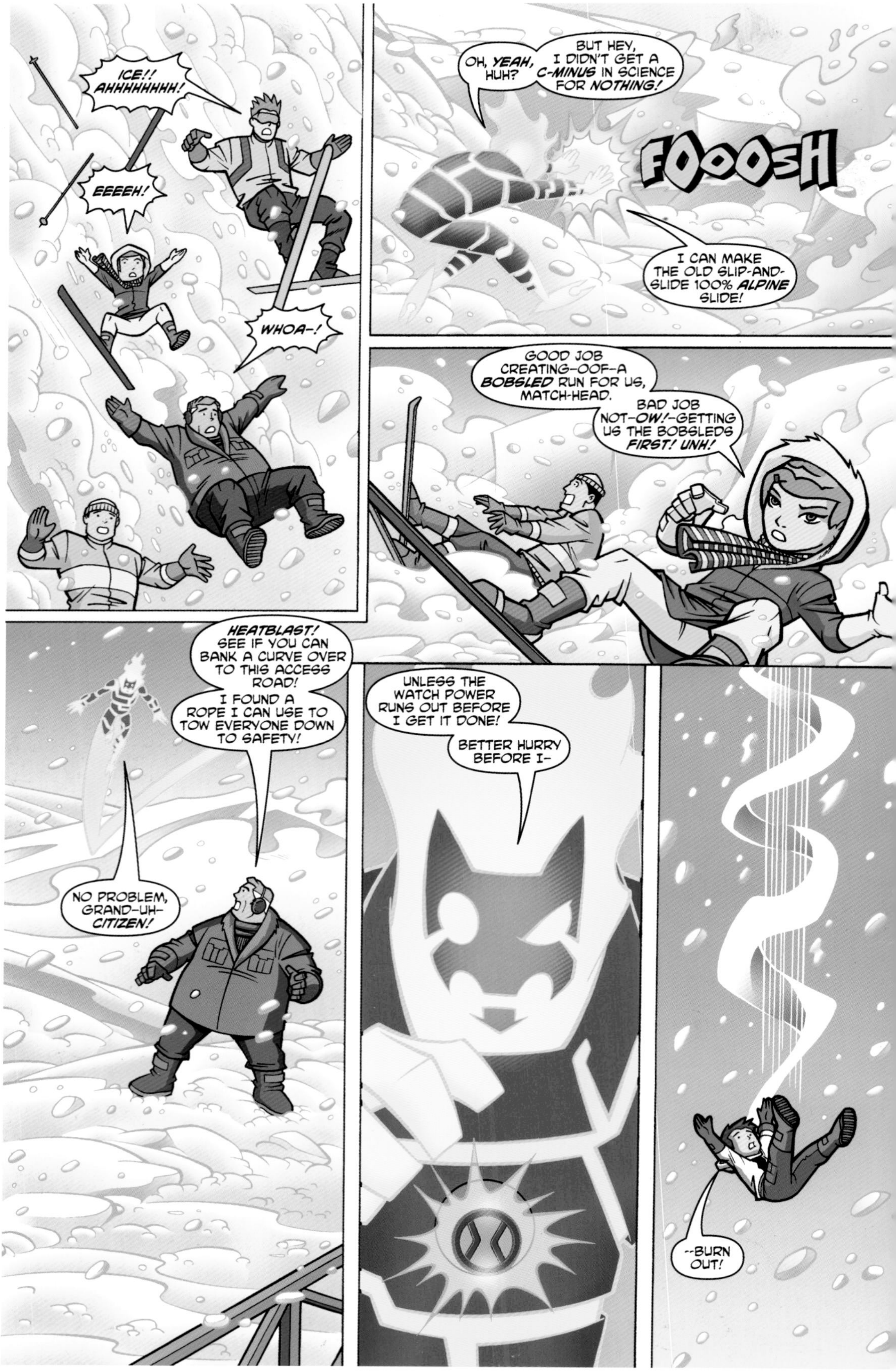
ICE!! AHHHHHHHH!
EEEEH!
WHOA-!
OH, YEAH, HUH?
BUT HEY, I DIDN'T GET A C-MINUS IN SCIENCE FOR NOTHING!
FOOOSH
I CAN MAKE THE OLD SLIP-AND-SLIDE 100% ALPINE SLIDE!
GOOD JOB CREATING--OOF--A BOBSLED RUN FOR US, MATCH-HEAD.
BAD JOB NOT--OW!--GETTING US THE BOBSLEDS FIRST! UNH!
HEATBLAST! SEE IF YOU CAN BANK A CURVE OVER TO THIS ACCESS ROAD!
I FOUND A ROPE I CAN USE TO TOW EVERYONE DOWN TO SAFETY!
NO PROBLEM, GRAND--UH--CITIZEN!
UNLESS THE WATCH POWER RUNS OUT BEFORE I GET IT DONE!
BETTER HURRY BEFORE I-
--BURN OUT!

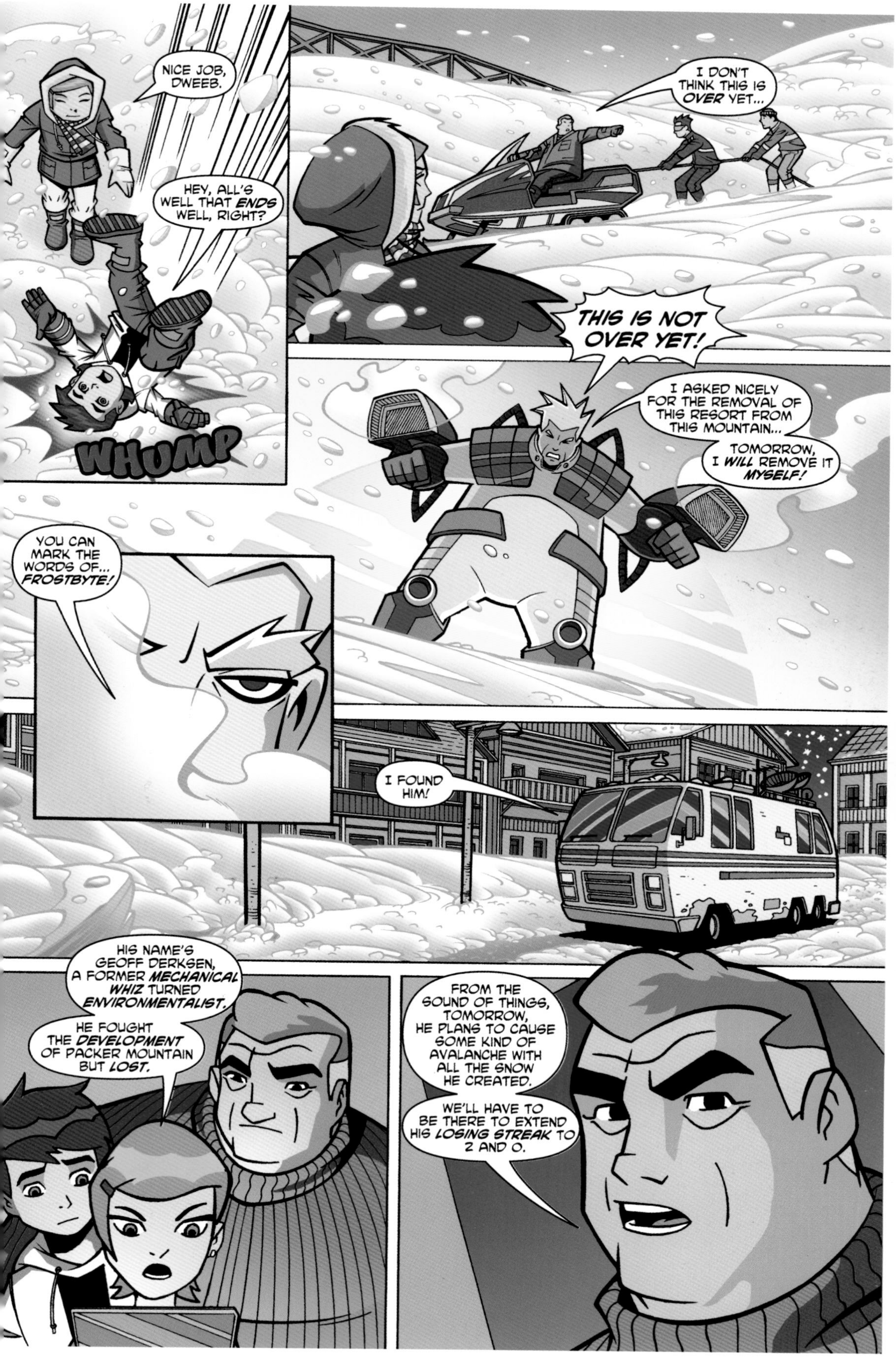
NICE JOB, DWEEB.
HEY, ALL'S WELL THAT *ENDS* WELL, RIGHT?
WHUMP
I DON'T THINK THIS IS *OVER* YET...
THIS IS NOT OVER YET!
I ASKED NICELY FOR THE REMOVAL OF THIS RESORT FROM THIS MOUNTAIN...
TOMORROW, I *WILL* REMOVE IT *MYSELF!*
YOU CAN MARK THE WORDS OF... *FROSTBYTE!*
I FOUND HIM!
HIS NAME'S GEOFF DERKSEN, A FORMER *MECHANICAL WHIZ* TURNED *ENVIRONMENTALIST.*
HE FOUGHT THE *DEVELOPMENT* OF PACKER MOUNTAIN BUT *LOST.*
FROM THE SOUND OF THINGS, TOMORROW, HE PLANS TO CAUSE SOME KIND OF AVALANCHE WITH ALL THE SNOW HE CREATED.
WE'LL HAVE TO BE THERE TO EXTEND HIS *LOSING STREAK* TO 2 AND 0.

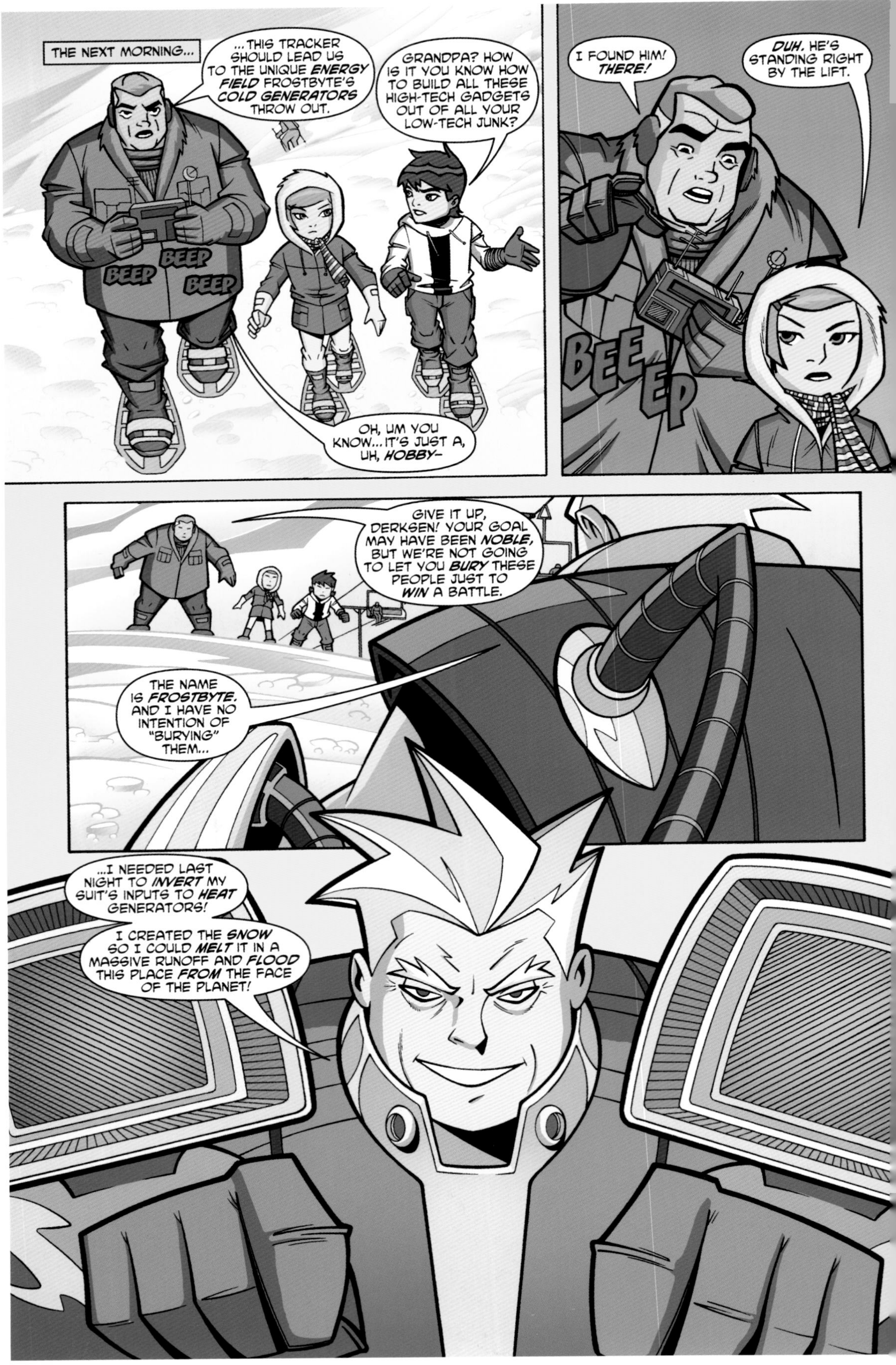

THE NEXT MORNING...
...THIS TRACKER SHOULD LEAD US TO THE UNIQUE ENERGY FIELD FROSTBYTE'S COLD GENERATORS THROW OUT.
GRANDPA? HOW IS IT YOU KNOW HOW TO BUILD ALL THESE HIGH-TECH GADGETS OUT OF ALL YOUR LOW-TECH JUNK?
BEEP BEEP BEEP
OH, UM YOU KNOW... IT'S JUST A, UH, HOBBY–
I FOUND HIM! THERE!
DUH. HE'S STANDING RIGHT BY THE LIFT.
BEEEP
GIVE IT UP, DERKSEN! YOUR GOAL MAY HAVE BEEN NOBLE, BUT WE'RE NOT GOING TO LET YOU BURY THESE PEOPLE JUST TO WIN A BATTLE.
THE NAME IS FROSTBYTE. AND I HAVE NO INTENTION OF "BURYING" THEM...
...I NEEDED LAST NIGHT TO INVERT MY SUIT'S INPUTS TO HEAT GENERATORS!
I CREATED THE SNOW SO I COULD MELT IT IN A MASSIVE RUNOFF AND FLOOD THIS PLACE FROM THE FACE OF THE PLANET!

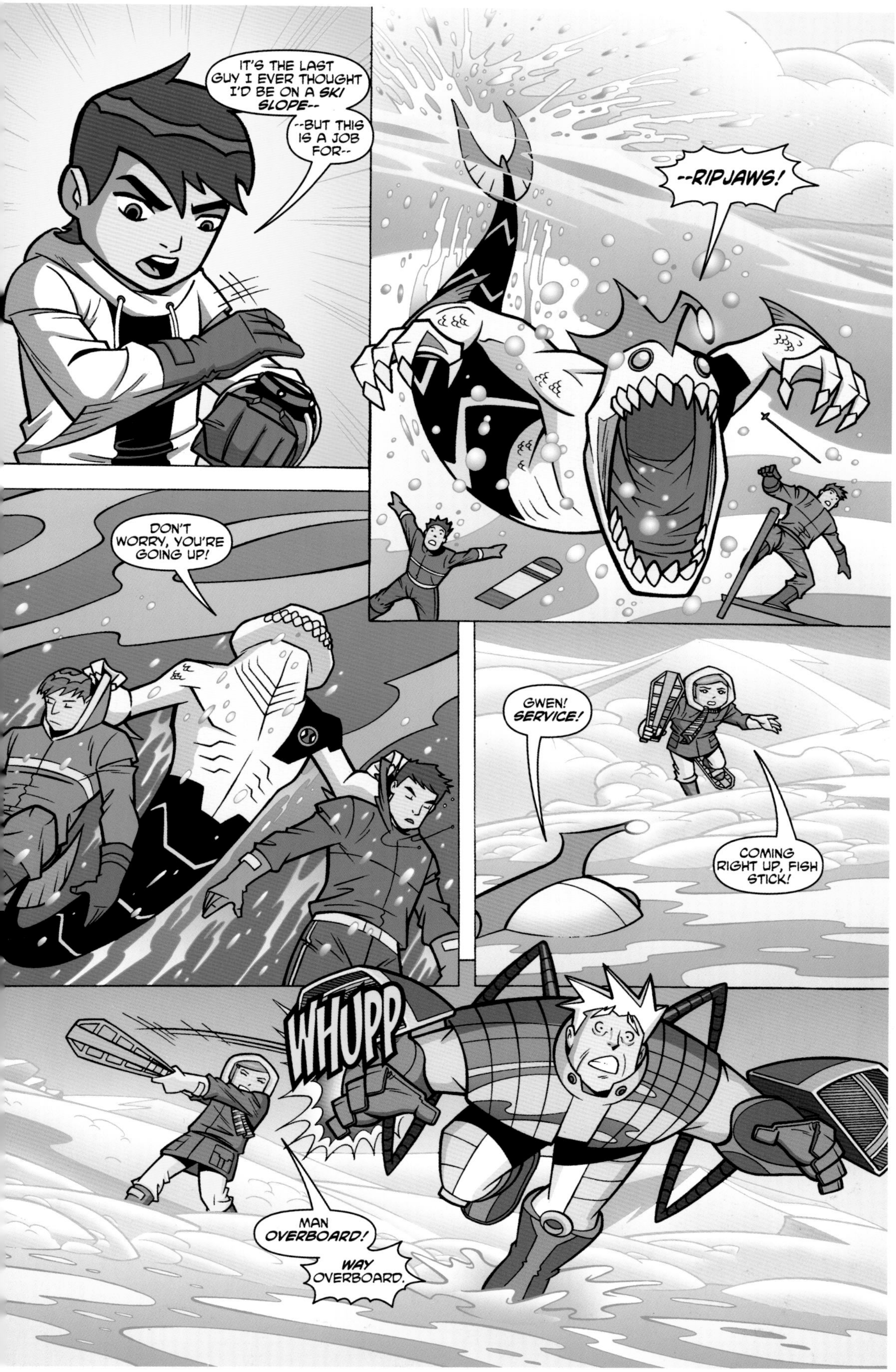

IT'S THE LAST GUY I EVER THOUGHT I'D BE ON A SKI SLOPE--
--BUT THIS IS A JOB FOR--
--RIPJAWS!
DON'T WORRY, YOU'RE GOING UP!
GWEN! SERVICE!
COMING RIGHT UP, FISH STICK!
WHUPP
MAN OVERBOARD!
WAY OVERBOARD.

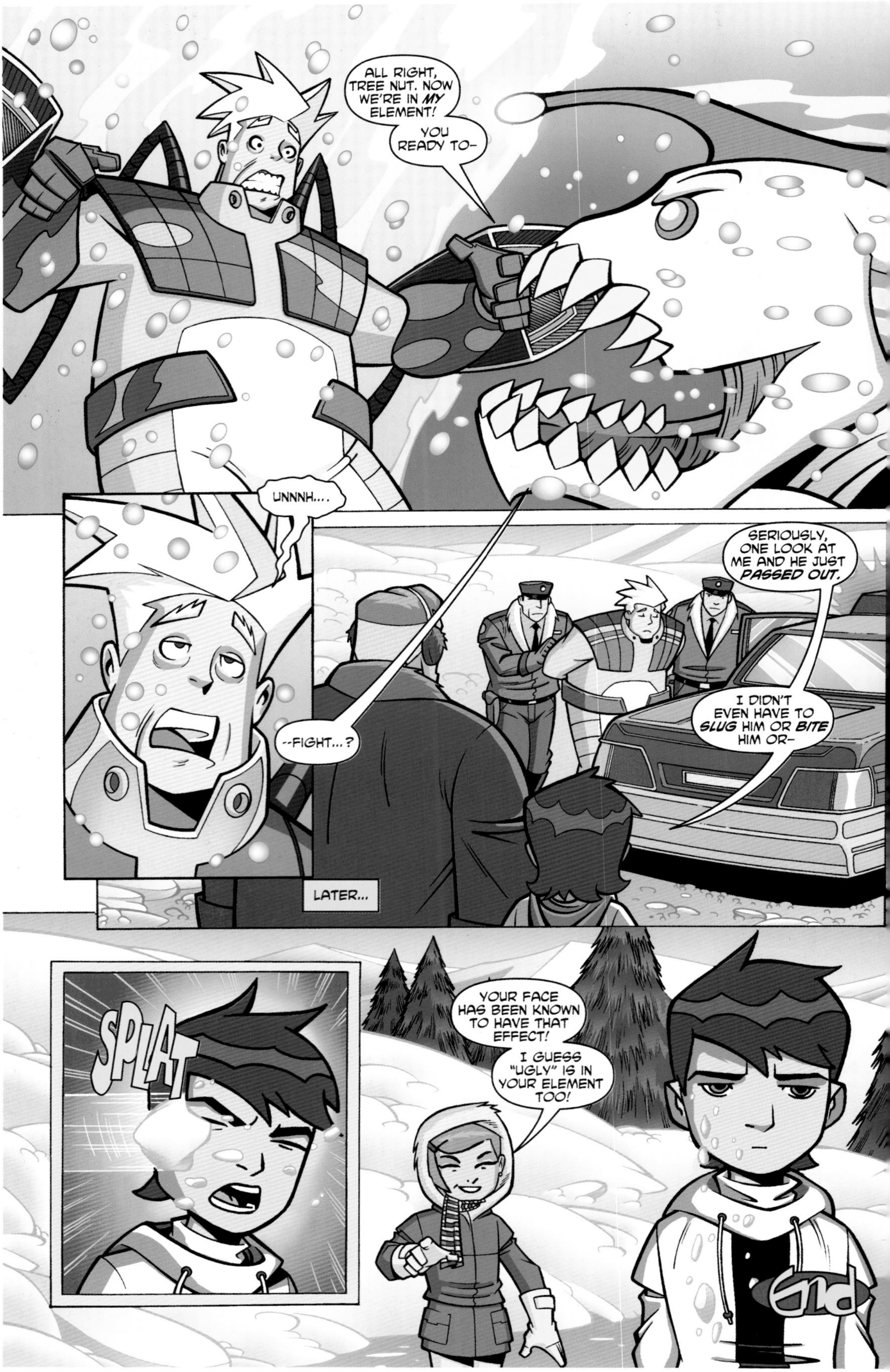
ALL RIGHT, TREE NUT. NOW WE'RE IN *MY* ELEMENT!
YOU READY TO–
UNNNH....
--FIGHT...?
LATER...
SERIOUSLY, ONE LOOK AT ME AND HE JUST *PASSED OUT.*
I DIDN'T EVEN HAVE TO *SLUG* HIM OR *BITE* HIM OR–
SPLAT
YOUR FACE HAS BEEN KNOWN TO HAVE THAT EFFECT!
I GUESS "UGLY" IS IN YOUR ELEMENT TOO!
END

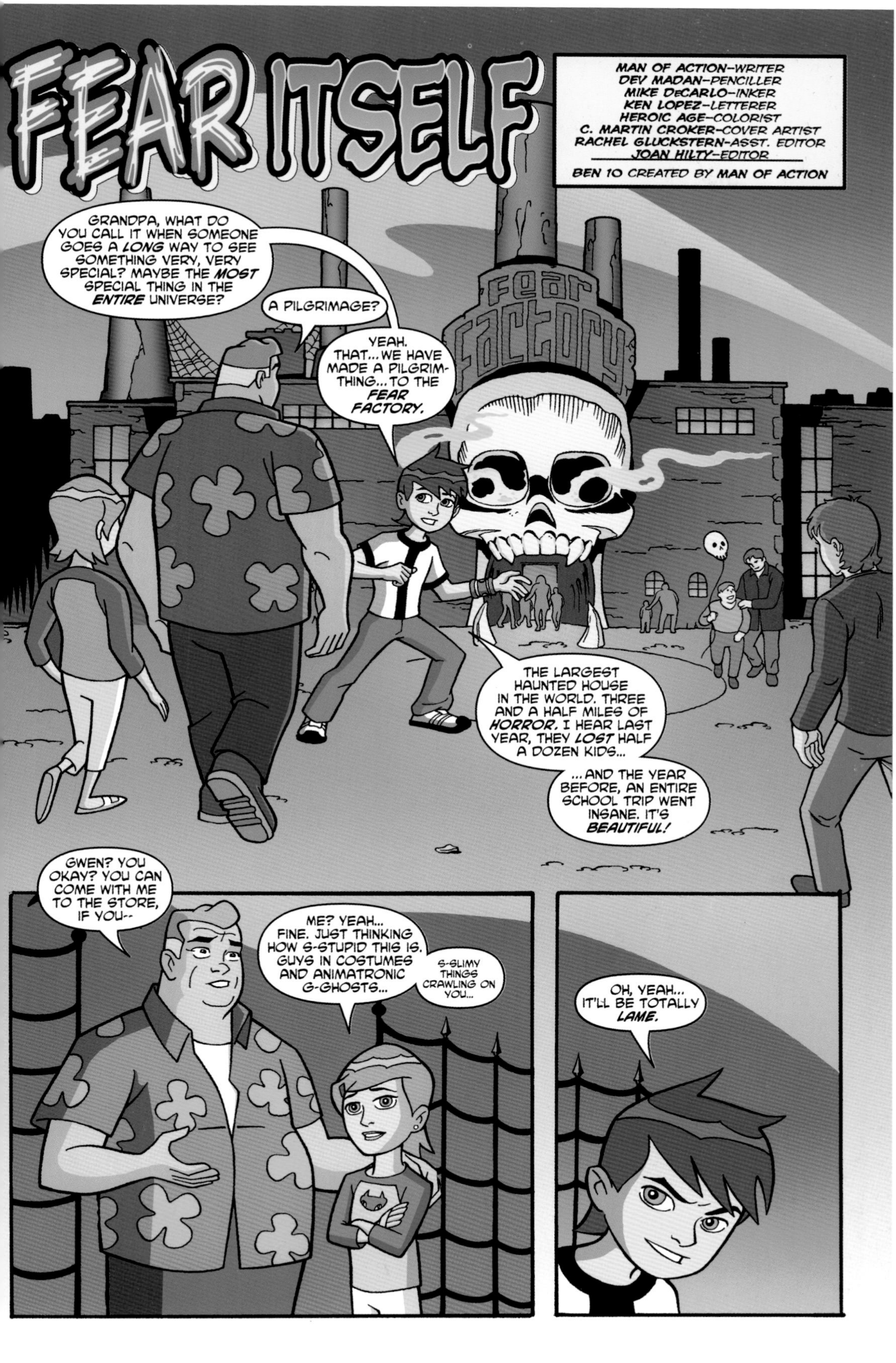

FEAR ITSELF
MAN OF ACTION–WRITER
DEV MADAN–PENCILLER
MIKE DeCARLO–INKER
KEN LOPEZ–LETTERER
HEROIC AGE–COLORIST
C. MARTIN CROKER–COVER ARTIST
RACHEL GLUCKSTERN–ASST. EDITOR
JOAN HILTY–EDITOR
BEN 10 CREATED BY MAN OF ACTION
GRANDPA, WHAT DO YOU CALL IT WHEN SOMEONE GOES A LONG WAY TO SEE SOMETHING VERY, VERY SPECIAL? MAYBE THE MOST SPECIAL THING IN THE ENTIRE UNIVERSE?
A PILGRIMAGE?
YEAH. THAT... WE HAVE MADE A PILGRIM-THING... TO THE FEAR FACTORY.
FEAR FACTORY
THE LARGEST HAUNTED HOUSE IN THE WORLD. THREE AND A HALF MILES OF HORROR. I HEAR LAST YEAR, THEY LOST HALF A DOZEN KIDS...
...AND THE YEAR BEFORE, AN ENTIRE SCHOOL TRIP WENT INSANE. IT'S BEAUTIFUL!
GWEN? YOU OKAY? YOU CAN COME WITH ME TO THE STORE, IF YOU--
ME? YEAH... FINE. JUST THINKING HOW S-STUPID THIS IS. GUYS IN COSTUMES AND ANIMATRONIC G-GHOSTS...
S-SLIMY THINGS CRAWLING ON YOU...
OH, YEAH... IT'LL BE TOTALLY LAME.

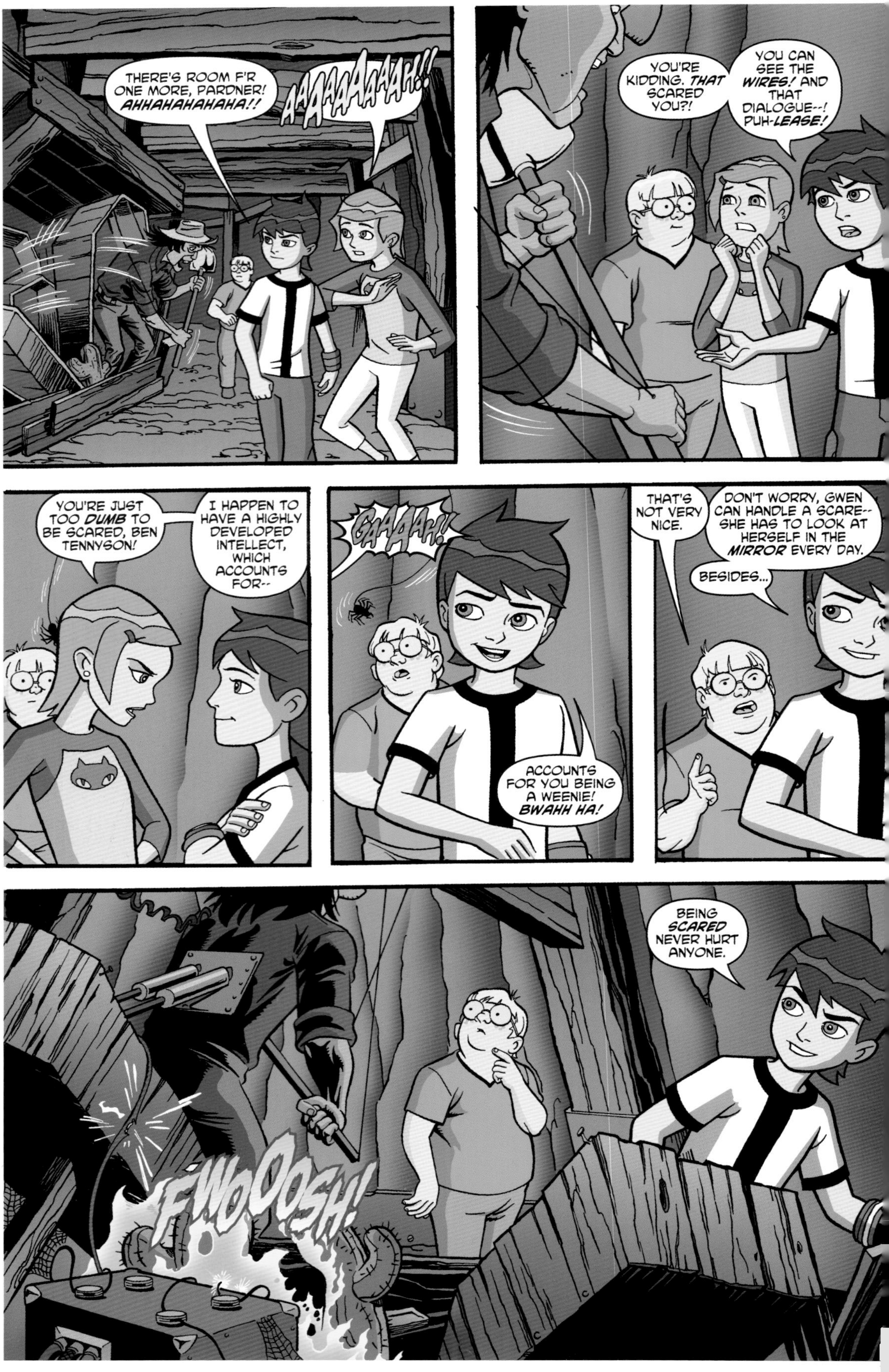
THERE'S ROOM F'R ONE MORE, PARDNER! AHHAHAHAHAHA!!
AAAAAAAAAAH!!
YOU'RE KIDDING. THAT SCARED YOU?!
YOU CAN SEE THE WIRES! AND THAT DIALOGUE--! PUH-LEASE!
YOU'RE JUST TOO DUMB TO BE SCARED, BEN TENNYSON!
I HAPPEN TO HAVE A HIGHLY DEVELOPED INTELLECT, WHICH ACCOUNTS FOR--
GAAAAH!
ACCOUNTS FOR YOU BEING A WEENIE! BWAHH HA!
THAT'S NOT VERY NICE.
DON'T WORRY, GWEN CAN HANDLE A SCARE-- SHE HAS TO LOOK AT HERSELF IN THE MIRROR EVERY DAY.
BESIDES...
BEING SCARED NEVER HURT ANYONE.
FWOOOSH!

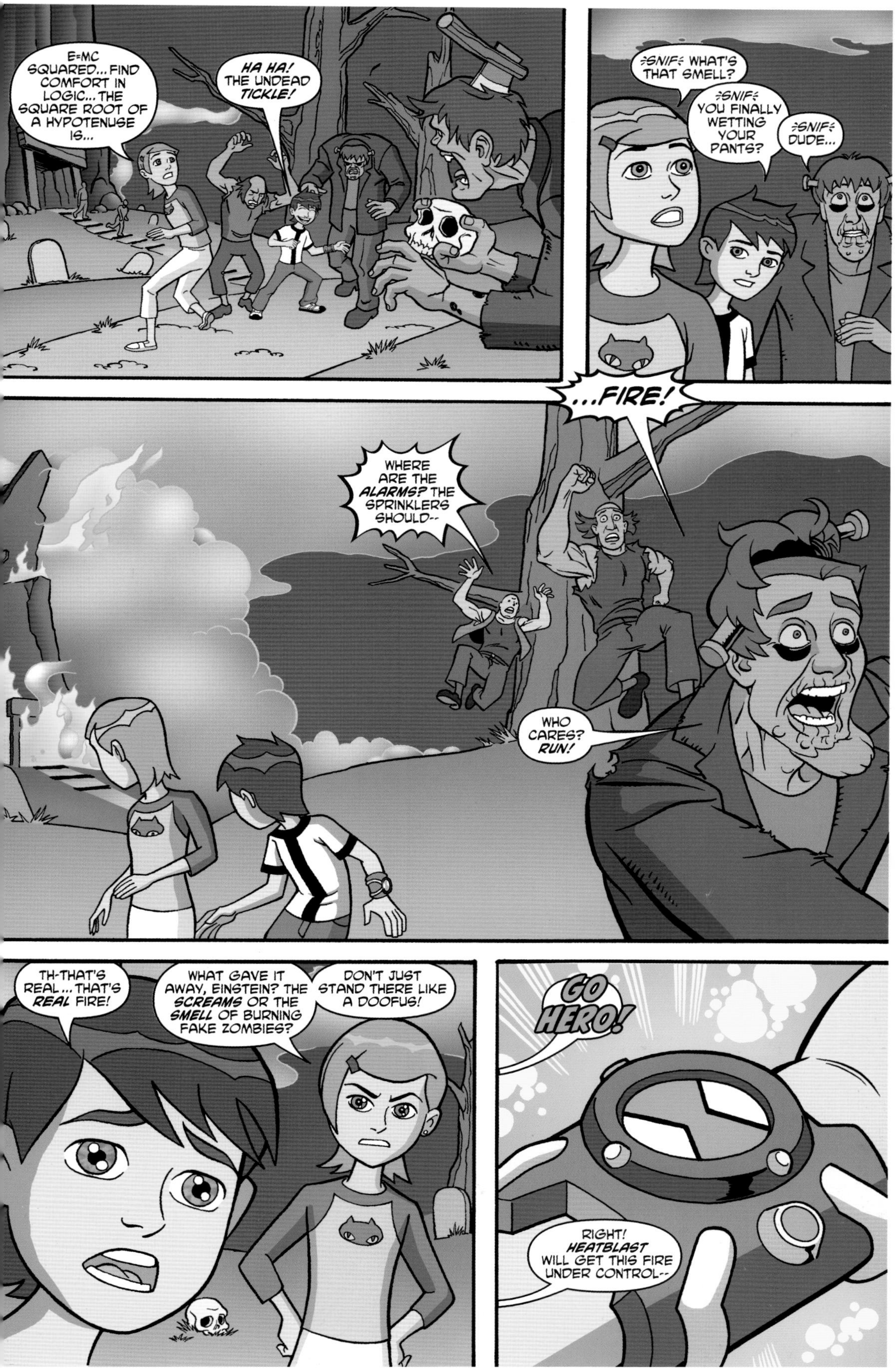
E=MC SQUARED... FIND COMFORT IN LOGIC... THE SQUARE ROOT OF A HYPOTENUSE IS...
HA HA! THE UNDEAD TICKLE!
SNIF WHAT'S THAT SMELL?
SNIF YOU FINALLY WETTING YOUR PANTS?
SNIF DUDE...
...FIRE!
WHERE ARE THE ALARMS? THE SPRINKLERS SHOULD--
WHO CARES? RUN!
TH-THAT'S REAL... THAT'S REAL FIRE!
WHAT GAVE IT AWAY, EINSTEIN? THE SCREAMS OR THE SMELL OF BURNING FAKE ZOMBIES?
DON'T JUST STAND THERE LIKE A DOOFUS!
GO HERO!
RIGHT! HEATBLAST WILL GET THIS FIRE UNDER CONTROL--

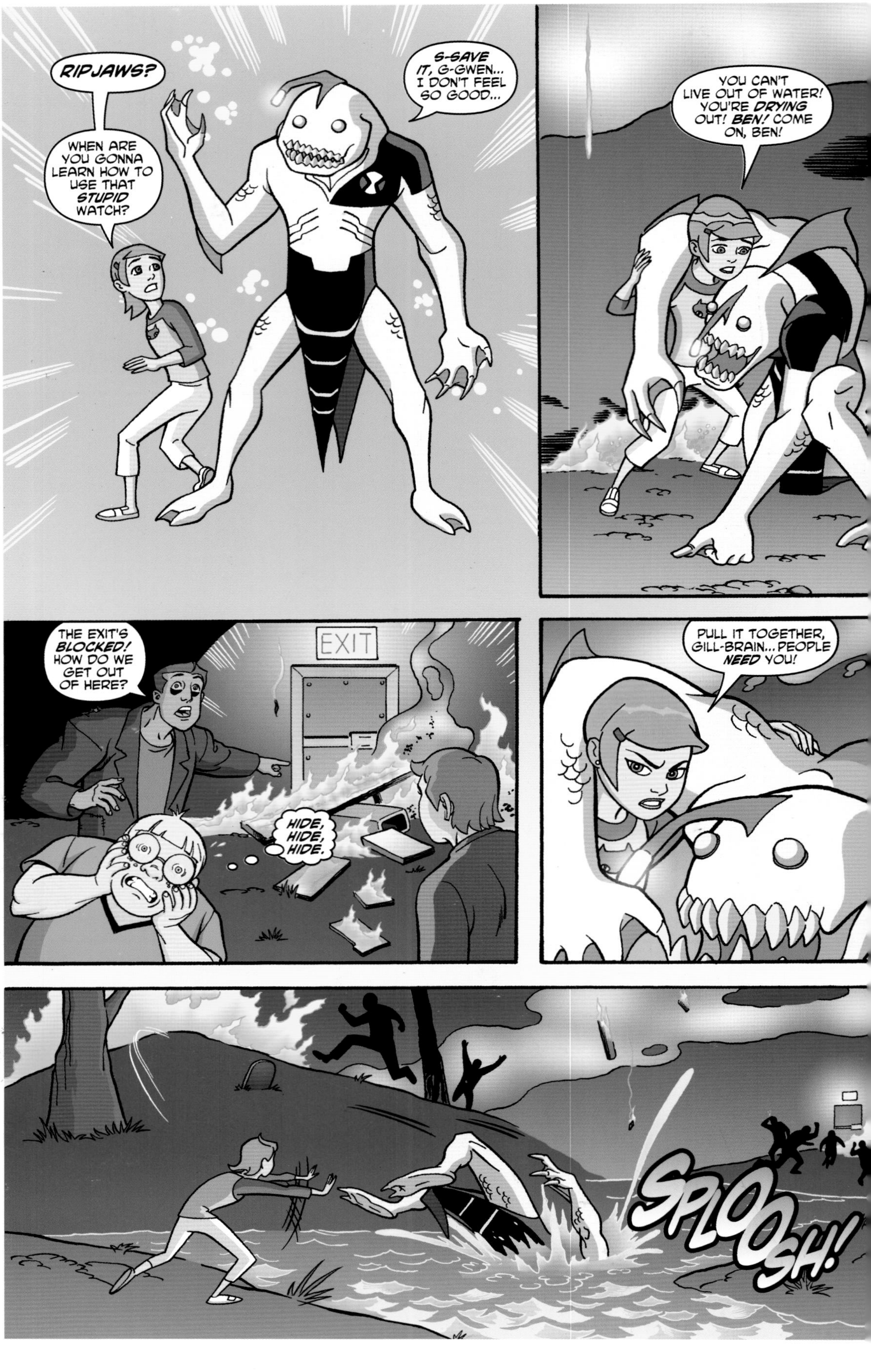
RIPJAWS?
WHEN ARE YOU GONNA LEARN HOW TO USE THAT STUPID WATCH?
S-SAVE IT, G-GWEN... I DON'T FEEL SO GOOD...
YOU CAN'T LIVE OUT OF WATER! YOU'RE DRYING OUT! BEN! COME ON, BEN!
THE EXIT'S BLOCKED! HOW DO WE GET OUT OF HERE?
EXIT
HIDE, HIDE, HIDE.
PULL IT TOGETHER, GILL-BRAIN... PEOPLE NEED YOU!
SPLOOSH!

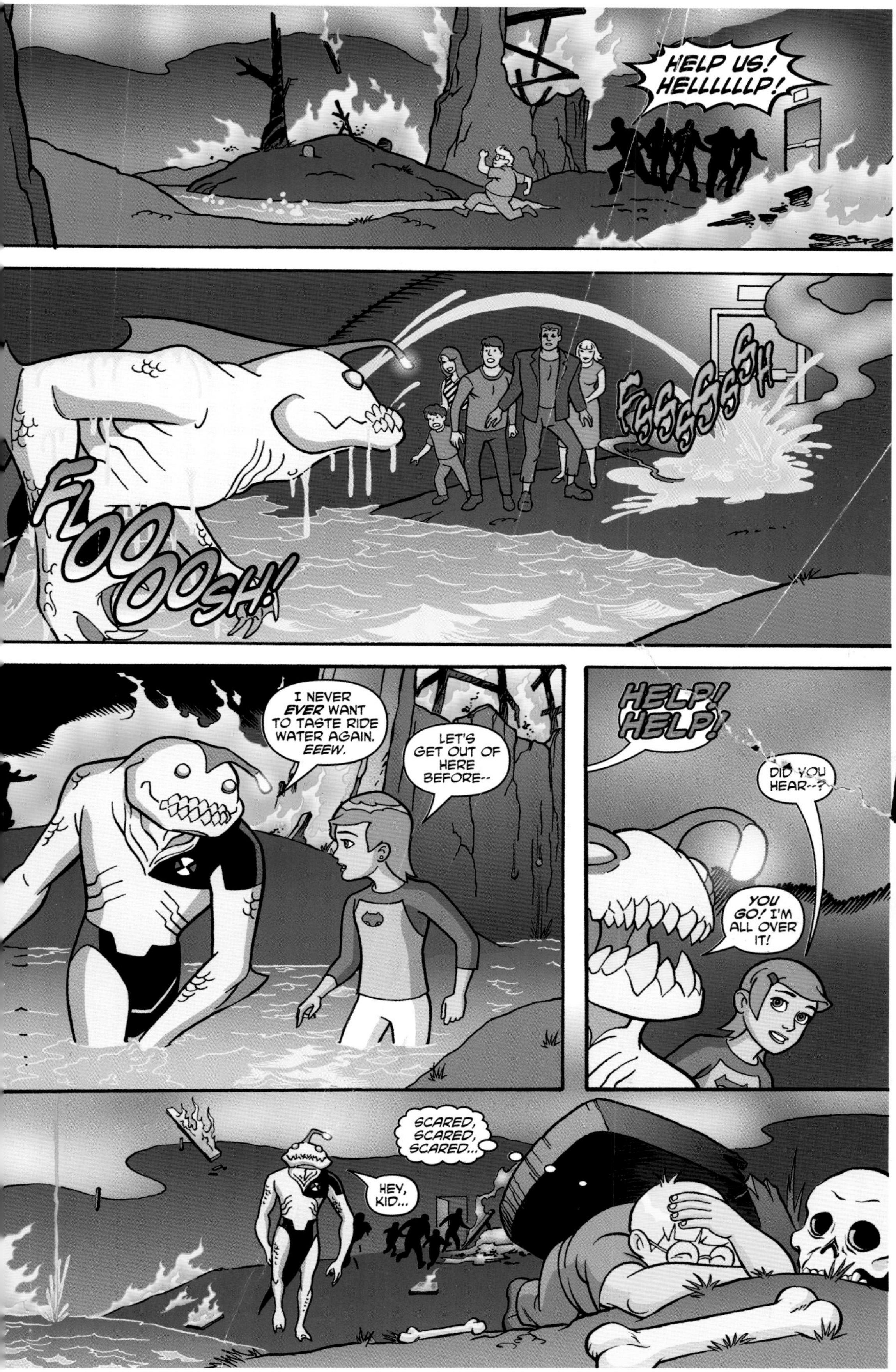

HELP US! HELLLLLLP!
FSSSSSSH
FLOOOOOSH!
I NEVER EVER WANT TO TASTE RIDE WATER AGAIN. EEEW.
LET'S GET OUT OF HERE BEFORE--
HELP! HELP!
DID YOU HEAR--?
YOU GO! I'M ALL OVER IT!
SCARED, SCARED, SCARED...
HEY, KID...

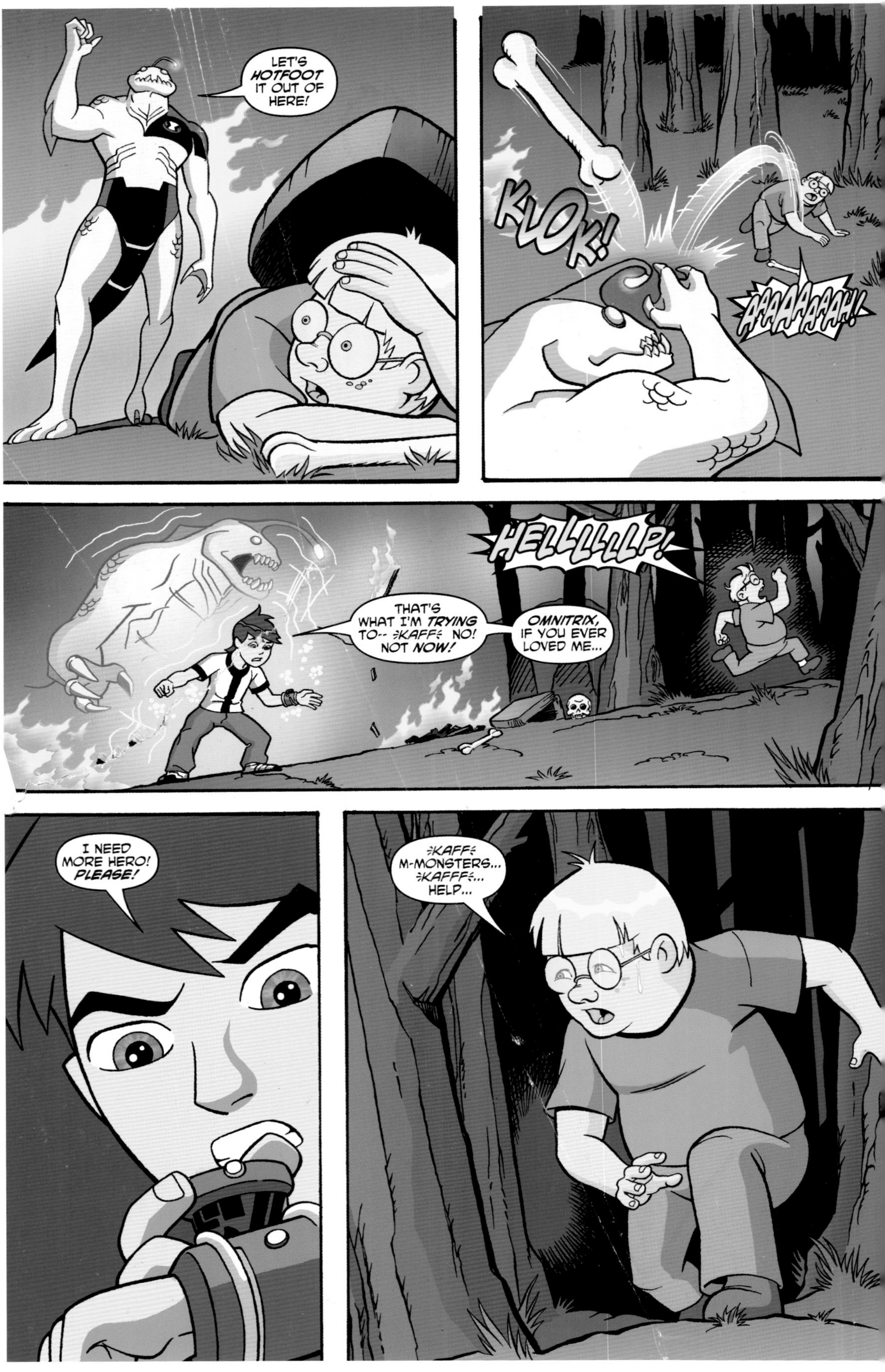
LET'S HOTFOOT IT OUT OF HERE!
KLOK!
AAAAAAAAH!
HELLLLLLLP!
THAT'S WHAT I'M TRYING TO-- KAFF NO! NOT NOW!
OMNITRIX, IF YOU EVER LOVED ME...
I NEED MORE HERO! PLEASE!
KAFF M-MONSTERS... KAFFF... HELP...

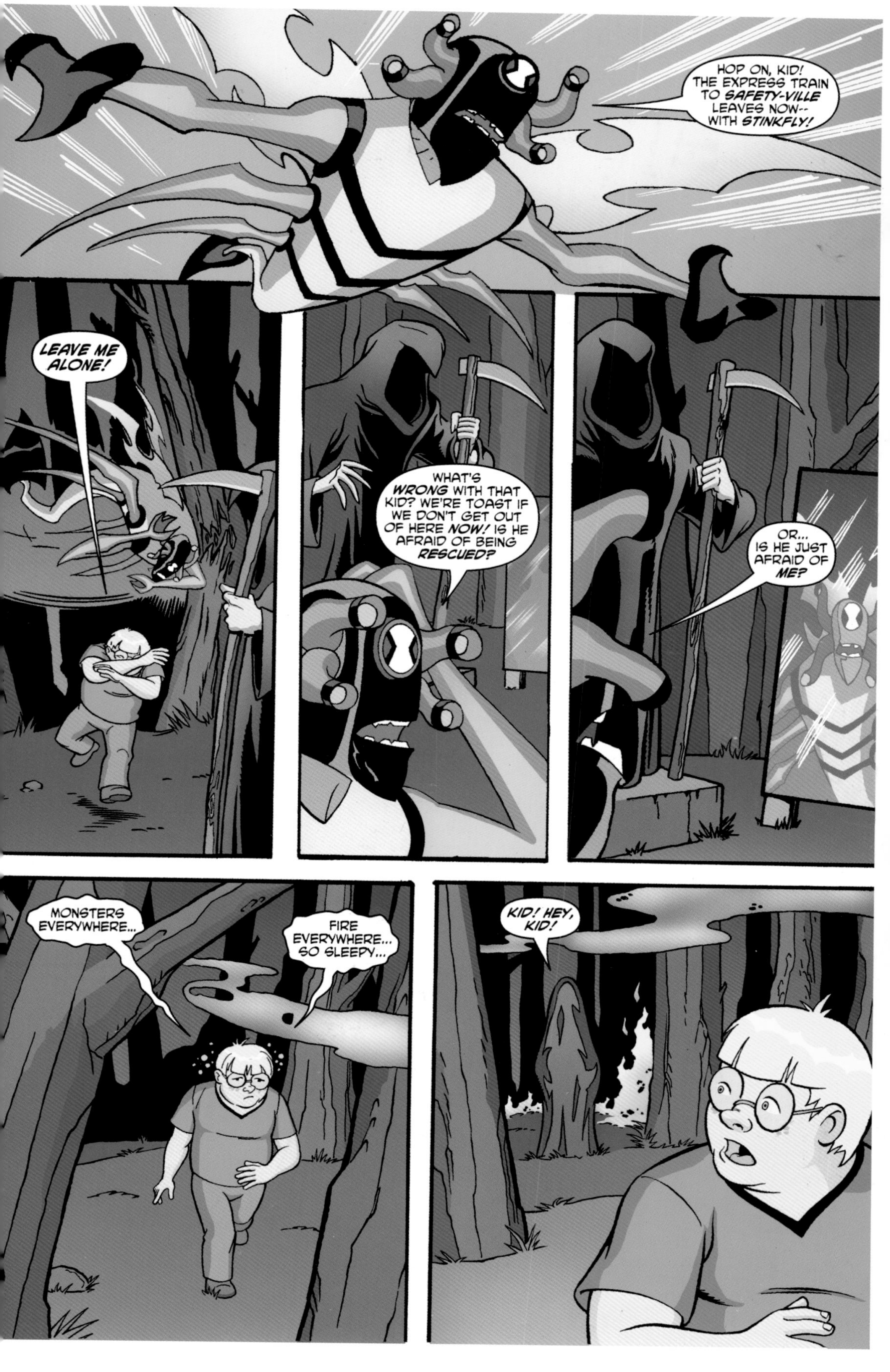
HOP ON, KID! THE EXPRESS TRAIN TO SAFETY-VILLE LEAVES NOW-- WITH STINKFLY!
LEAVE ME ALONE!
WHAT'S WRONG WITH THAT KID? WE'RE TOAST IF WE DON'T GET OUT OF HERE NOW! IS HE AFRAID OF BEING RESCUED?
OR... IS HE JUST AFRAID OF ME?
MONSTERS EVERYWHERE...
FIRE EVERYWHERE... SO SLEEPY...
KID! HEY, KID!

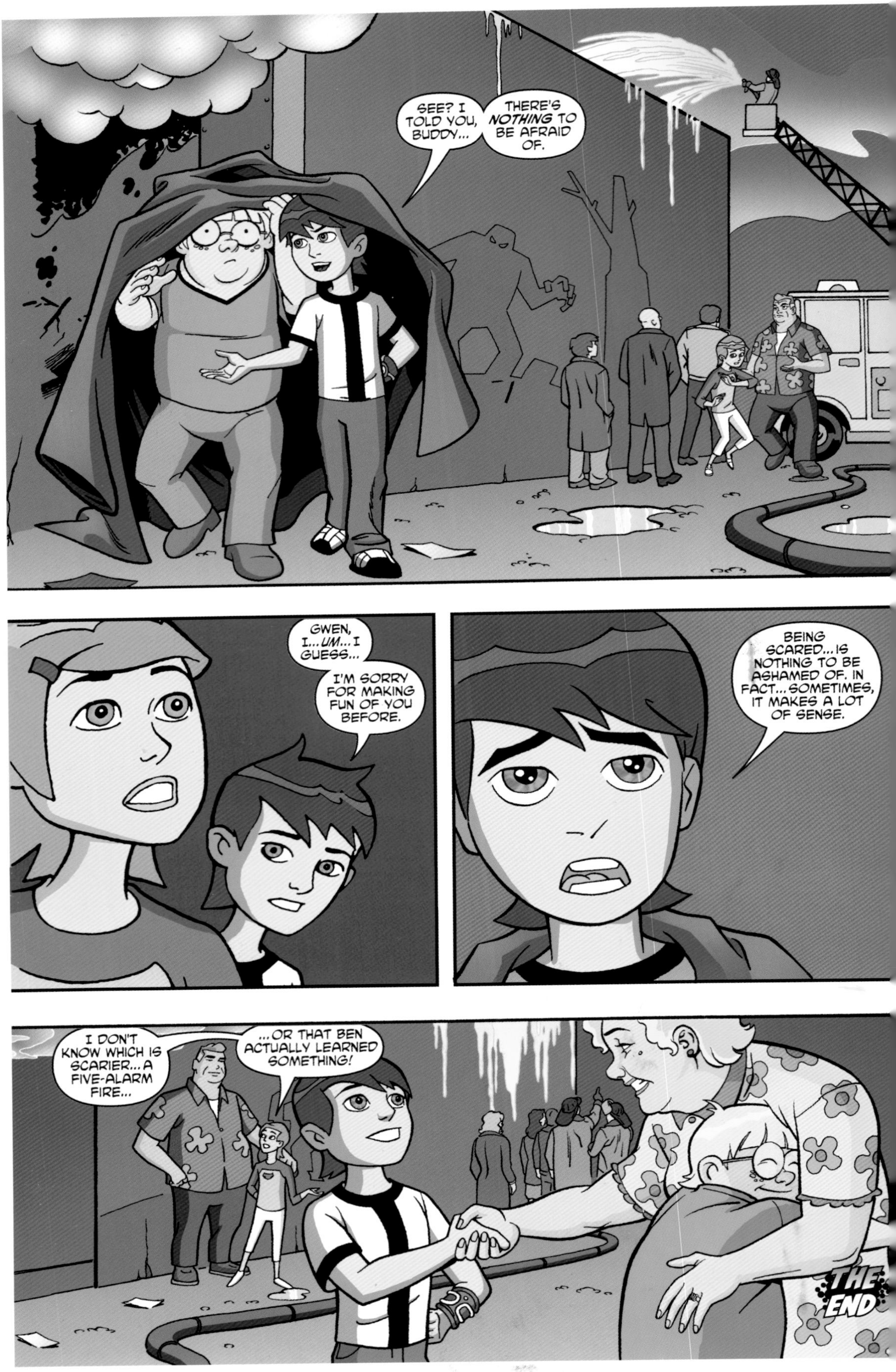
SEE? I TOLD YOU, BUDDY...
THERE'S *NOTHING* TO BE AFRAID OF.
GWEN, I... *UM*... I GUESS...
I'M SORRY FOR MAKING FUN OF YOU BEFORE.
BEING SCARED... IS NOTHING TO BE ASHAMED OF. IN FACT... SOMETIMES, IT MAKES A LOT OF SENSE.
I DON'T KNOW WHICH IS SCARIER... A FIVE-ALARM FIRE...
...OR THAT BEN ACTUALLY LEARNED SOMETHING!
THE END

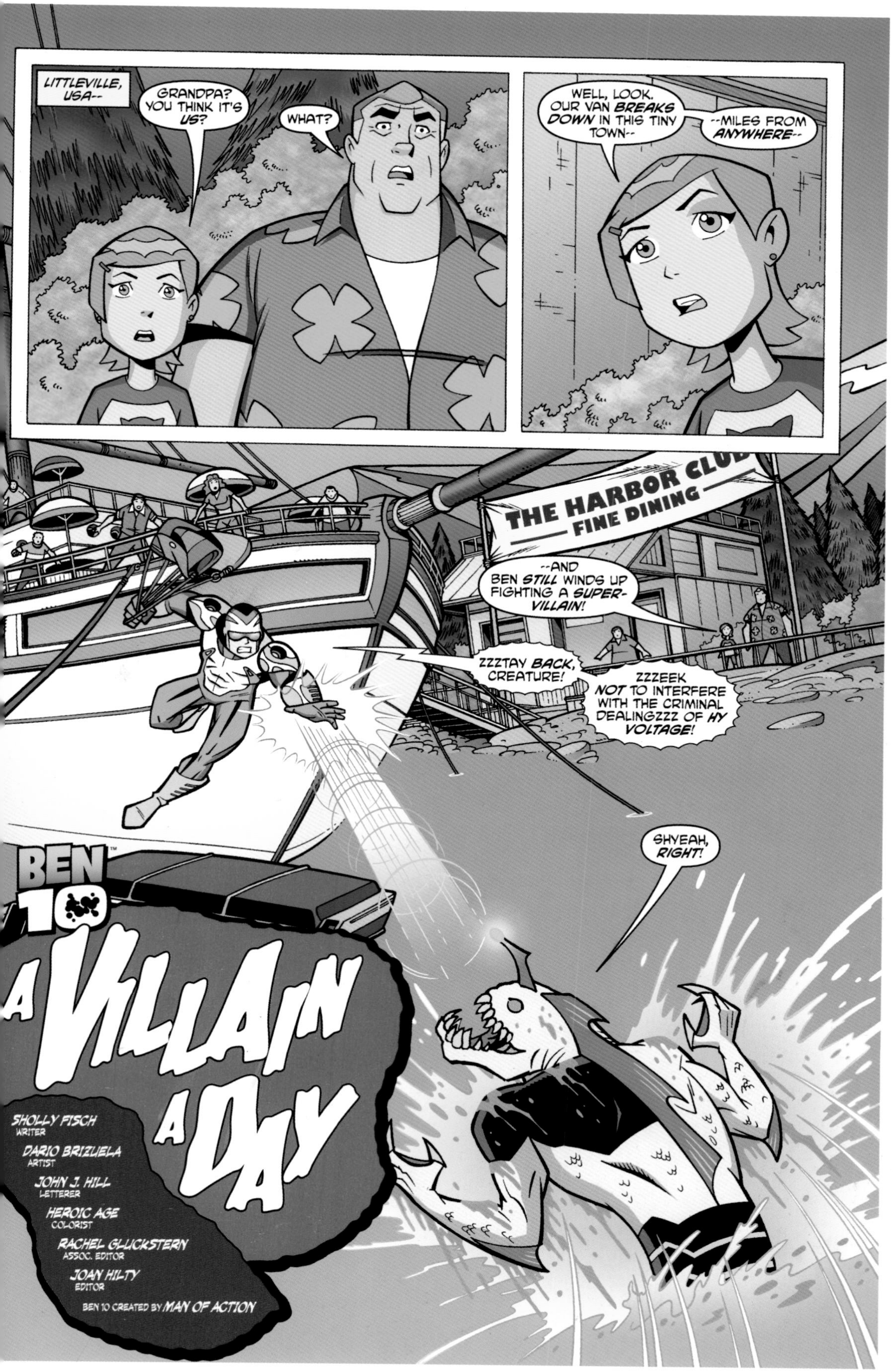
LITTLEVILLE, USA--
GRANDPA? YOU THINK IT'S US?
WHAT?
WELL, LOOK. OUR VAN BREAKS DOWN IN THIS TINY TOWN--
--MILES FROM ANYWHERE--
THE HARBOR CLUB
FINE DINING
--AND BEN STILL WINDS UP FIGHTING A SUPER-VILLAIN!
ZZZTAY BACK, CREATURE!
ZZZEEK NOT TO INTERFERE WITH THE CRIMINAL DEALINGZZZ OF HY VOLTAGE!
SHYEAH, RIGHT!
BEN 10
A VILLAIN A DAY
SHOLLY FISCH WRITER
DARIO BRIZUELA ARTIST
JOHN J. HILL LETTERER
HEROIC AGE COLORIST
RACHEL GLUCKSTERN ASSOC. EDITOR
JOAN HILTY EDITOR
BEN 10 CREATED BY MAN OF ACTION

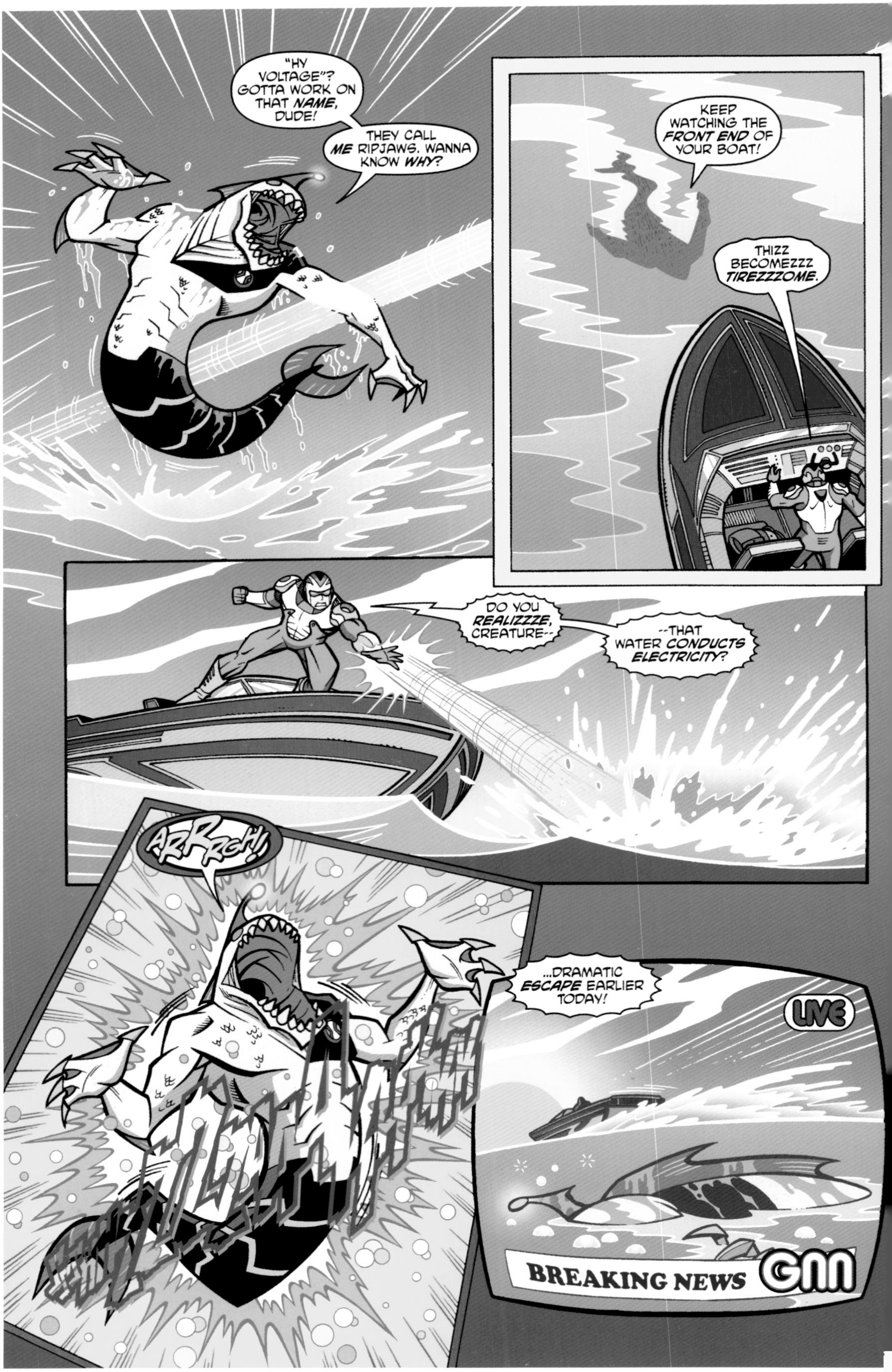
"HY VOLTAGE"? GOTTA WORK ON THAT NAME, DUDE!
THEY CALL ME RIPJAWS. WANNA KNOW WHY?
KEEP WATCHING THE FRONT END OF YOUR BOAT!
THIZZ BECOMEZZZ TIREZZZOME.
DO YOU REALIZZZE, CREATURE--
--THAT WATER CONDUCTS ELECTRICITY?
ARRRGH!
...DRAMATIC ESCAPE EARLIER TODAY!
LIVE
BREAKING NEWS
GNN

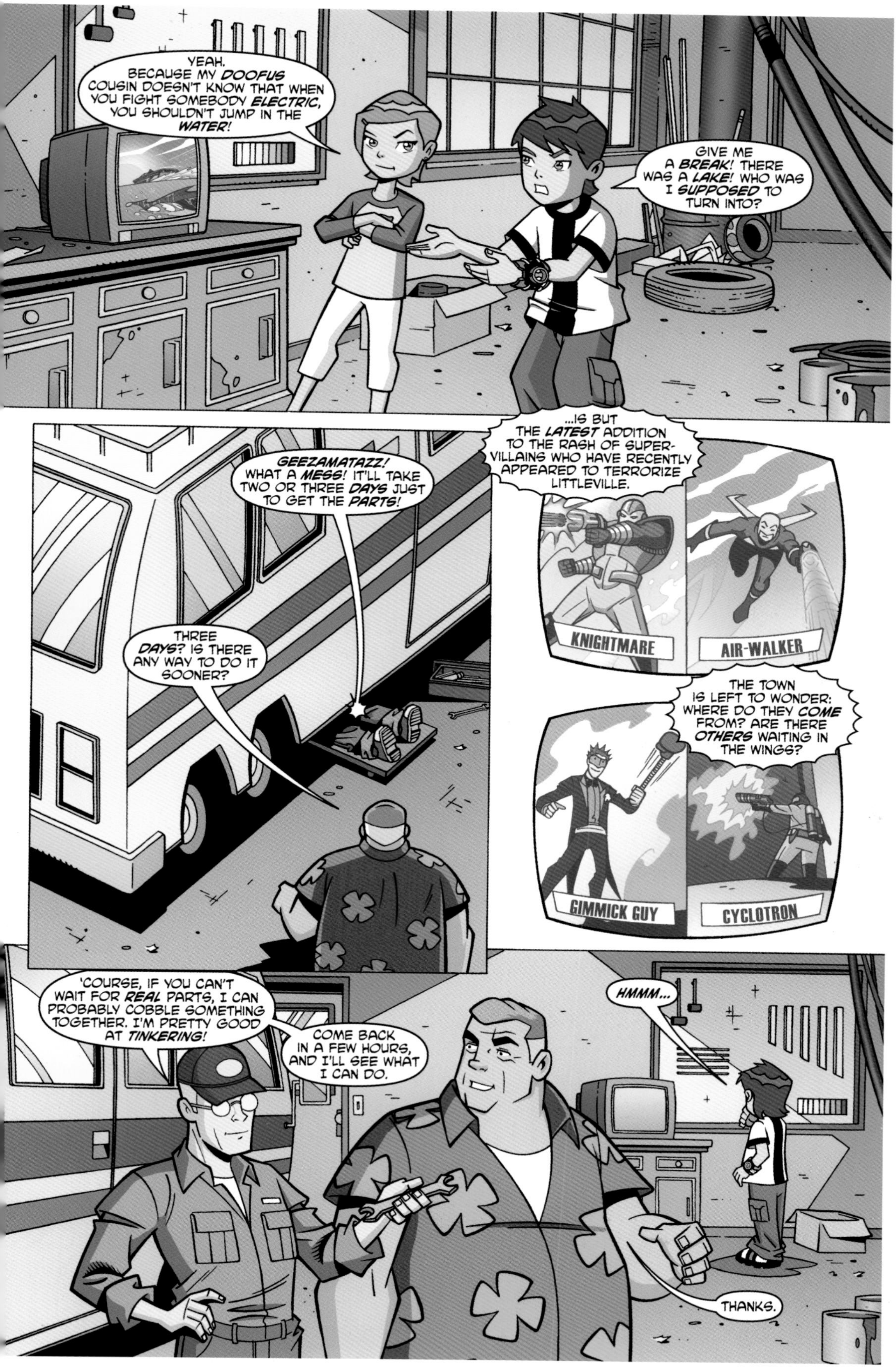
YEAH. BECAUSE MY DOOFUS COUSIN DOESN'T KNOW THAT WHEN YOU FIGHT SOMEBODY ELECTRIC, YOU SHOULDN'T JUMP IN THE WATER!
GIVE ME A BREAK! THERE WAS A LAKE! WHO WAS I SUPPOSED TO TURN INTO?
GEEZAMATAZZ! WHAT A MESS! IT'LL TAKE TWO OR THREE DAYS JUST TO GET THE PARTS!
THREE DAYS? IS THERE ANY WAY TO DO IT SOONER?
...IS BUT THE LATEST ADDITION TO THE RASH OF SUPER-VILLAINS WHO HAVE RECENTLY APPEARED TO TERRORIZE LITTLEVILLE.
KNIGHTMARE
AIR-WALKER
THE TOWN IS LEFT TO WONDER: WHERE DO THEY COME FROM? ARE THERE OTHERS WAITING IN THE WINGS?
GIMMICK GUY
CYCLOTRON
'COURSE, IF YOU CAN'T WAIT FOR REAL PARTS, I CAN PROBABLY COBBLE SOMETHING TOGETHER. I'M PRETTY GOOD AT TINKERING!
COME BACK IN A FEW HOURS, AND I'LL SEE WHAT I CAN DO.
HMMM...
THANKS.

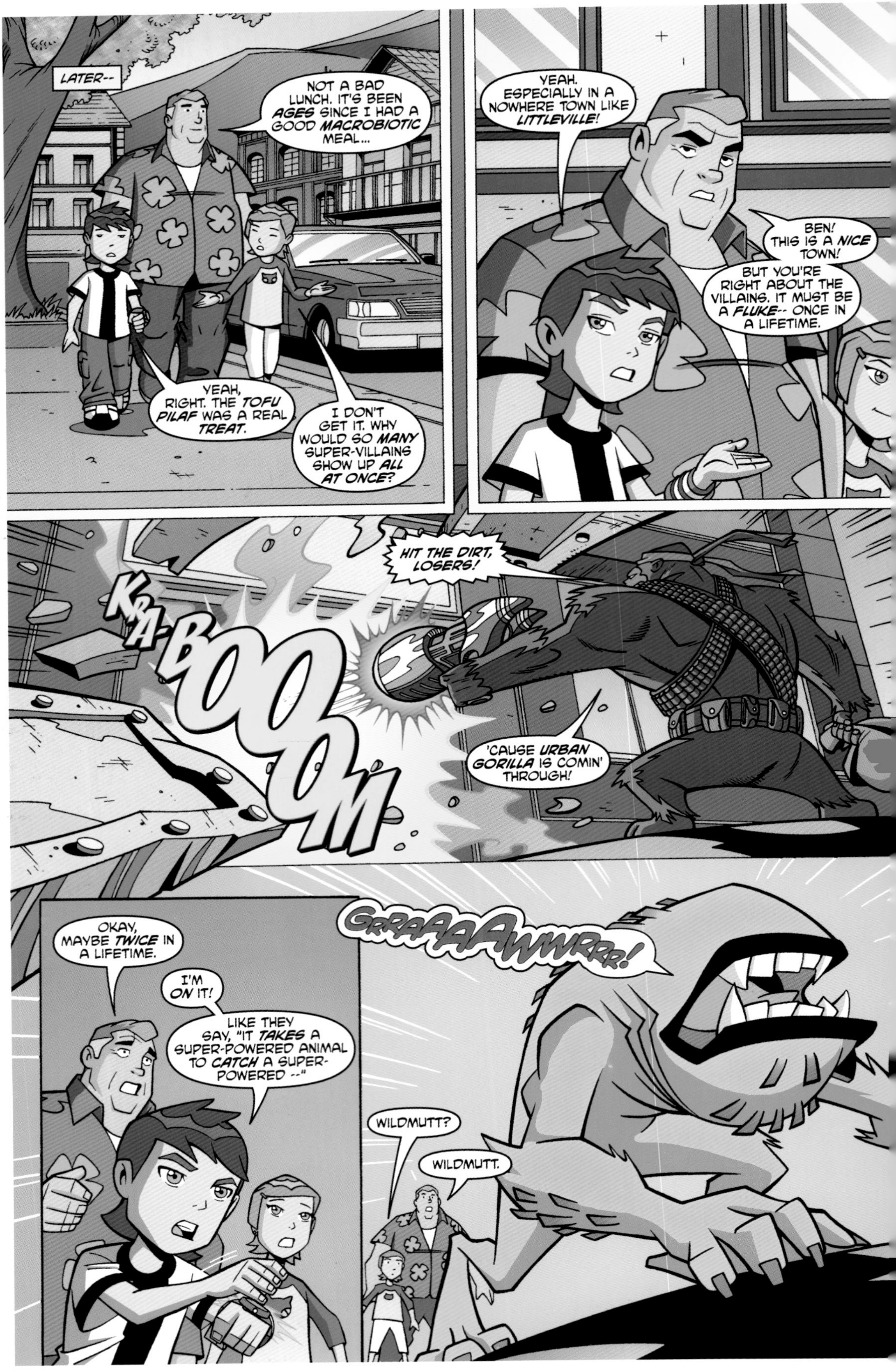
LATER--
NOT A BAD LUNCH. IT'S BEEN AGES SINCE I HAD A GOOD MACROBIOTIC MEAL...
YEAH, RIGHT. THE TOFU PILAF WAS A REAL TREAT.
I DON'T GET IT. WHY WOULD SO MANY SUPER-VILLAINS SHOW UP ALL AT ONCE?
YEAH. ESPECIALLY IN A NOWHERE TOWN LIKE LITTLEVILLE!
BEN! THIS IS A NICE TOWN!
BUT YOU'RE RIGHT ABOUT THE VILLAINS. IT MUST BE A FLUKE-- ONCE IN A LIFETIME.
HIT THE DIRT, LOSERS!
KRA-BOOOOM!
'CAUSE URBAN GORILLA IS COMIN' THROUGH!
OKAY, MAYBE TWICE IN A LIFETIME.
I'M ON IT!
LIKE THEY SAY, "IT TAKES A SUPER-POWERED ANIMAL TO CATCH A SUPER-POWERED --"
GRRAAAAWWRRR!
WILDMUTT?
WILDMUTT.

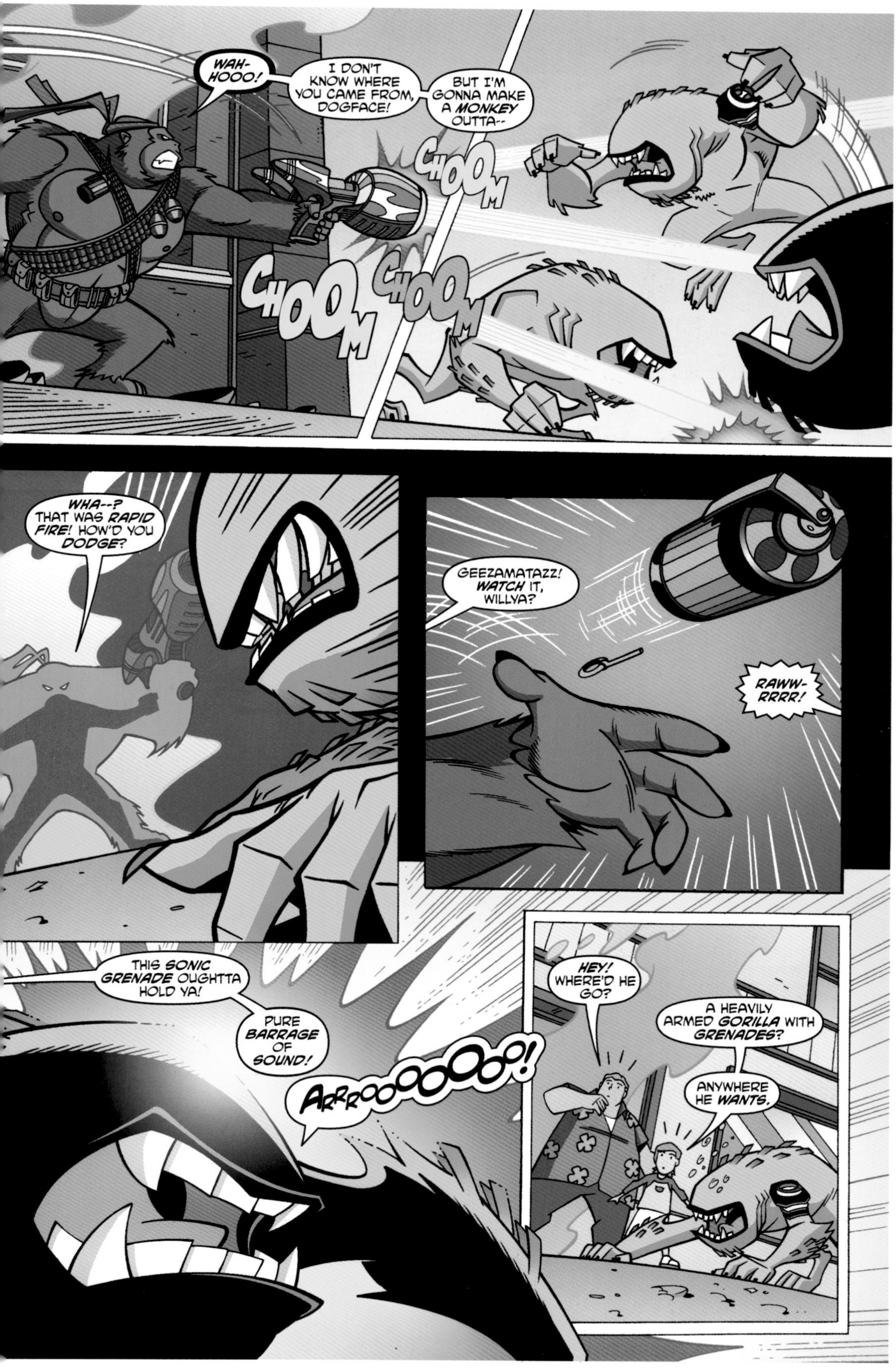
WAH-HOOO!
I DON'T KNOW WHERE YOU CAME FROM, DOGFACE!
BUT I'M GONNA MAKE A MONKEY OUTTA--
CHOOM
CHOOM
CHOOM
WHA--? THAT WAS RAPID FIRE! HOW'D YOU DODGE?
GEEZAMATAZZ! WATCH IT, WILLYA?
RAWW-RRRR!
THIS SONIC GRENADE OUGHTTA HOLD YA!
PURE BARRAGE OF SOUND!
ARRROOOOOOOO!
HEY! WHERE'D HE GO?
A HEAVILY ARMED GORILLA WITH GRENADES?
ANYWHERE HE WANTS.

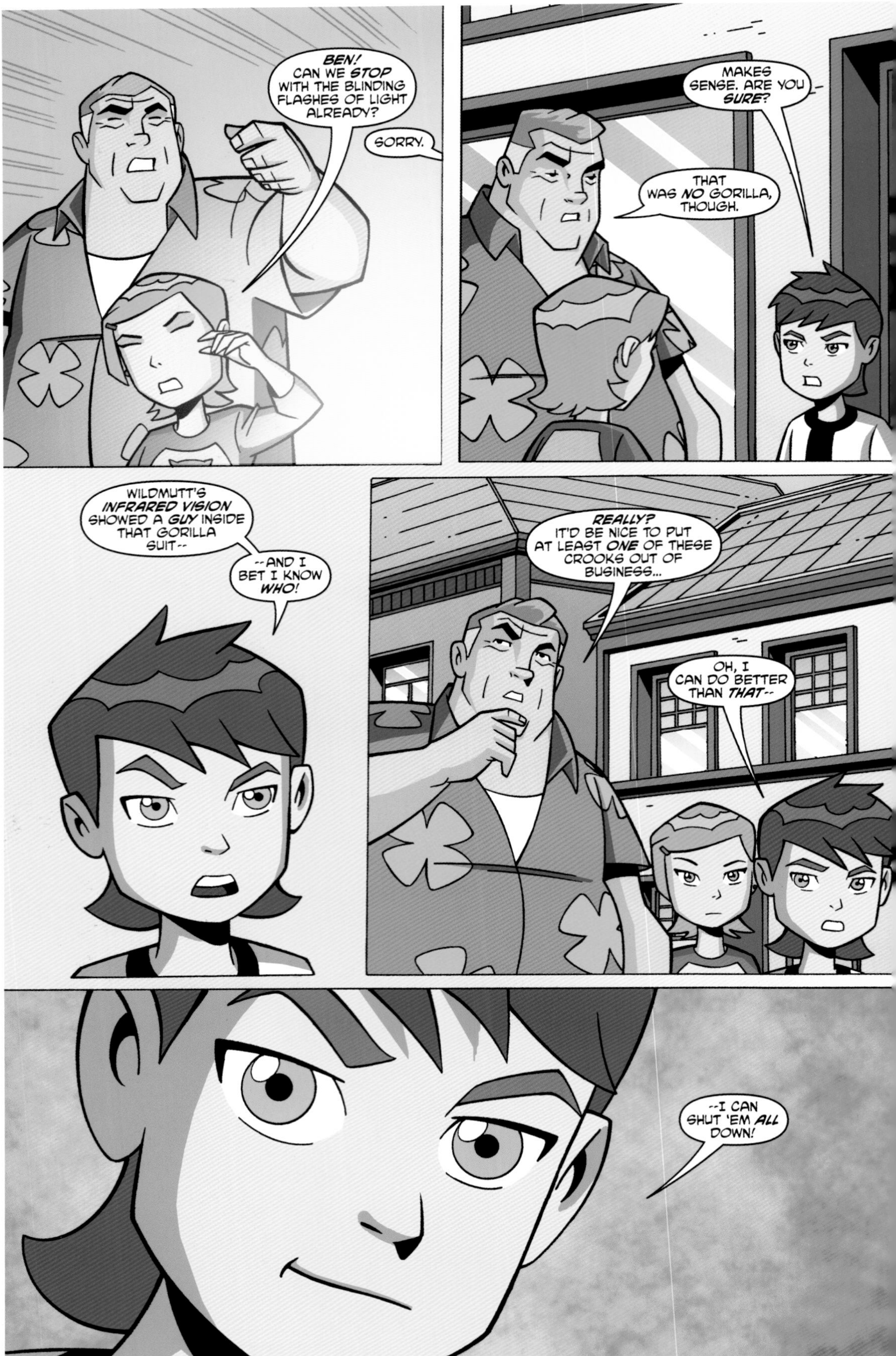
BEN! CAN WE STOP WITH THE BLINDING FLASHES OF LIGHT ALREADY?
SORRY.
MAKES SENSE. ARE YOU SURE?
THAT WAS NO GORILLA, THOUGH.
WILDMUTT'S INFRARED VISION SHOWED A GUY INSIDE THAT GORILLA SUIT--
--AND I BET I KNOW WHO!
REALLY? IT'D BE NICE TO PUT AT LEAST ONE OF THESE CROOKS OUT OF BUSINESS...
OH, I CAN DO BETTER THAN THAT--
--I CAN SHUT 'EM ALL DOWN!

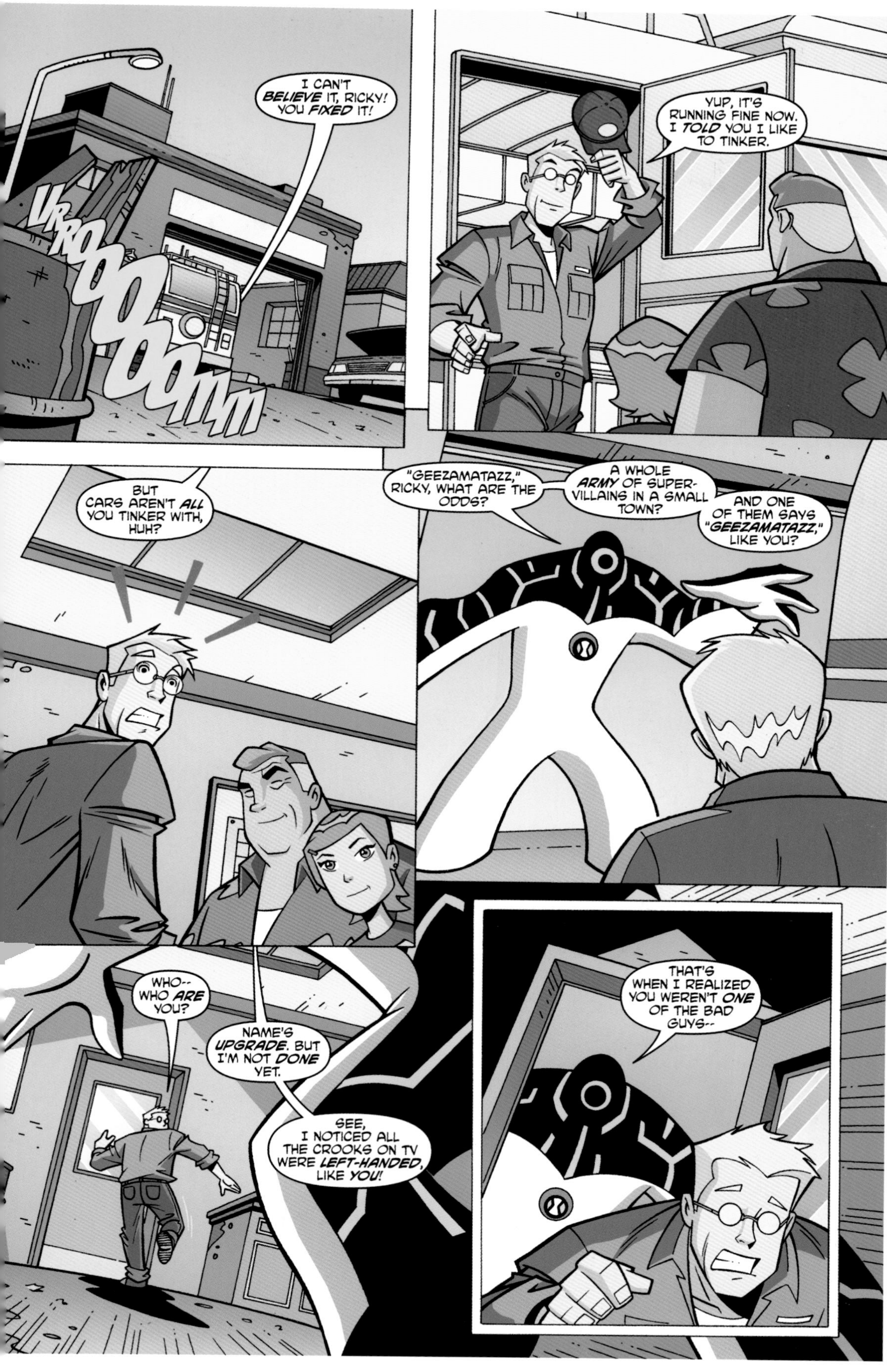
I CAN'T BELIEVE IT, RICKY! YOU FIXED IT!
VRROOOOOOMM
YUP, IT'S RUNNING FINE NOW. I TOLD YOU I LIKE TO TINKER.
BUT CARS AREN'T ALL YOU TINKER WITH, HUH?
"GEEZAMATAZZ," RICKY, WHAT ARE THE ODDS?
A WHOLE ARMY OF SUPER-VILLAINS IN A SMALL TOWN?
AND ONE OF THEM SAYS "GEEZAMATAZZ," LIKE YOU?
WHO-- WHO ARE YOU?
NAME'S UPGRADE. BUT I'M NOT DONE YET.
SEE, I NOTICED ALL THE CROOKS ON TV WERE LEFT-HANDED, LIKE YOU!
THAT'S WHEN I REALIZED YOU WEREN'T ONE OF THE BAD GUYS--

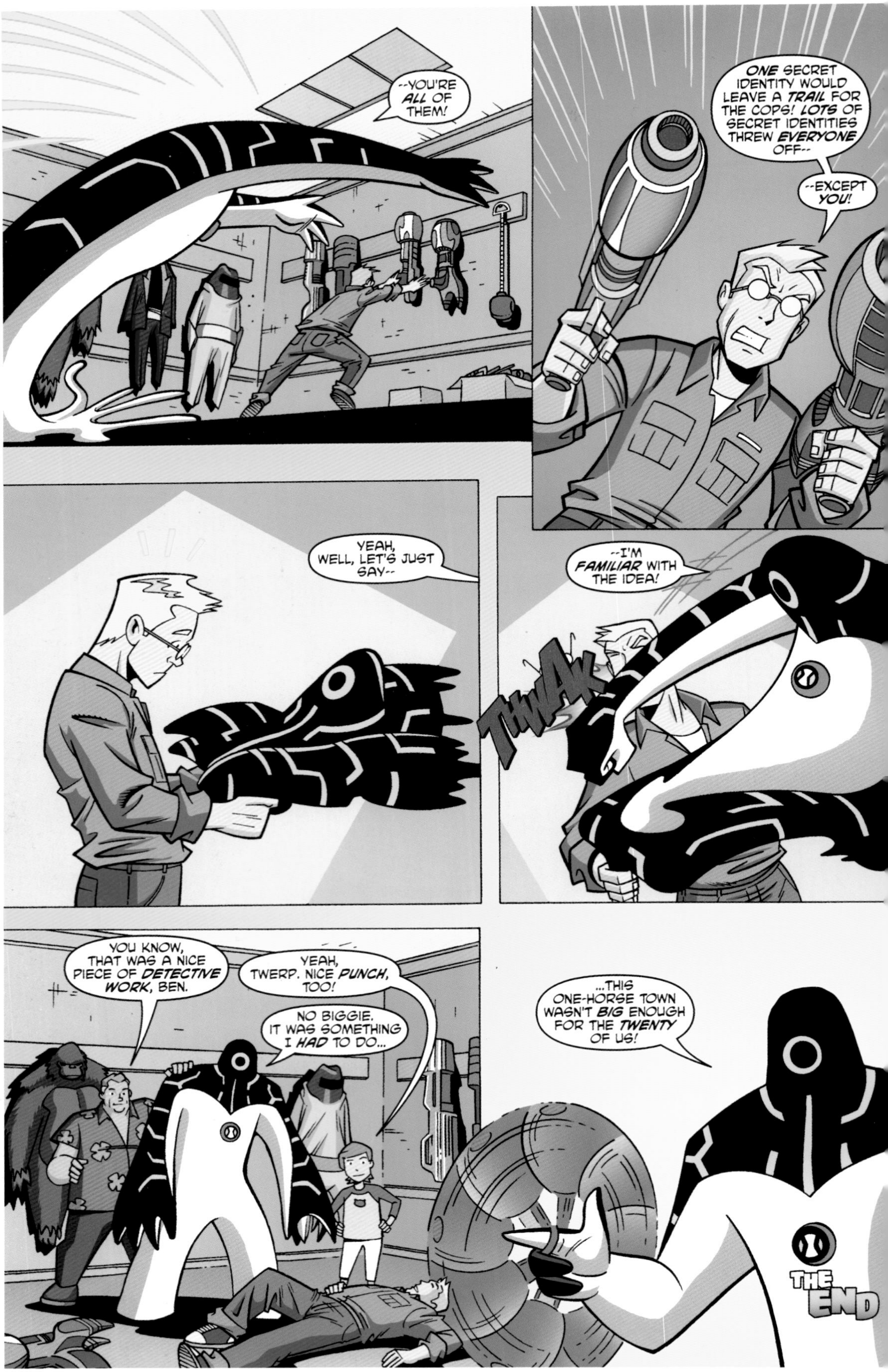
--YOU'RE ALL OF THEM!
ONE SECRET IDENTITY WOULD LEAVE A TRAIL FOR THE COPS! LOTS OF SECRET IDENTITIES THREW EVERYONE OFF--
--EXCEPT YOU!
YEAH, WELL, LET'S JUST SAY--
--I'M FAMILIAR WITH THE IDEA!
THWAK
YOU KNOW, THAT WAS A NICE PIECE OF DETECTIVE WORK, BEN.
YEAH, TWERP. NICE PUNCH, TOO!
NO BIGGIE. IT WAS SOMETHING I HAD TO DO...
...THIS ONE-HORSE TOWN WASN'T BIG ENOUGH FOR THE TWENTY OF US!
THE END

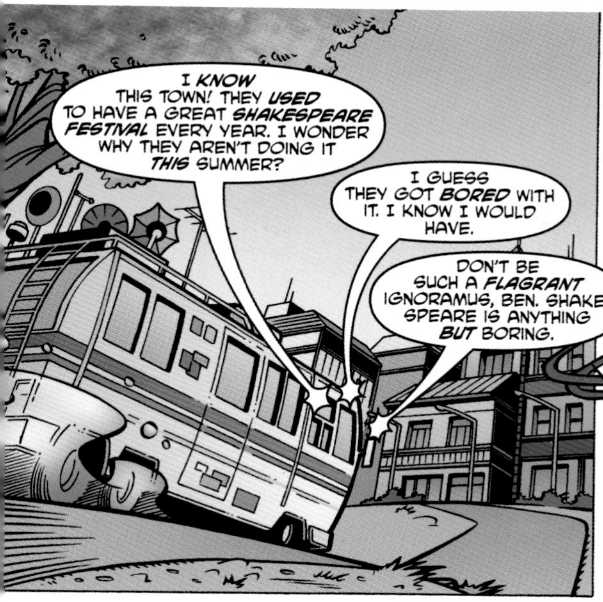
I KNOW THIS TOWN! THEY USED TO HAVE A GREAT SHAKESPEARE FESTIVAL EVERY YEAR. I WONDER WHY THEY AREN'T DOING IT THIS SUMMER?
I GUESS THEY GOT BORED WITH IT. I KNOW I WOULD HAVE.
DON'T BE SUCH A FLAGRANT IGNORAMUS, BEN. SHAKE-SPEARE IS ANYTHING BUT BORING.

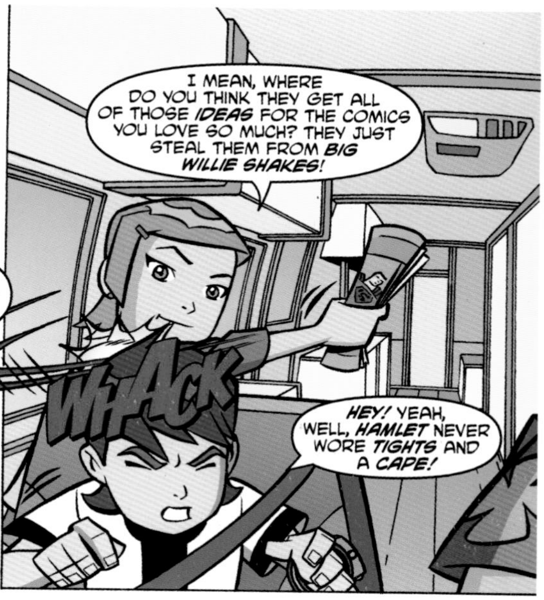
I MEAN, WHERE DO YOU THINK THEY GET ALL OF THOSE IDEAS FOR THE COMICS YOU LOVE SO MUCH? THEY JUST STEAL THEM FROM BIG WILLIE SHAKES!
WHACK
HEY! YEAH, WELL, HAMLET NEVER WORE TIGHTS AND A CAPE!

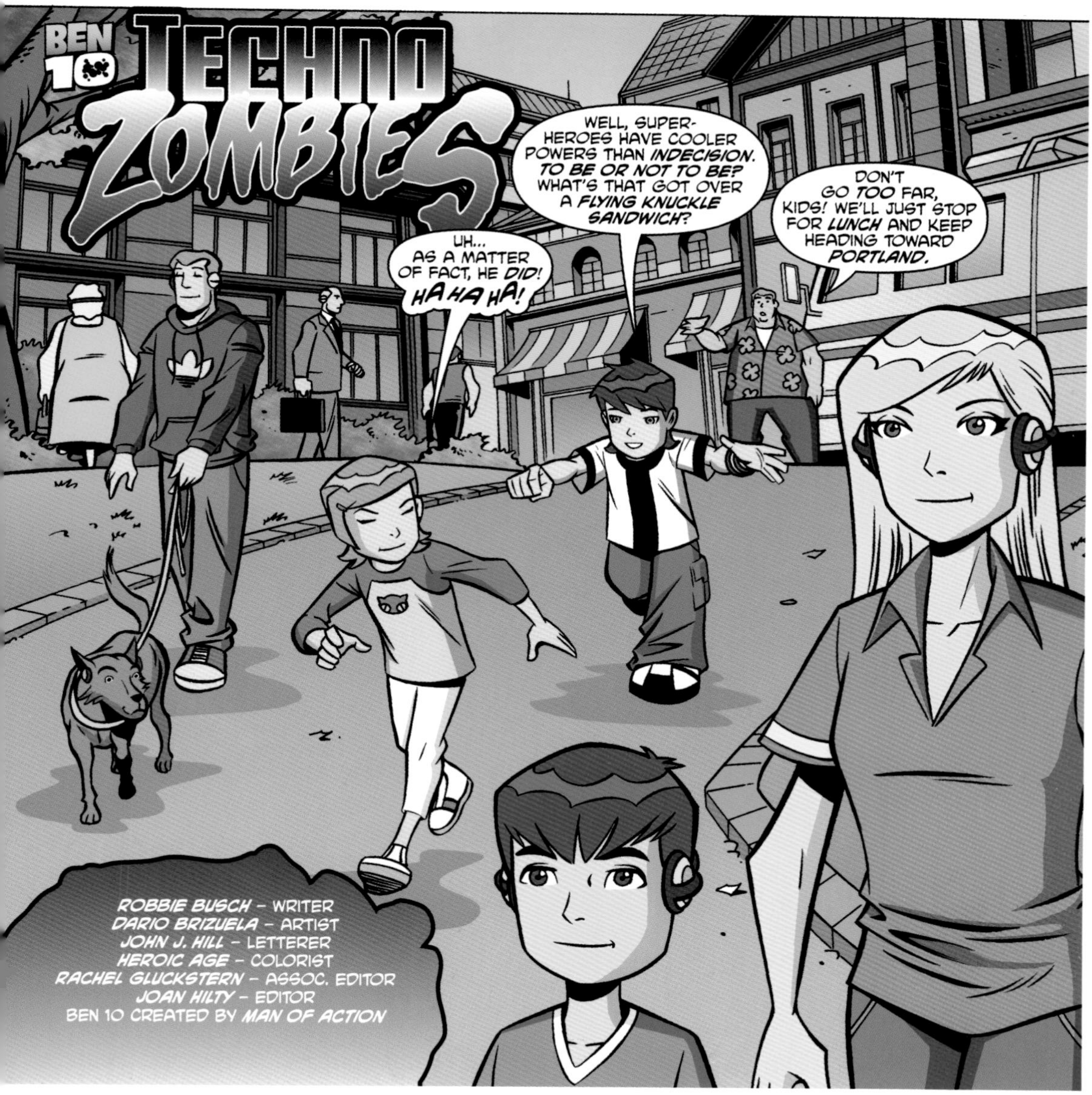
BEN 10
TECHNO ZOMBIES
WELL, SUPER-HEROES HAVE COOLER POWERS THAN INDECISION. TO BE OR NOT TO BE? WHAT'S THAT GOT OVER A FLYING KNUCKLE SANDWICH?
UH... AS A MATTER OF FACT, HE DID! HA HA HA!
DON'T GO TOO FAR, KIDS! WE'LL JUST STOP FOR LUNCH AND KEEP HEADING TOWARD PORTLAND.
ROBBIE BUSCH – WRITER
DARIO BRIZUELA – ARTIST
JOHN J. HILL – LETTERER
HEROIC AGE – COLORIST
RACHEL GLUCKSTERN – ASSOC. EDITOR
JOAN HILTY – EDITOR
BEN 10 CREATED BY MAN OF ACTION

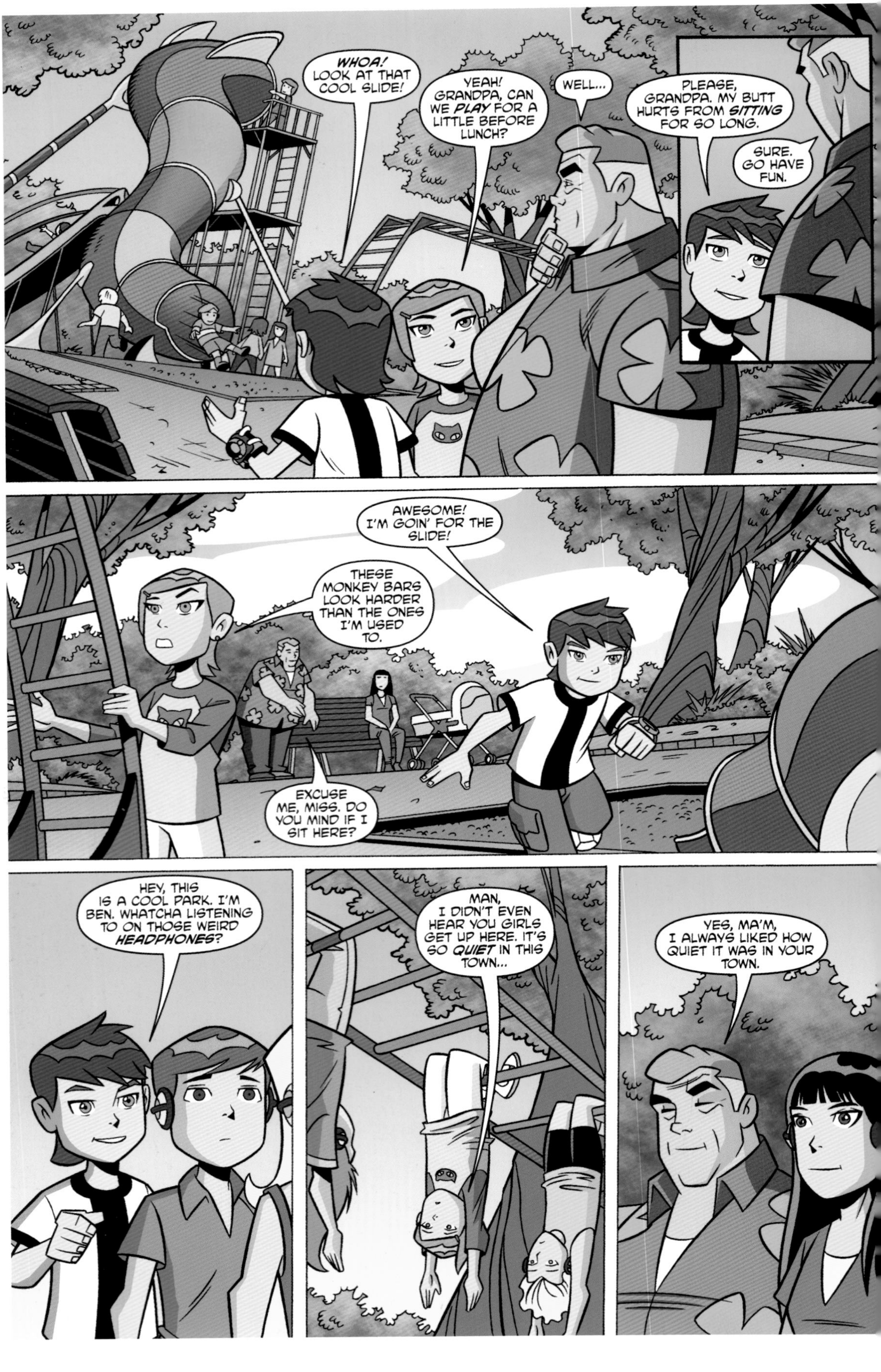
WHOA! LOOK AT THAT COOL SLIDE!
YEAH! GRANDPA, CAN WE PLAY FOR A LITTLE BEFORE LUNCH?
WELL...
PLEASE, GRANDPA. MY BUTT HURTS FROM SITTING FOR SO LONG.
SURE. GO HAVE FUN.
AWESOME! I'M GOIN' FOR THE SLIDE!
THESE MONKEY BARS LOOK HARDER THAN THE ONES I'M USED TO.
EXCUSE ME, MISS. DO YOU MIND IF I SIT HERE?
HEY, THIS IS A COOL PARK. I'M BEN. WHATCHA LISTENING TO ON THOSE WEIRD HEADPHONES?
MAN, I DIDN'T EVEN HEAR YOU GIRLS GET UP HERE. IT'S SO QUIET IN THIS TOWN...
YES, MA'M, I ALWAYS LIKED HOW QUIET IT WAS IN YOUR TOWN.

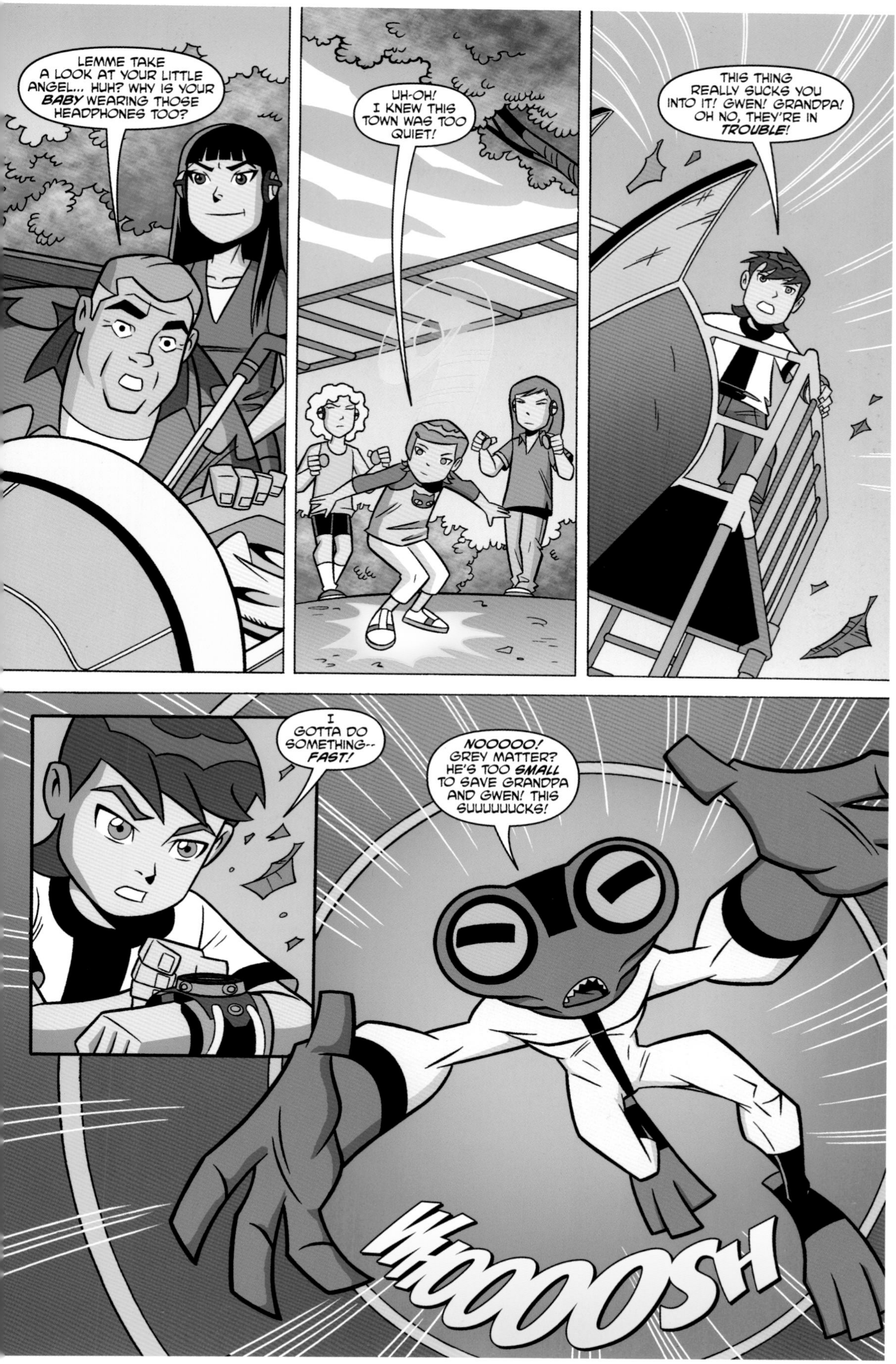
LEMME TAKE A LOOK AT YOUR LITTLE ANGEL... HUH? WHY IS YOUR BABY WEARING THOSE HEADPHONES TOO?
UH-OH! I KNEW THIS TOWN WAS TOO QUIET!
THIS THING REALLY SUCKS YOU INTO IT! GWEN! GRANDPA! OH NO, THEY'RE IN TROUBLE!
I GOTTA DO SOMETHING-- FAST!
NOOOOO! GREY MATTER? HE'S TOO SMALL TO SAVE GRANDPA AND GWEN! THIS SUUUUUUCKS!
WHOOOOSH

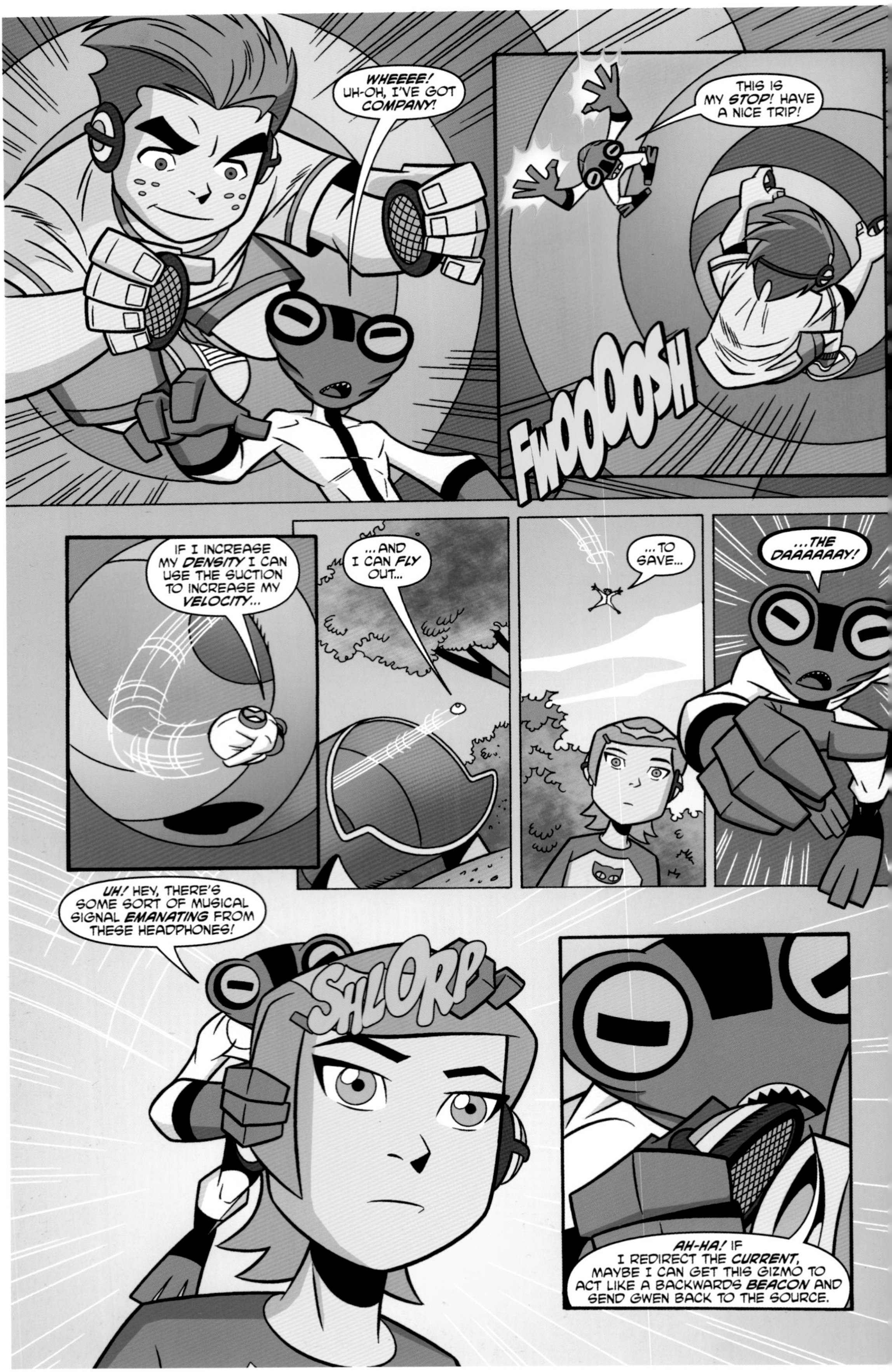

WHEEEE! UH-OH, I'VE GOT COMPANY!
THIS IS MY STOP! HAVE A NICE TRIP!
FWOOOOSH
IF I INCREASE MY DENSITY I CAN USE THE SUCTION TO INCREASE MY VELOCITY...
...AND I CAN FLY OUT...
...TO SAVE...
...THE DAAAAAAY!
UH! HEY, THERE'S SOME SORT OF MUSICAL SIGNAL EMANATING FROM THESE HEADPHONES!
SHLORP
AH-HA! IF I REDIRECT THE CURRENT, MAYBE I CAN GET THIS GIZMO TO ACT LIKE A BACKWARDS BEACON AND SEND GWEN BACK TO THE SOURCE.

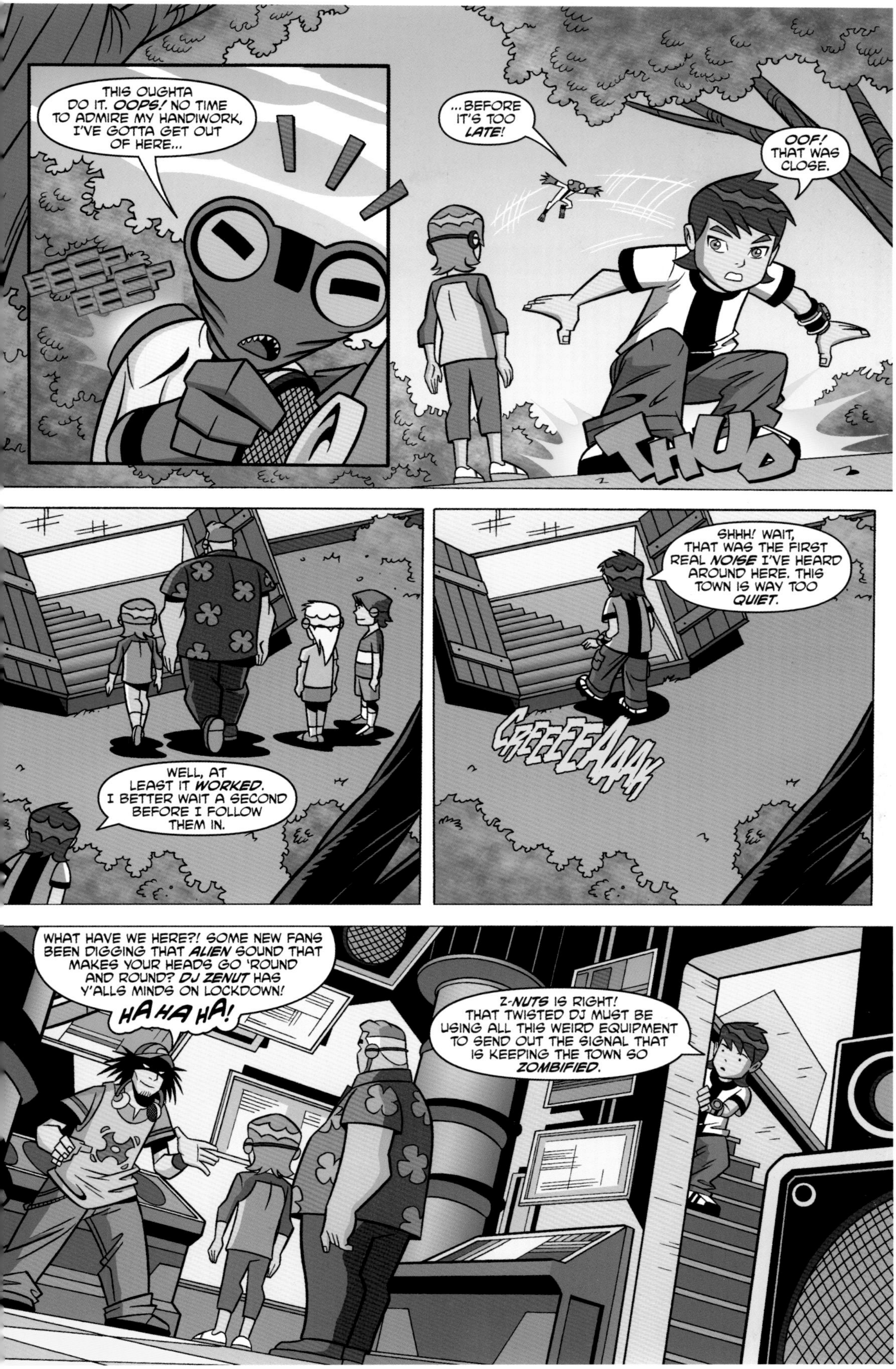
THIS OUGHTA DO IT. OOPS! NO TIME TO ADMIRE MY HANDIWORK, I'VE GOTTA GET OUT OF HERE...
BEEEP BEEEP
...BEFORE IT'S TOO LATE!
OOF! THAT WAS CLOSE.
THUD
WELL, AT LEAST IT WORKED. I BETTER WAIT A SECOND BEFORE I FOLLOW THEM IN.
SHHH! WAIT, THAT WAS THE FIRST REAL NOISE I'VE HEARD AROUND HERE. THIS TOWN IS WAY TOO QUIET.
CREEEEAAAK
WHAT HAVE WE HERE?! SOME NEW FANS BEEN DIGGING THAT ALIEN SOUND THAT MAKES YOUR HEADS GO 'ROUND AND ROUND? DJ ZENUT HAS Y'ALLS MINDS ON LOCKDOWN!
HA HA HA!
Z-NUTS IS RIGHT! THAT TWISTED DJ MUST BE USING ALL THIS WEIRD EQUIPMENT TO SEND OUT THE SIGNAL THAT IS KEEPING THE TOWN SO ZOMBIFIED.

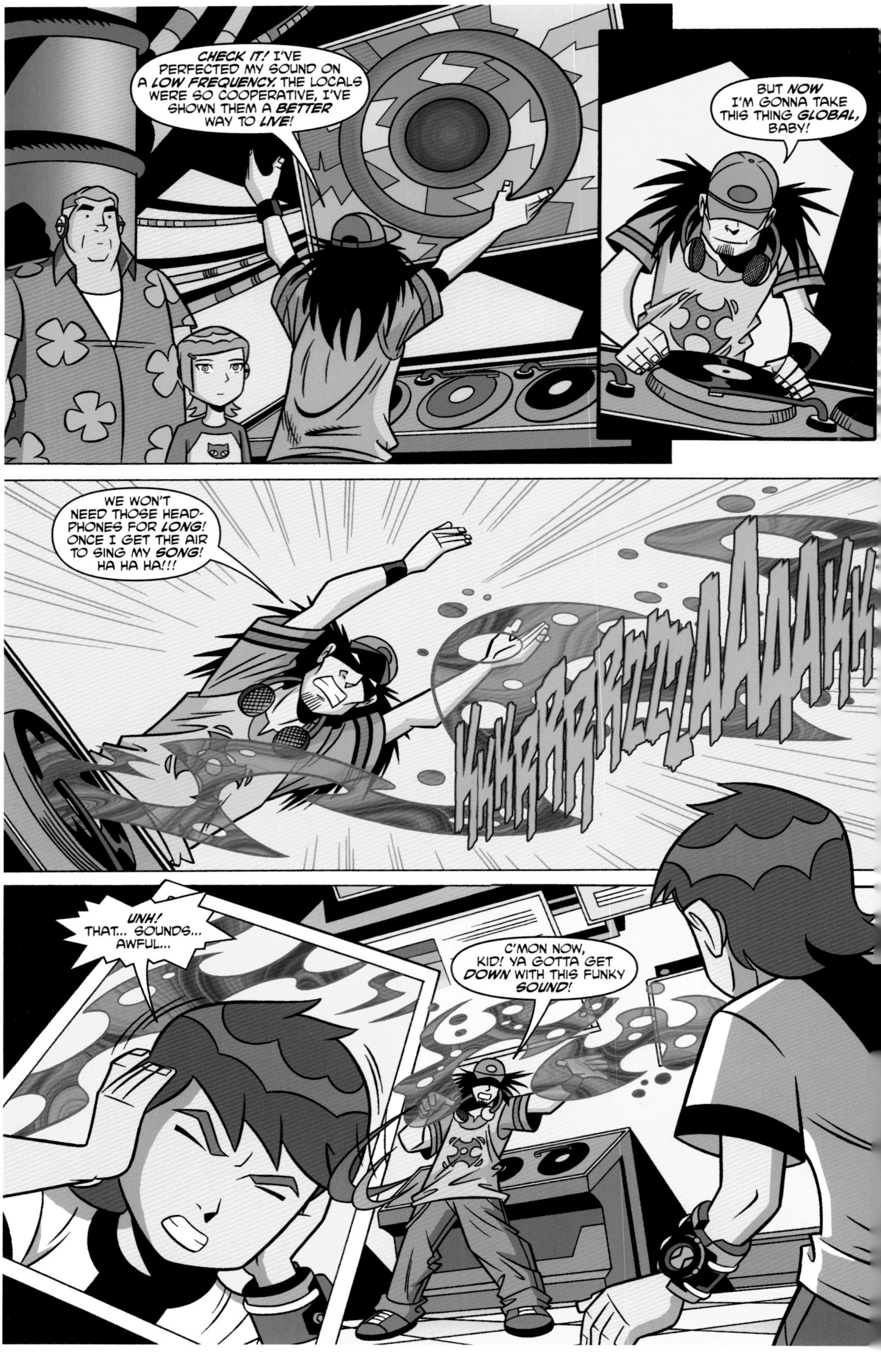
CHECK IT! I'VE PERFECTED MY SOUND ON A LOW FREQUENCY. THE LOCALS WERE SO COOPERATIVE, I'VE SHOWN THEM A BETTER WAY TO LIVE!
BUT NOW I'M GONNA TAKE THIS THING GLOBAL, BABY!
WE WON'T NEED THOSE HEAD-PHONES FOR LONG! ONCE I GET THE AIR TO SING MY SONG! HA HA HA!!!
KKKRRRRZZZZAAAAKK
UNH! THAT... SOUNDS... AWFUL...
C'MON NOW, KID! YA GOTTA GET DOWN WITH THIS FUNKY SOUND!

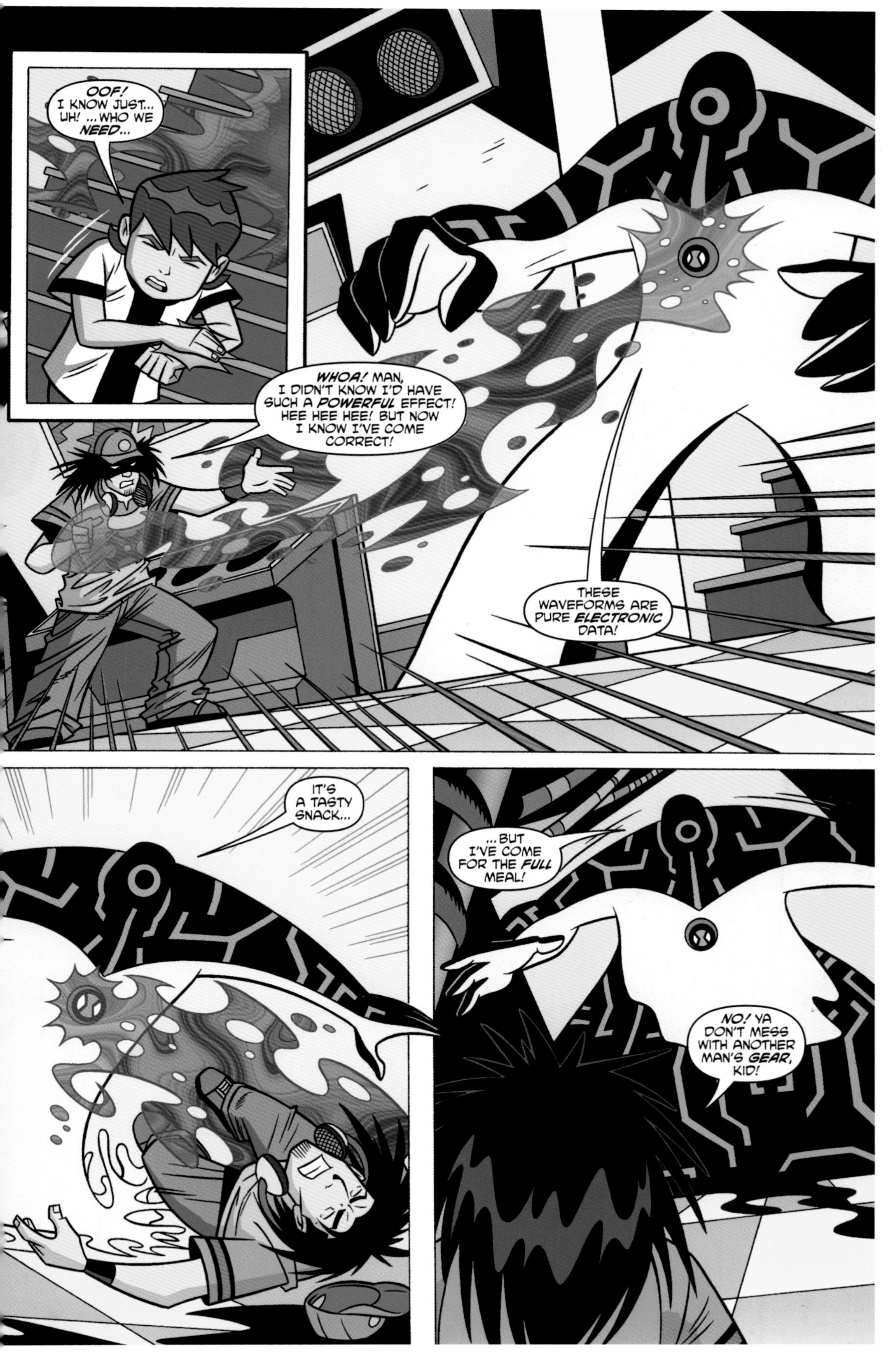
OOF! I KNOW JUST... UH! ...WHO WE NEED...
WHOA! MAN, I DIDN'T KNOW I'D HAVE SUCH A POWERFUL EFFECT! HEE HEE HEE! BUT NOW I KNOW I'VE COME CORRECT!
THESE WAVEFORMS ARE PURE ELECTRONIC DATA!
IT'S A TASTY SNACK...
...BUT I'VE COME FOR THE FULL MEAL!
NO! YA DON'T MESS WITH ANOTHER MAN'S GEAR, KID!

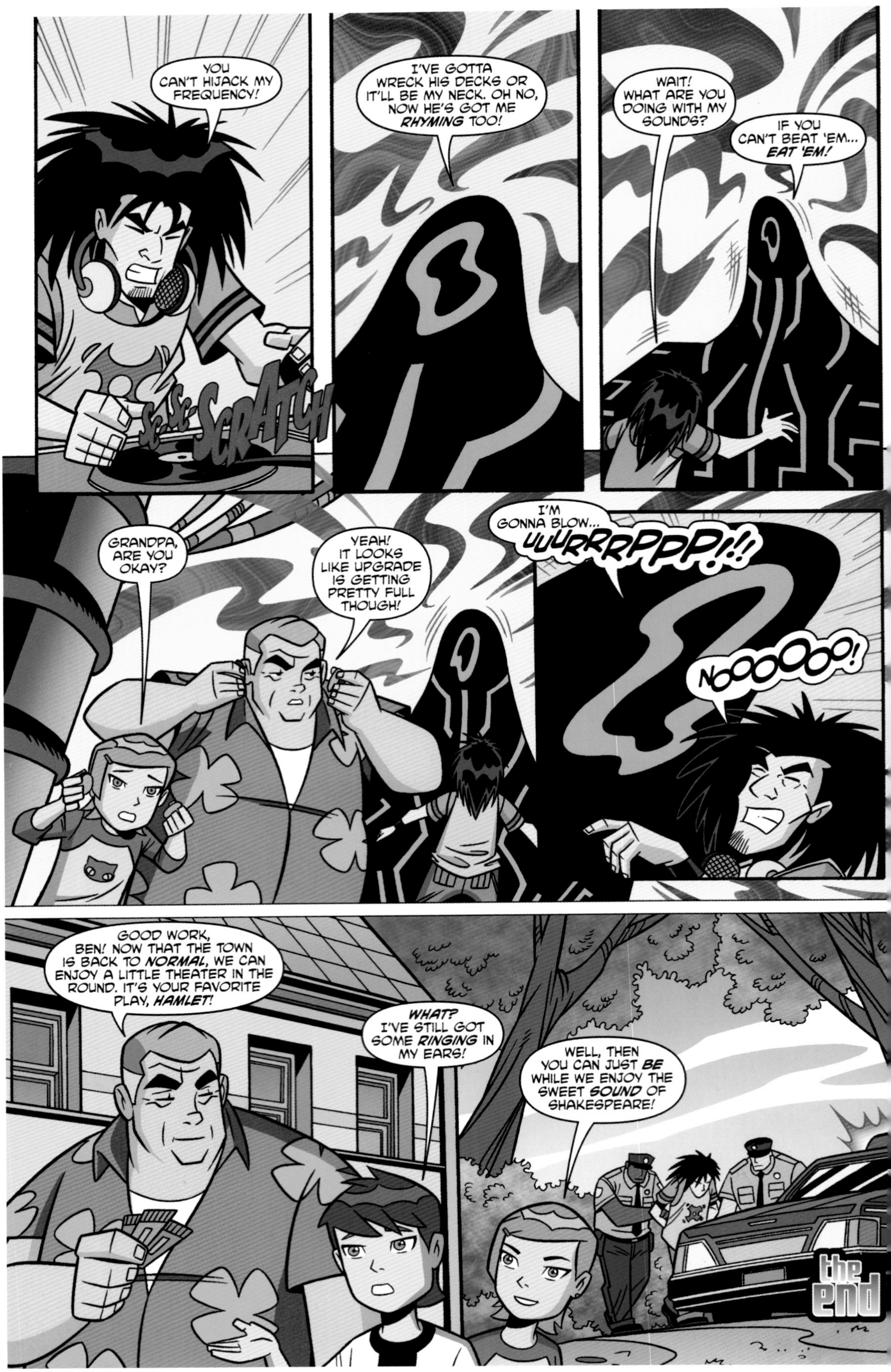

YOU CAN'T HIJACK MY FREQUENCY!
SC SC SCRATCH
I'VE GOTTA WRECK HIS DECKS OR IT'LL BE MY NECK. OH NO, NOW HE'S GOT ME *RHYMING* TOO!
WAIT! WHAT ARE YOU DOING WITH MY SOUNDS?
IF YOU CAN'T BEAT 'EM... *EAT 'EM!*
GRANDPA, ARE YOU OKAY?
YEAH! IT LOOKS LIKE UPGRADE IS GETTING PRETTY FULL THOUGH!
I'M GONNA BLOW... UUURRRPPPP!!!
NOOOOOOO!
GOOD WORK, BEN! NOW THAT THE TOWN IS BACK TO *NORMAL*, WE CAN ENJOY A LITTLE THEATER IN THE ROUND. IT'S YOUR FAVORITE PLAY, *HAMLET!*
WHAT? I'VE STILL GOT SOME *RINGING* IN MY EARS!
WELL, THEN YOU CAN JUST *BE* WHILE WE ENJOY THE SWEET *SOUND* OF SHAKESPEARE!
the end

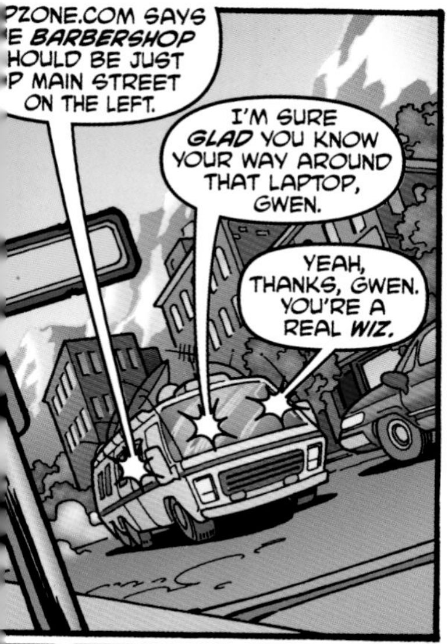
PZONE.COM SAYS
E BARBERSHOP
HOULD BE JUST
P MAIN STREET
ON THE LEFT.
I'M SURE GLAD YOU KNOW YOUR WAY AROUND THAT LAPTOP, GWEN.
YEAH, THANKS, GWEN. YOU'RE A REAL WIZ.

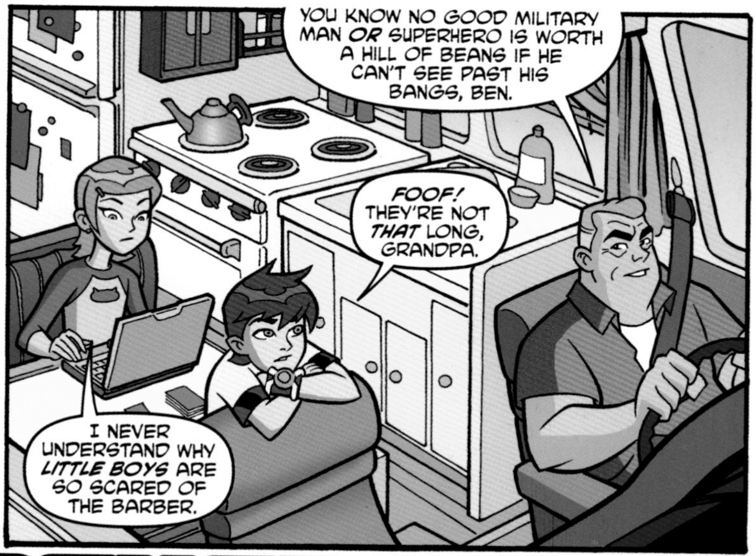
YOU KNOW NO GOOD MILITARY MAN OR SUPERHERO IS WORTH A HILL OF BEANS IF HE CAN'T SEE PAST HIS BANGS, BEN.
FOOF! THEY'RE NOT THAT LONG, GRANDPA.
I NEVER UNDERSTAND WHY LITTLE BOYS ARE SO SCARED OF THE BARBER.

BARBERSHOP BLUES

BBIE BUSCH WRITER · TRAVIS KOTZEBUE PENCILLER · MIKE DECARLO INKER · MIKE SELLERS LETTERER · HEROIC AGE COLORIST · RACHEL GLUCKSTERN ASSOC. EDITOR · JOAN HILTY EDITOR

BEN 10 CREATED BY MAN OF ACTION

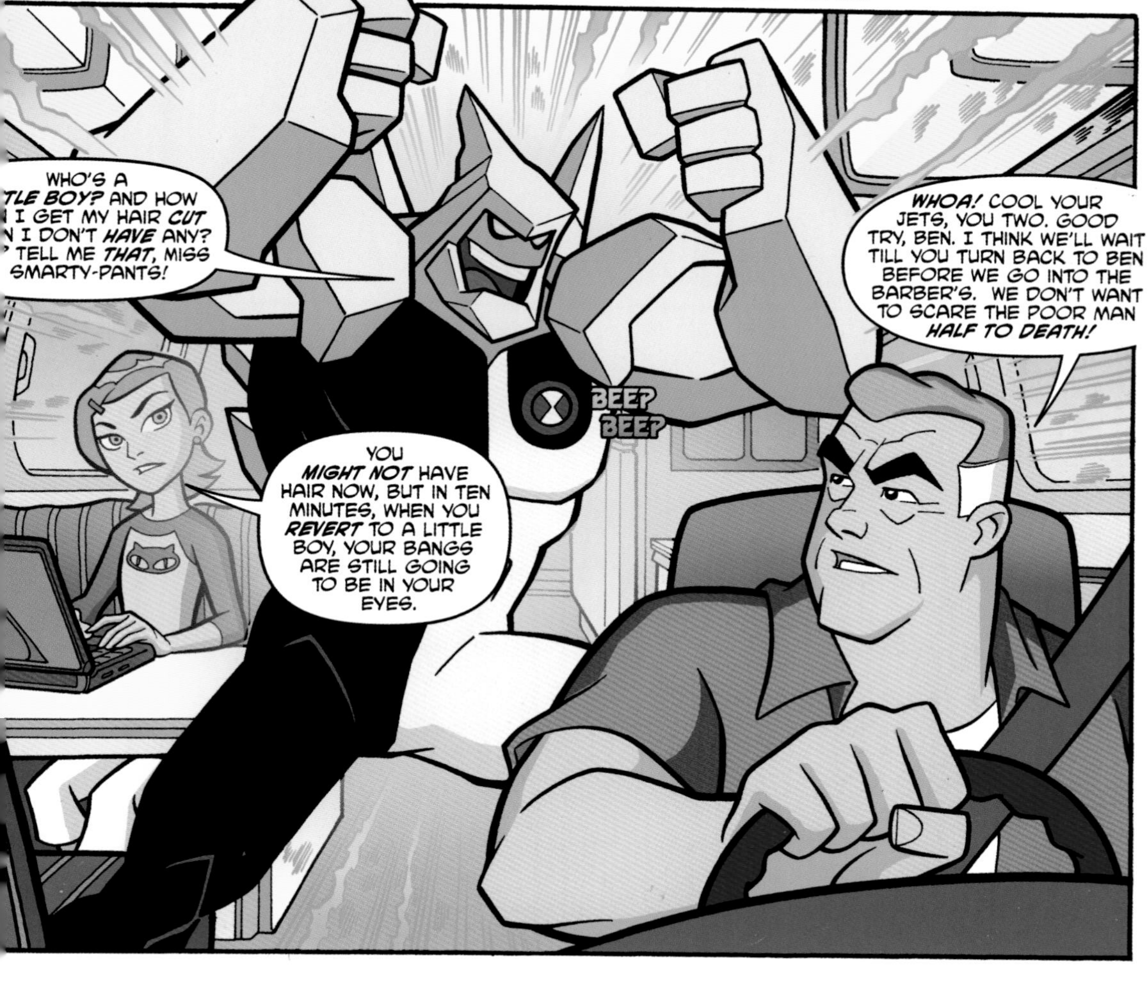
WHO'S A
TLE BOY? AND HOW
I GET MY HAIR CUT
N I DON'T HAVE ANY?
' TELL ME THAT, MISS
SMARTY-PANTS!
WHOA! COOL YOUR JETS, YOU TWO. GOOD TRY, BEN. I THINK WE'LL WAIT TILL YOU TURN BACK TO BEN BEFORE WE GO INTO THE BARBER'S. WE DON'T WANT TO SCARE THE POOR MAN HALF TO DEATH!
BEEP
BEEP
YOU MIGHT NOT HAVE HAIR NOW, BUT IN TEN MINUTES, WHEN YOU REVERT TO A LITTLE BOY, YOUR BANGS ARE STILL GOING TO BE IN YOUR EYES.

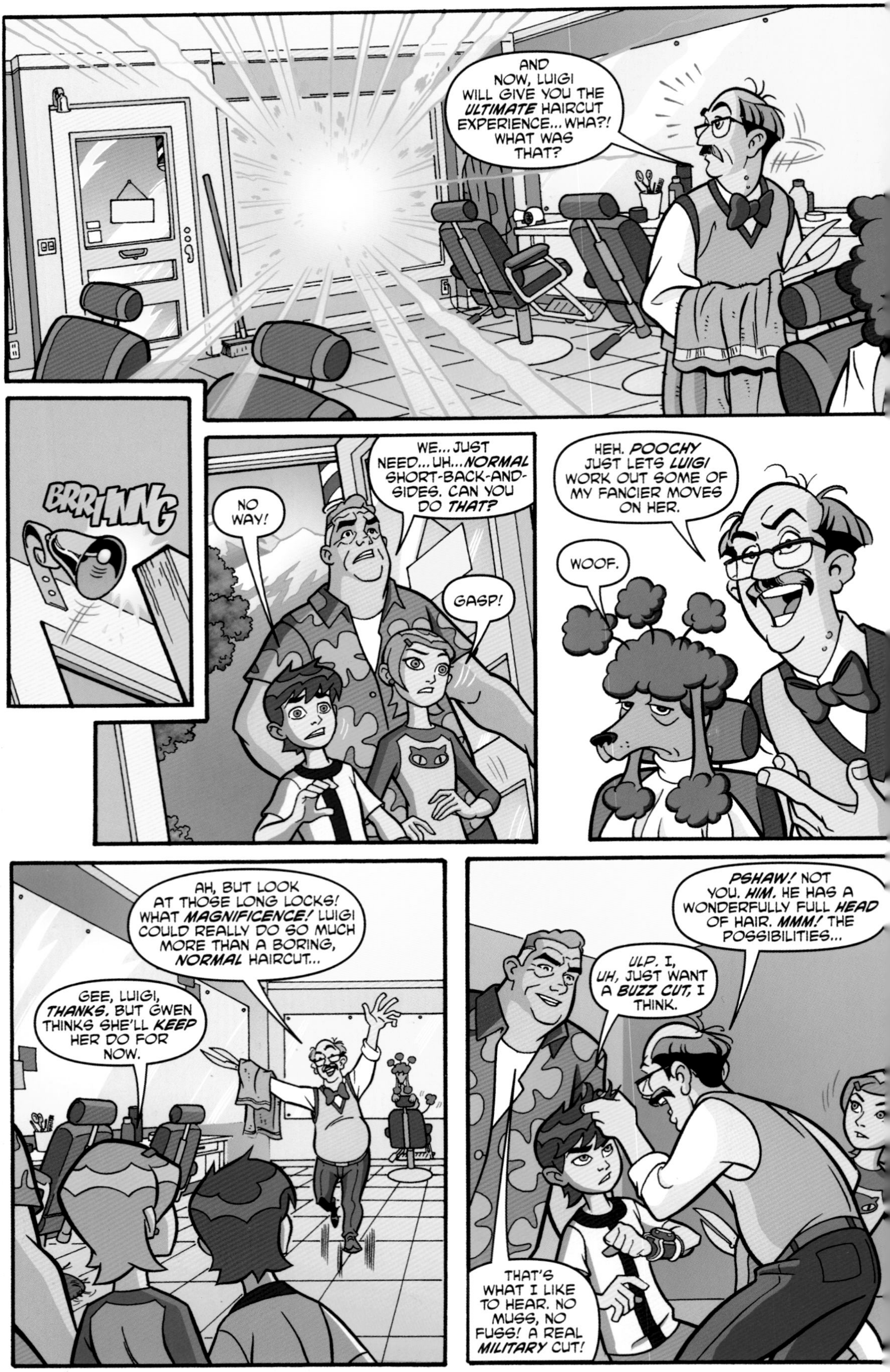
AND NOW, LUIGI WILL GIVE YOU THE *ULTIMATE* HAIRCUT EXPERIENCE... WHA?! WHAT WAS THAT?
BRRIIINNG
NO WAY!
WE... JUST NEED... UH... *NORMAL* SHORT-BACK-AND-SIDES. CAN YOU DO *THAT?*
GASP!
HEH. *POOCHY* JUST LETS *LUIGI* WORK OUT SOME OF MY FANCIER MOVES ON HER.
WOOF.
AH, BUT LOOK AT THOSE LONG LOCKS! WHAT *MAGNIFICENCE!* LUIGI COULD REALLY DO SO MUCH MORE THAN A BORING, *NORMAL* HAIRCUT...
GEE, LUIGI, *THANKS.* BUT GWEN THINKS SHE'LL *KEEP* HER DO FOR NOW.
PSHAW! NOT YOU. *HIM.* HE HAS A WONDERFULLY FULL *HEAD* OF HAIR. *MMM!* THE POSSIBILITIES...
ULP. I, *UH,* JUST WANT A *BUZZ CUT,* I THINK.
THAT'S WHAT I LIKE TO HEAR. NO MUSS, NO FUSS! A REAL *MILITARY* CUT!

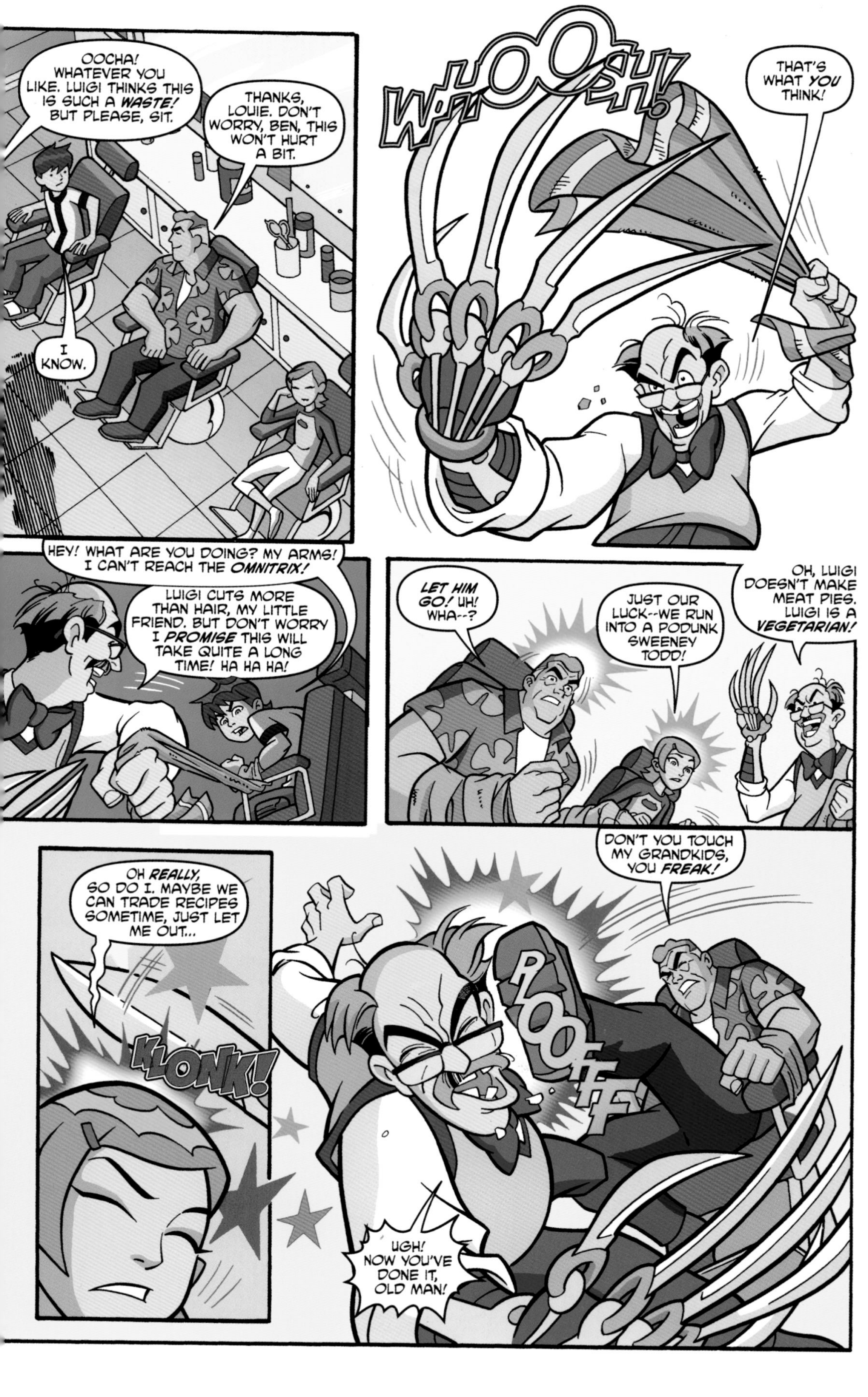
OOCHA! WHATEVER YOU LIKE. LUIGI THINKS THIS IS SUCH A WASTE! BUT PLEASE, SIT.
THANKS, LOUIE. DON'T WORRY, BEN, THIS WON'T HURT A BIT.
I KNOW.
WHOOOSH!
THAT'S WHAT YOU THINK!
HEY! WHAT ARE YOU DOING? MY ARMS! I CAN'T REACH THE OMNITRIX!
LUIGI CUTS MORE THAN HAIR, MY LITTLE FRIEND. BUT DON'T WORRY I PROMISE THIS WILL TAKE QUITE A LONG TIME! HA HA HA!
LET HIM GO! UH! WHA--?
JUST OUR LUCK--WE RUN INTO A PODUNK SWEENEY TODD!
OH, LUIGI DOESN'T MAKE MEAT PIES. LUIGI IS A VEGETARIAN!
OH REALLY, SO DO I. MAYBE WE CAN TRADE RECIPES SOMETIME, JUST LET ME OUT...
KLONK!
DON'T YOU TOUCH MY GRANDKIDS, YOU FREAK!
ROOFFF
UGH! NOW YOU'VE DONE IT, OLD MAN!

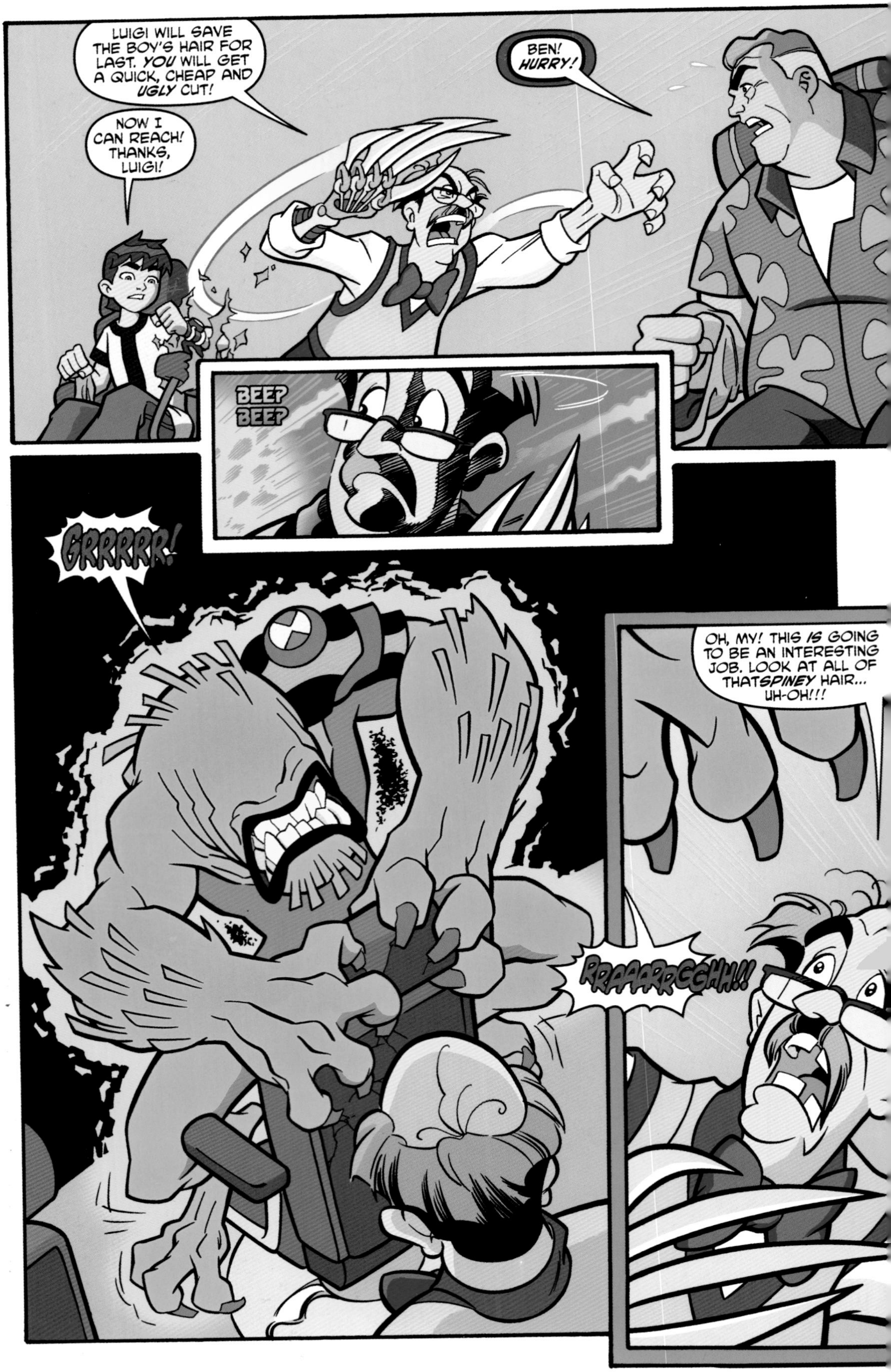
LUIGI WILL SAVE THE BOY'S HAIR FOR LAST. YOU WILL GET A QUICK, CHEAP AND UGLY CUT!
NOW I CAN REACH! THANKS, LUIGI!
BEN! HURRY!
BEEP BEEP
GRRRRR!
OH, MY! THIS IS GOING TO BE AN INTERESTING JOB. LOOK AT ALL OF THATSPINEY HAIR... UH-OH!!!
RRAAARRGGHH!!

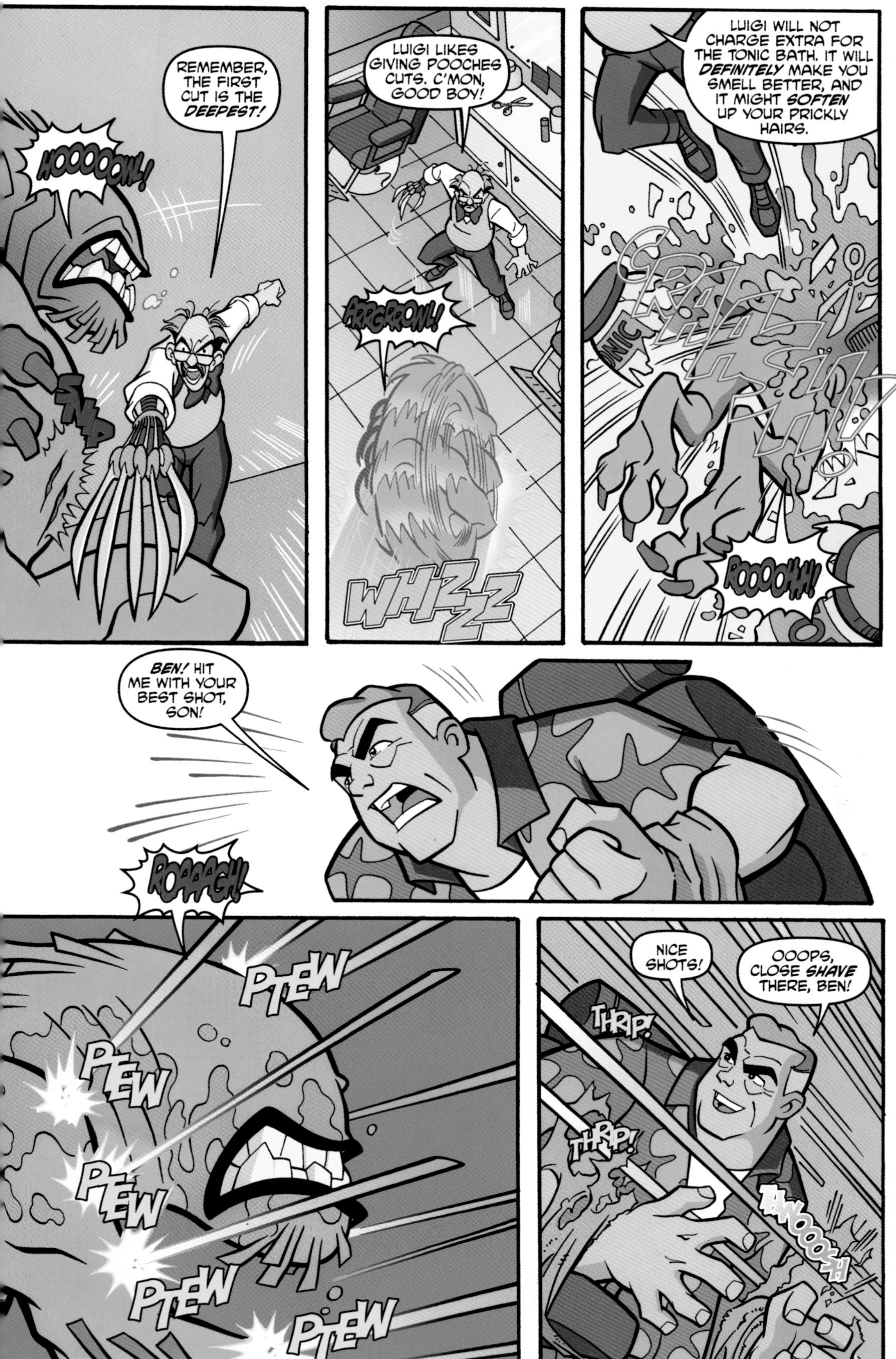

REMEMBER, THE FIRST CUT IS THE DEEPEST!
HOOOOOWL!
SNIP
LUIGI LIKES GIVING POOCHES CUTS. C'MON, GOOD BOY!
ARRGRROWL!
WHIZZZ
LUIGI WILL NOT CHARGE EXTRA FOR THE TONIC BATH. IT WILL DEFINITELY MAKE YOU SMELL BETTER, AND IT MIGHT SOFTEN UP YOUR PRICKLY HAIRS.
CRASH!
ROOOOHH!
BEN! HIT ME WITH YOUR BEST SHOT, SON!
ROAAAGH!
PTEW
PTEW
PTEW
PTEW
PTEW
NICE SHOTS!
OOOPS, CLOSE SHAVE THERE, BEN!
THRIP!
THRIP!
THWOOOSH

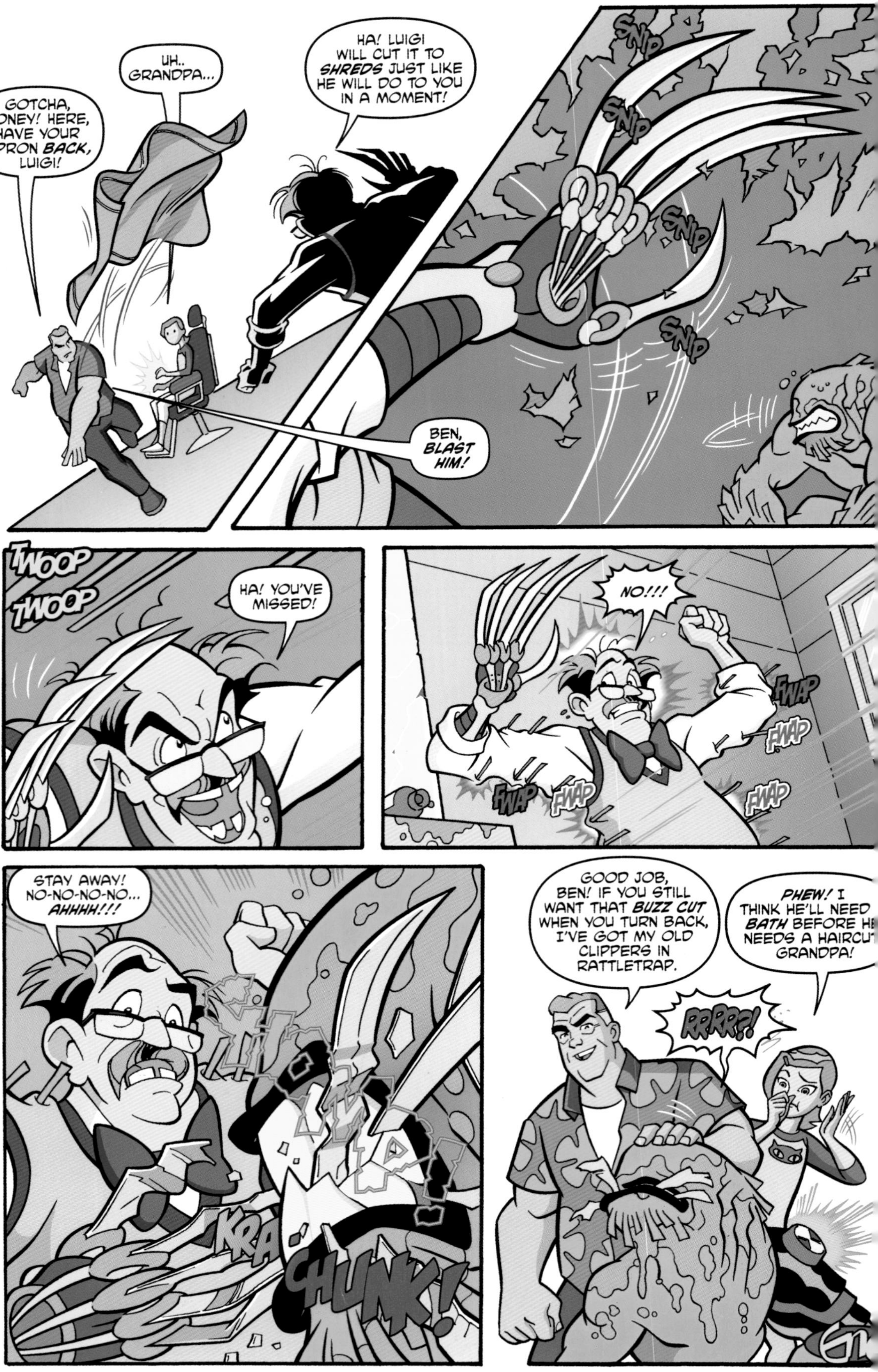

GOTCHA, HONEY! HERE, HAVE YOUR APRON *BACK*, LUIGI!
UH.. GRANDPA...
HA! LUIGI WILL CUT IT TO *SHREDS* JUST LIKE HE WILL DO TO YOU IN A MOMENT!
SNIP
SNIP
SNIP
SNIP
BEN, *BLAST HIM!*
TWOOP
TWOOP
HA! YOU'VE MISSED!
NO!!!
FWAP
FWAP
FWAP
FWAP
FWAP
STAY AWAY! NO-NO-NO-NO... *AHHHH!!!*
KRA-
CHUNK!
GOOD JOB, BEN! IF YOU STILL WANT THAT *BUZZ CUT* WHEN YOU TURN BACK, I'VE GOT MY OLD CLIPPERS IN RATTLETRAP.
PHEW! I THINK HE'LL NEED *BATH* BEFORE H NEEDS A HAIRCU GRANDPA!
RRRR?!

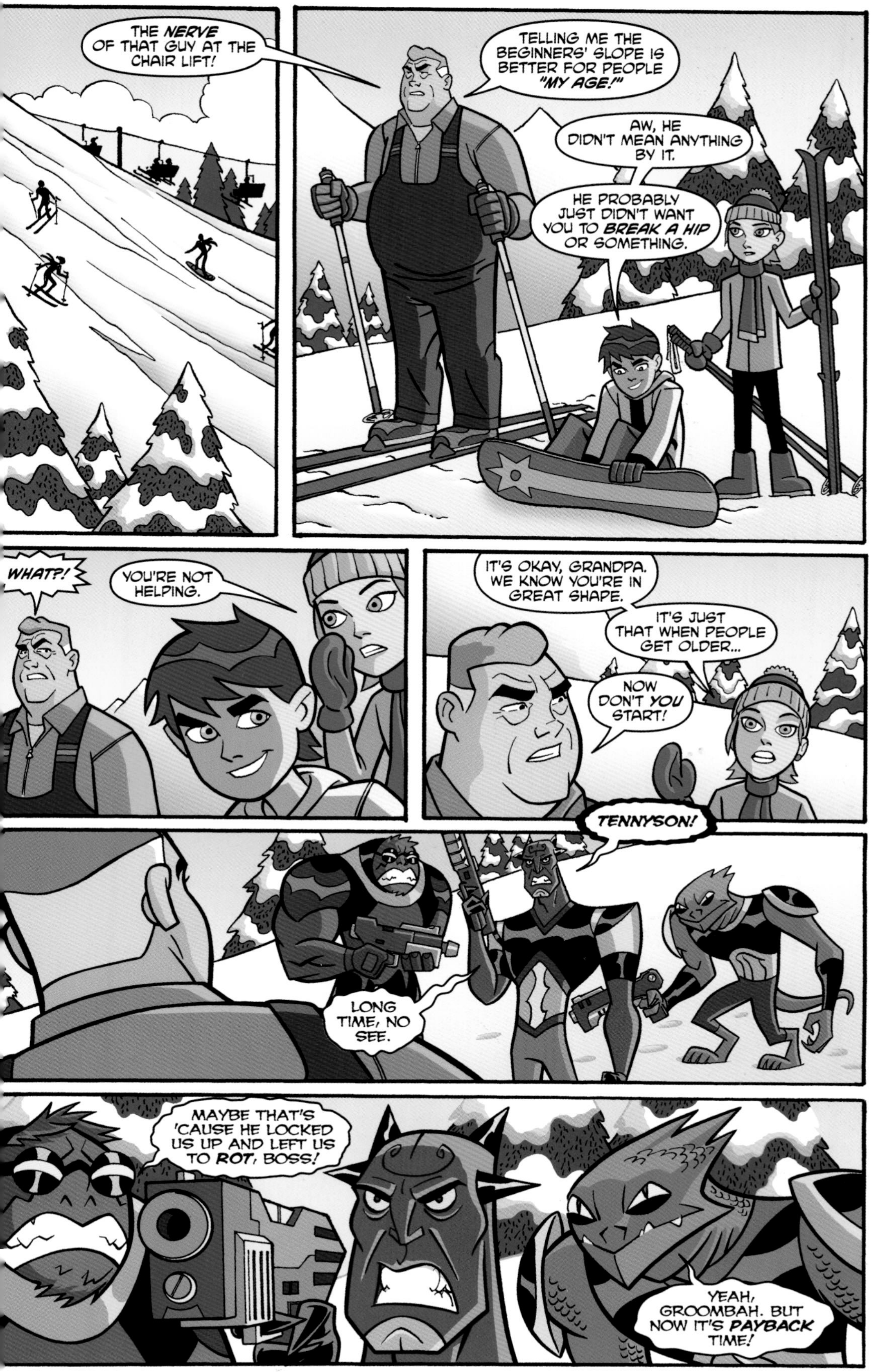
THE NERVE OF THAT GUY AT THE CHAIR LIFT!
TELLING ME THE BEGINNERS' SLOPE IS BETTER FOR PEOPLE "MY AGE!"
AW, HE DIDN'T MEAN ANYTHING BY IT.
HE PROBABLY JUST DIDN'T WANT YOU TO BREAK A HIP OR SOMETHING.
WHAT?!
YOU'RE NOT HELPING.
IT'S OKAY, GRANDPA. WE KNOW YOU'RE IN GREAT SHAPE.
IT'S JUST THAT WHEN PEOPLE GET OLDER...
NOW DON'T YOU START!
TENNYSON!
LONG TIME, NO SEE.
MAYBE THAT'S 'CAUSE HE LOCKED US UP AND LEFT US TO ROT, BOSS!
YEAH, GROOMBAH. BUT NOW IT'S PAYBACK TIME!

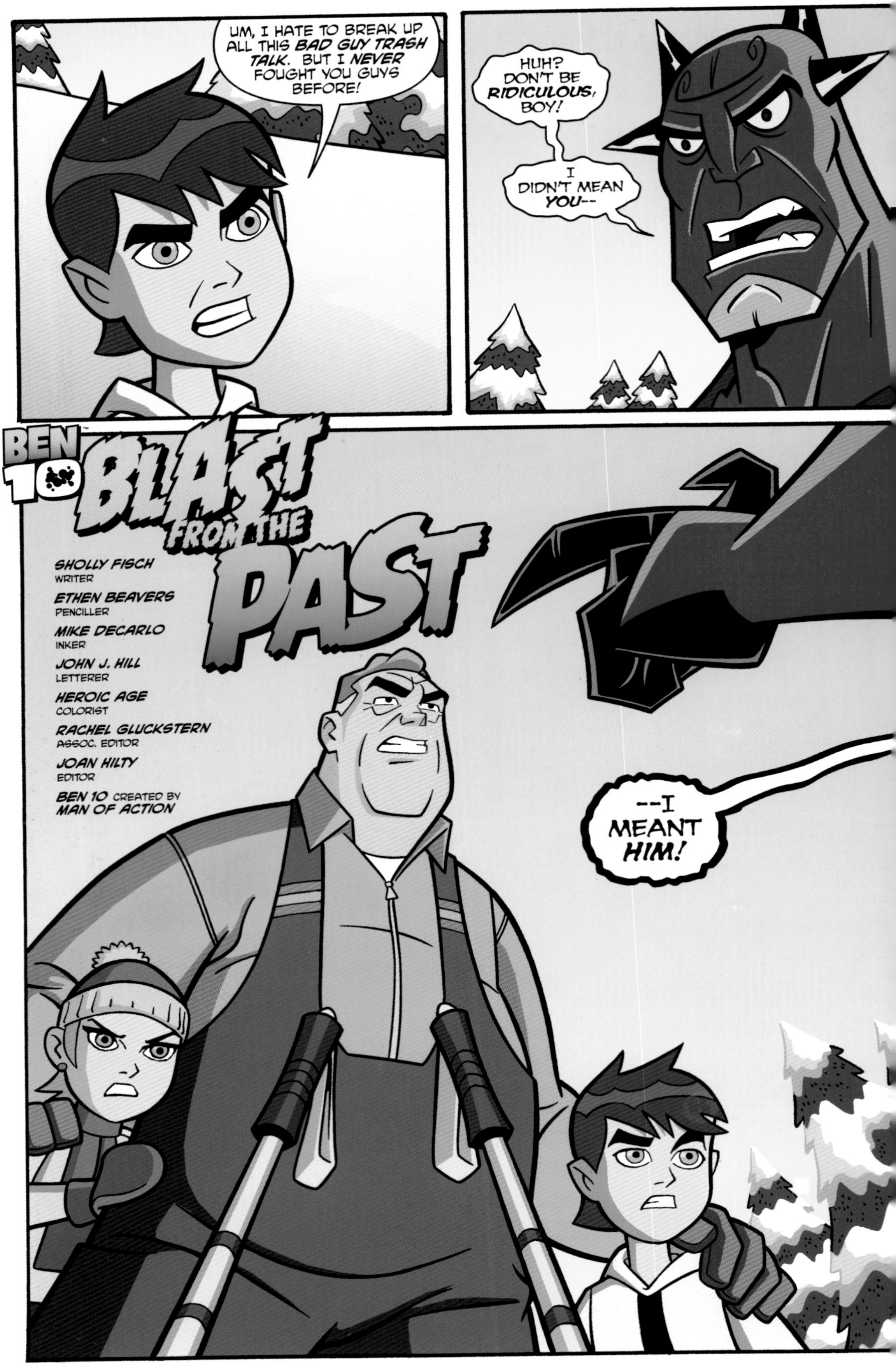
UM, I HATE TO BREAK UP ALL THIS BAD GUY TRASH TALK. BUT I NEVER FOUGHT YOU GUYS BEFORE!
HUH? DON'T BE RIDICULOUS, BOY!
I DIDN'T MEAN YOU--
BEN 10
BLAST FROM THE PAST
SHOLLY FISCH WRITER
ETHEN BEAVERS PENCILLER
MIKE DECARLO INKER
JOHN J. HILL LETTERER
HEROIC AGE COLORIST
RACHEL GLUCKSTERN ASSOC. EDITOR
JOAN HILTY EDITOR
BEN 10 CREATED BY MAN OF ACTION
--I MEANT HIM!

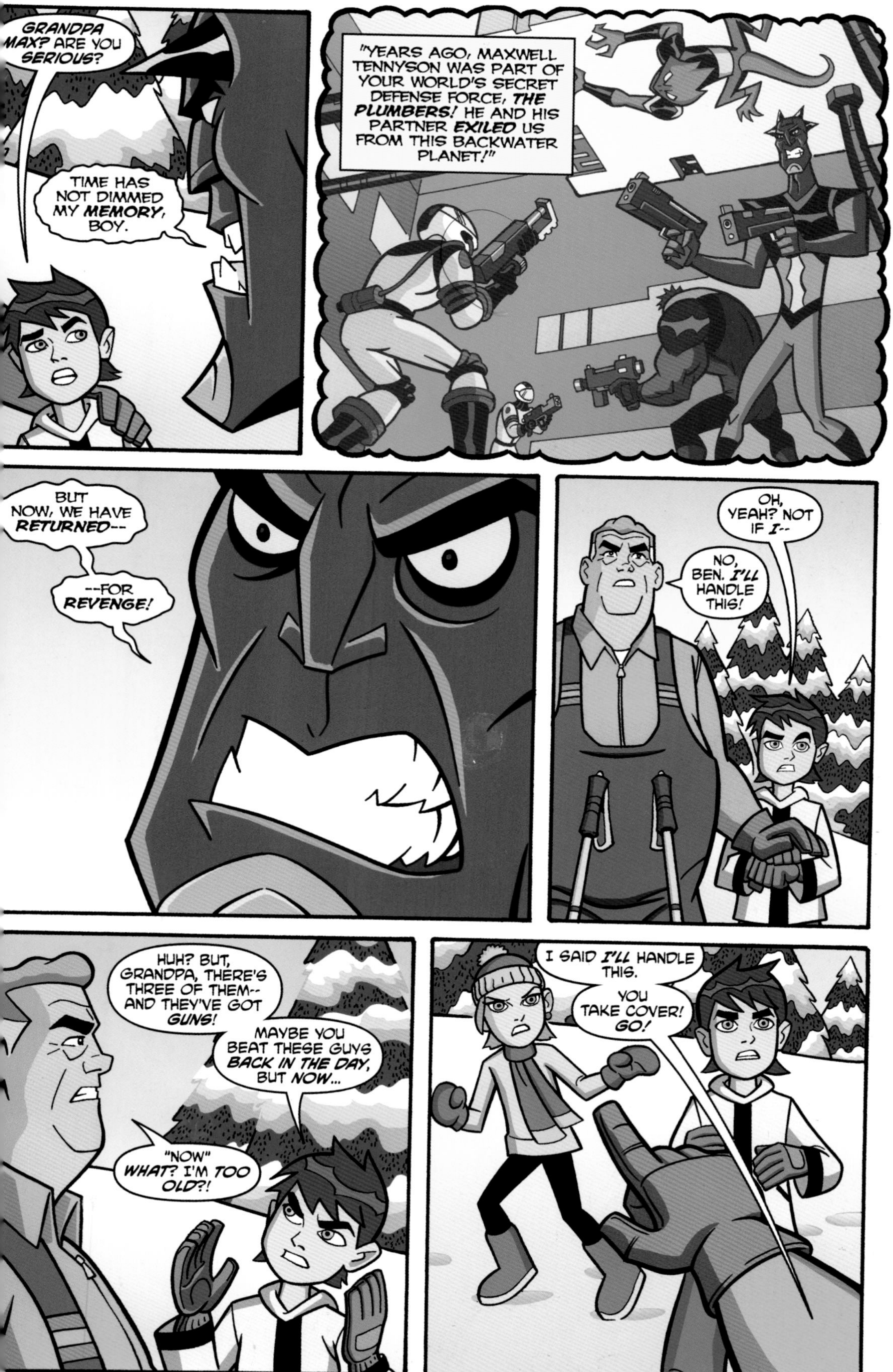
GRANDPA MAX? ARE YOU SERIOUS?
TIME HAS NOT DIMMED MY MEMORY, BOY.
"YEARS AGO, MAXWELL TENNYSON WAS PART OF YOUR WORLD'S SECRET DEFENSE FORCE, THE PLUMBERS! HE AND HIS PARTNER EXILED US FROM THIS BACKWATER PLANET!"
BUT NOW, WE HAVE RETURNED--
--FOR REVENGE!
OH, YEAH? NOT IF I--
NO, BEN. I'LL HANDLE THIS!
HUH? BUT, GRANDPA, THERE'S THREE OF THEM-- AND THEY'VE GOT GUNS!
MAYBE YOU BEAT THESE GUYS BACK IN THE DAY, BUT NOW...
"NOW" WHAT? I'M TOO OLD?!
I SAID I'LL HANDLE THIS.
YOU TAKE COVER! GO!

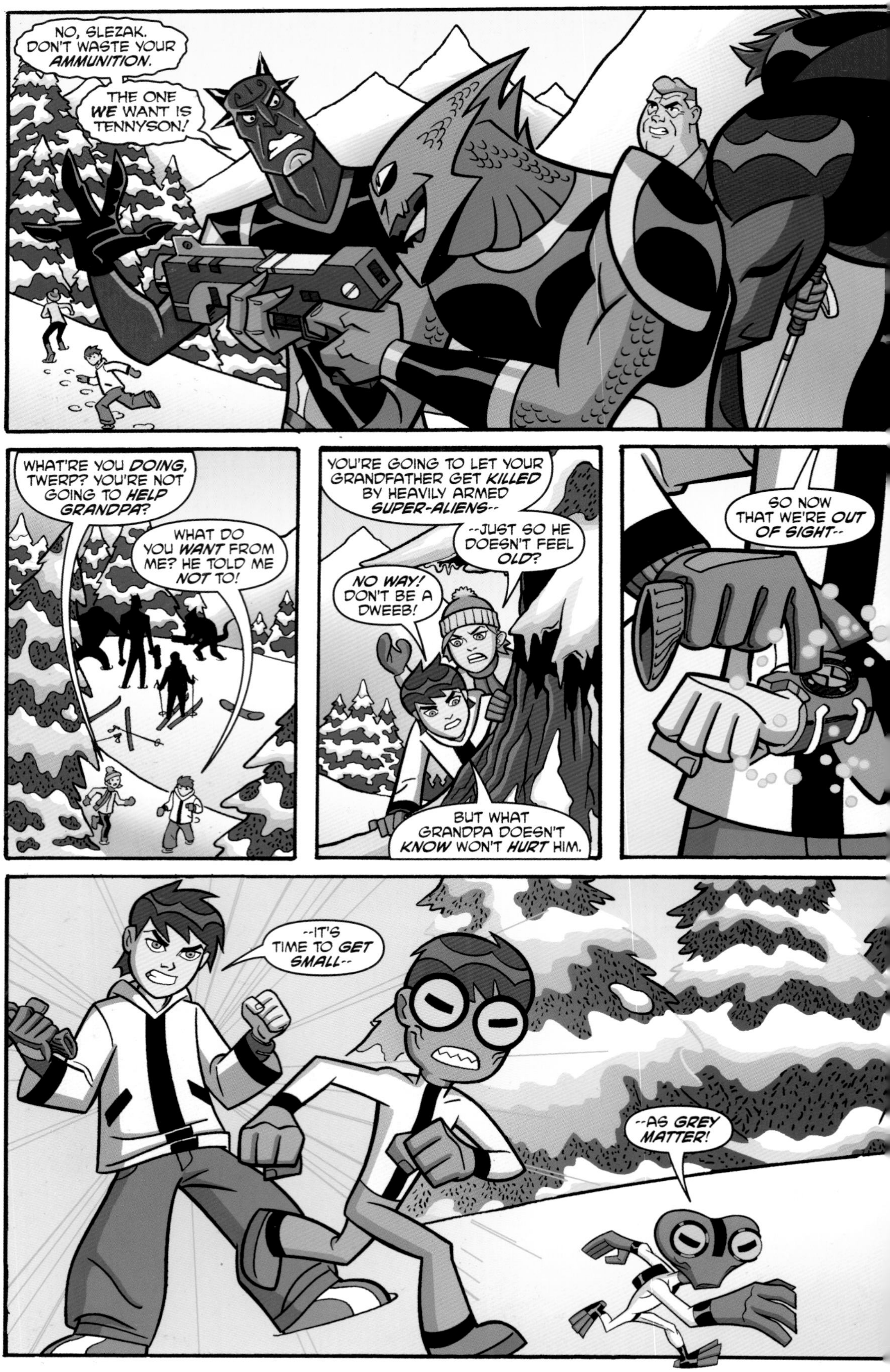
NO, SLEZAK. DON'T WASTE YOUR AMMUNITION.
THE ONE WE WANT IS TENNYSON!
WHAT'RE YOU DOING, TWERP? YOU'RE NOT GOING TO HELP GRANDPA?
WHAT DO YOU WANT FROM ME? HE TOLD ME NOT TO!
YOU'RE GOING TO LET YOUR GRANDFATHER GET KILLED BY HEAVILY ARMED SUPER-ALIENS--
--JUST SO HE DOESN'T FEEL OLD?
NO WAY! DON'T BE A DWEEB!
BUT WHAT GRANDPA DOESN'T KNOW WON'T HURT HIM.
SO NOW THAT WE'RE OUT OF SIGHT--
--IT'S TIME TO GET SMALL--
--AS GREY MATTER!

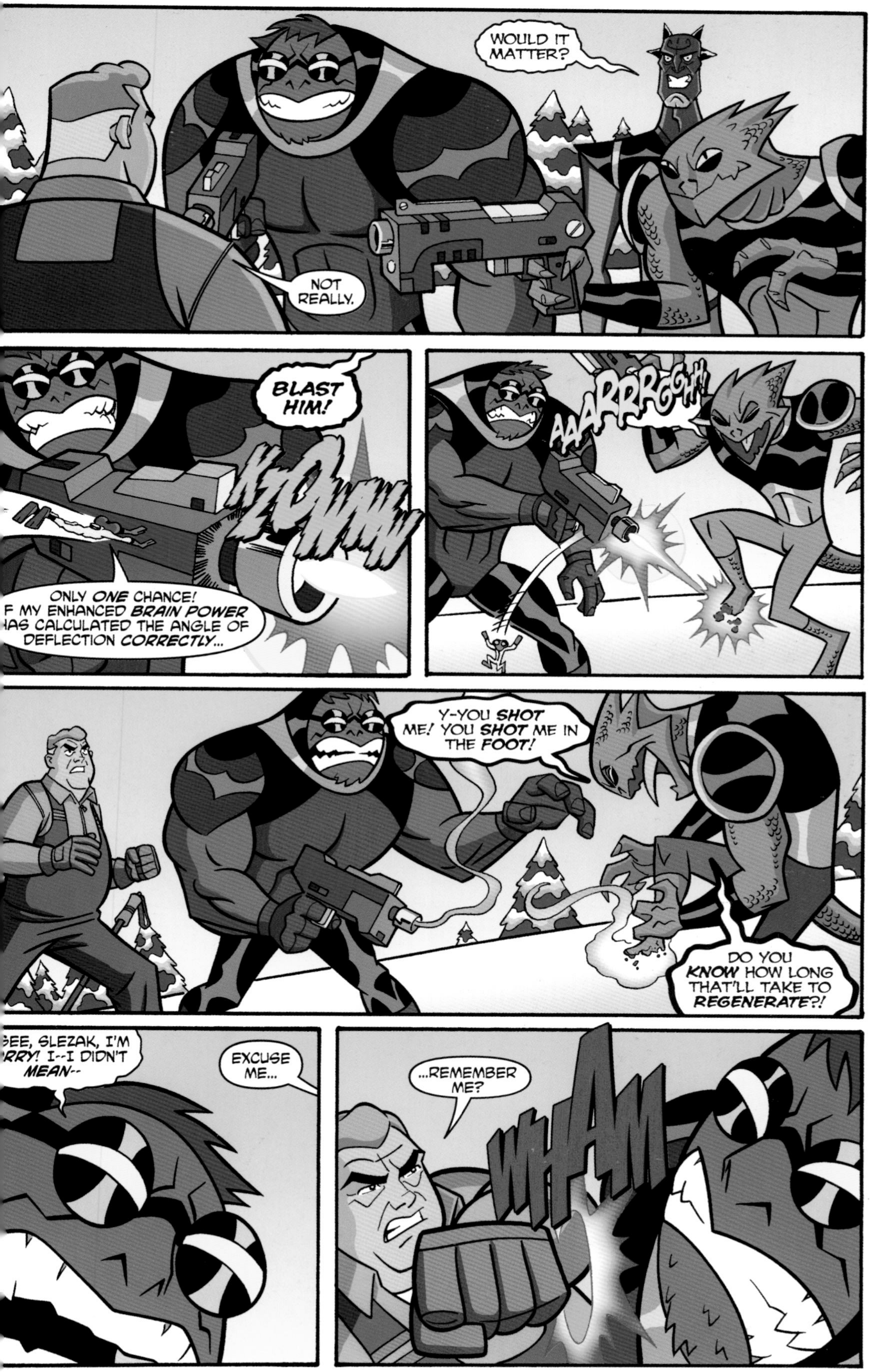
WOULD IT MATTER?
NOT REALLY.
BLAST HIM!
KROWWW
ONLY ONE CHANCE! F MY ENHANCED BRAIN POWER HAS CALCULATED THE ANGLE OF DEFLECTION CORRECTLY...
AAARRRGGH!
Y-YOU SHOT ME! YOU SHOT ME IN THE FOOT!
DO YOU KNOW HOW LONG THAT'LL TAKE TO REGENERATE?!
GEE, SLEZAK, I'M RRY! I--I DIDN'T MEAN--
EXCUSE ME...
...REMEMBER ME?
WHAM

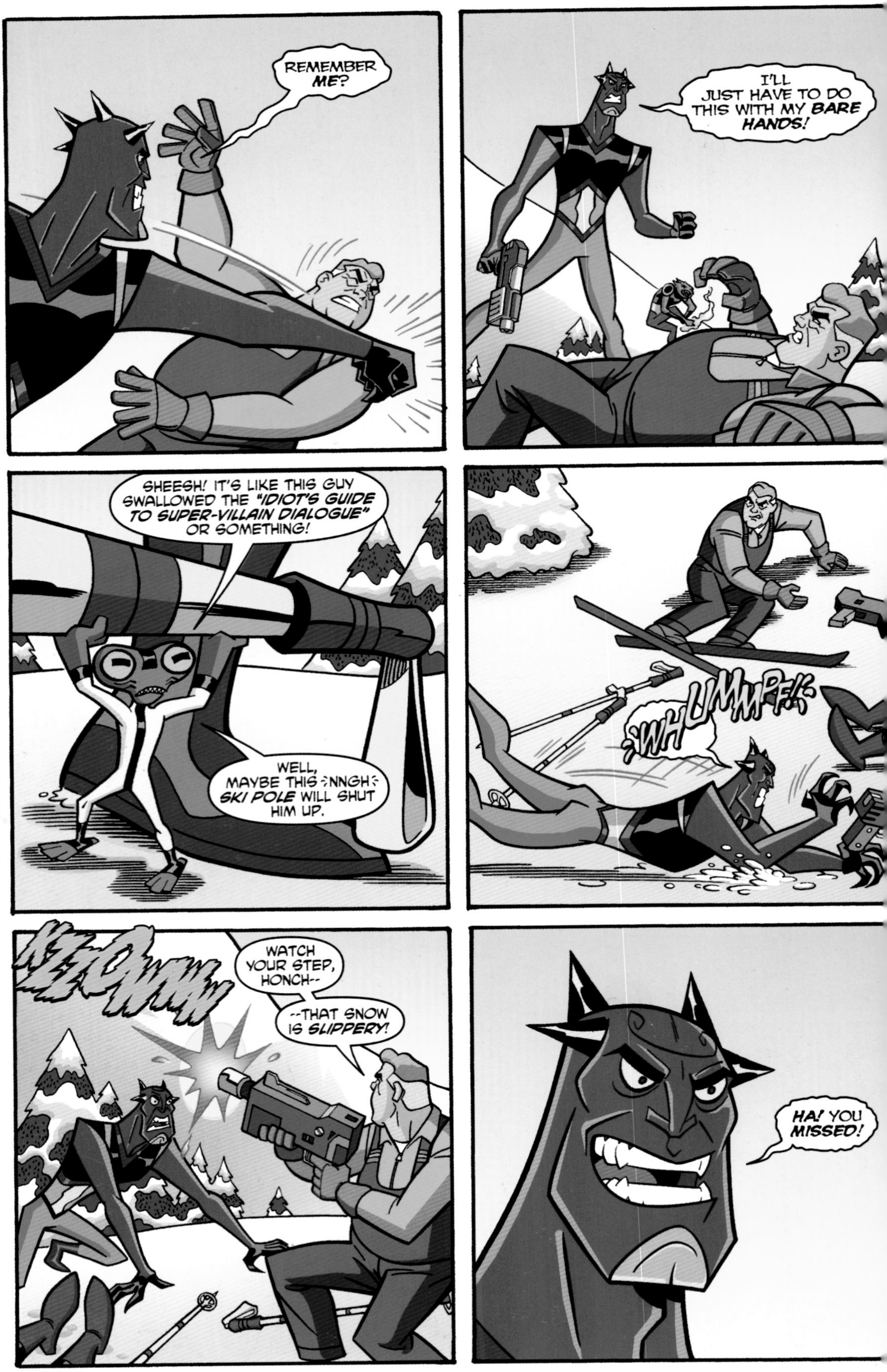
REMEMBER ME?
I'LL JUST HAVE TO DO THIS WITH MY BARE HANDS!
SHEESH! IT'S LIKE THIS GUY SWALLOWED THE "IDIOT'S GUIDE TO SUPER-VILLAIN DIALOGUE" OR SOMETHING!
WELL, MAYBE THIS -NNGH- SKI POLE WILL SHUT HIM UP.
WHUMMPF!!
WATCH YOUR STEP, HONCH--
--THAT SNOW IS SLIPPERY!
HA! YOU MISSED!

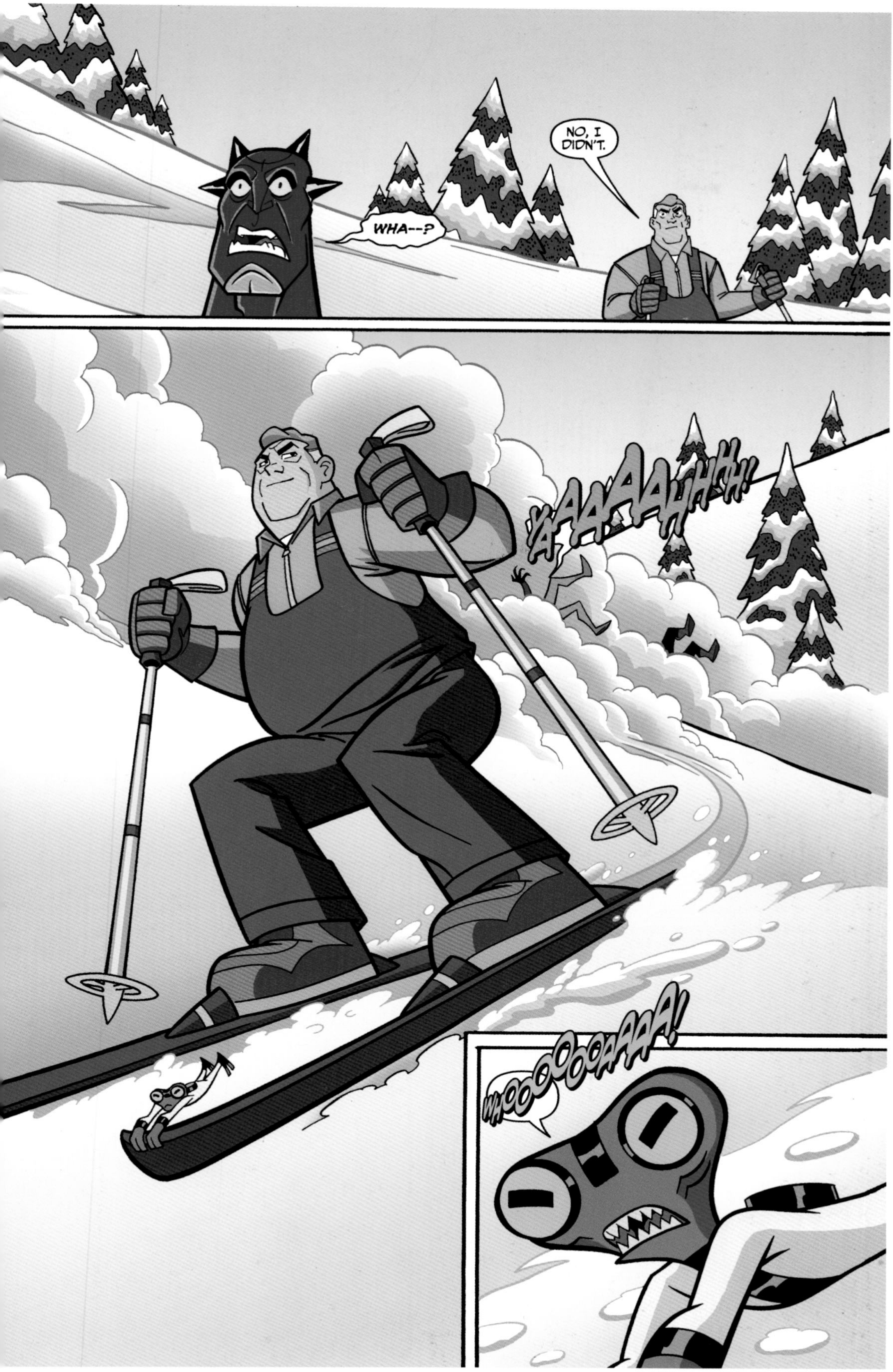
NO, I DIDN'T.
WHA--?
YAAAAAHHHH!
WHOOOOOOOAAAA!

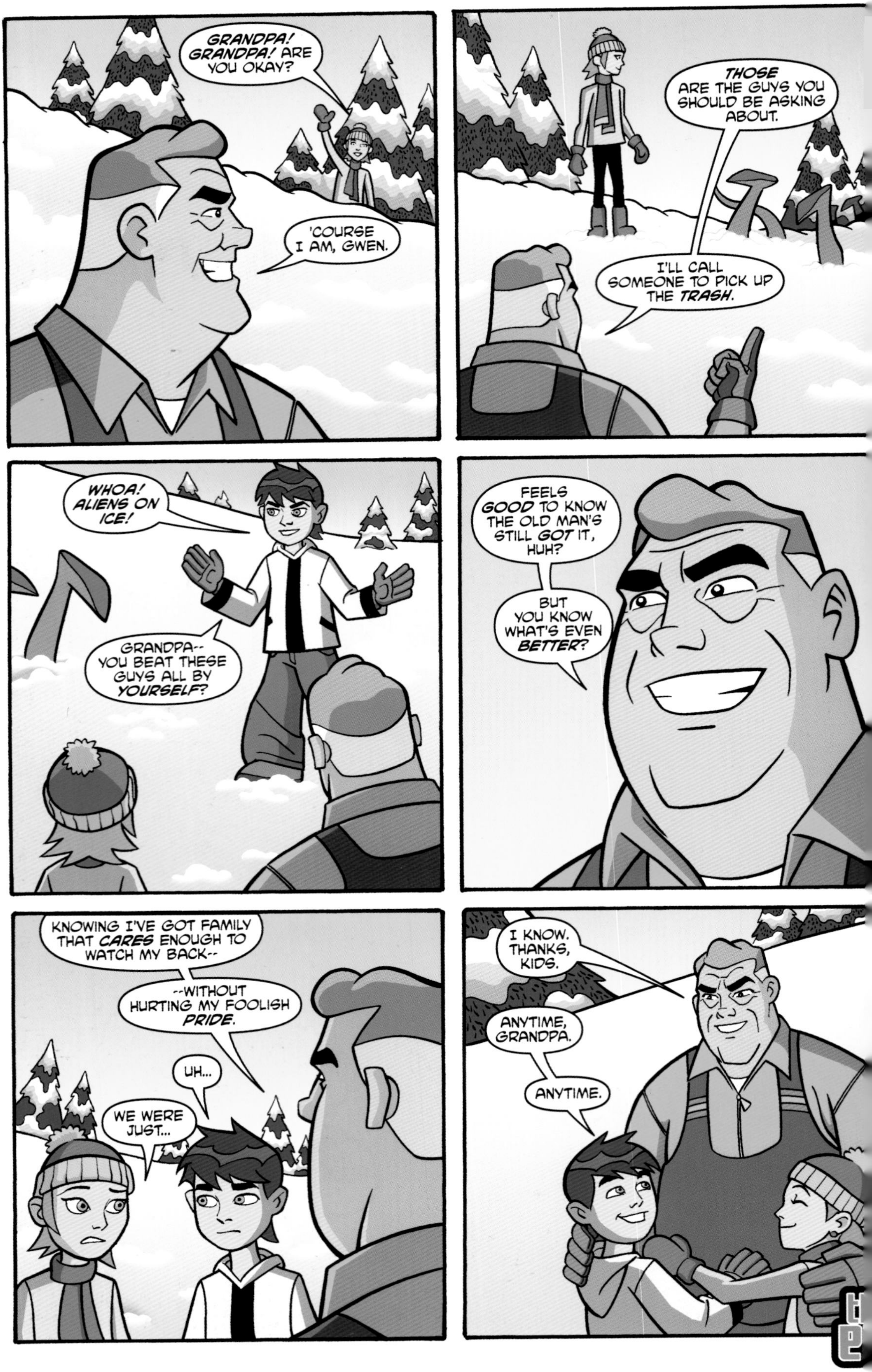
GRANDPA! GRANDPA! ARE YOU OKAY?
'COURSE I AM, GWEN.
THOSE ARE THE GUYS YOU SHOULD BE ASKING ABOUT.
I'LL CALL SOMEONE TO PICK UP THE TRASH.
WHOA! ALIENS ON ICE!
GRANDPA-- YOU BEAT THESE GUYS ALL BY YOURSELF?
FEELS GOOD TO KNOW THE OLD MAN'S STILL GOT IT, HUH?
BUT YOU KNOW WHAT'S EVEN BETTER?
KNOWING I'VE GOT FAMILY THAT CARES ENOUGH TO WATCH MY BACK--
--WITHOUT HURTING MY FOOLISH PRIDE.
UH...
WE WERE JUST...
I KNOW. THANKS, KIDS.
ANYTIME, GRANDPA.
ANYTIME.

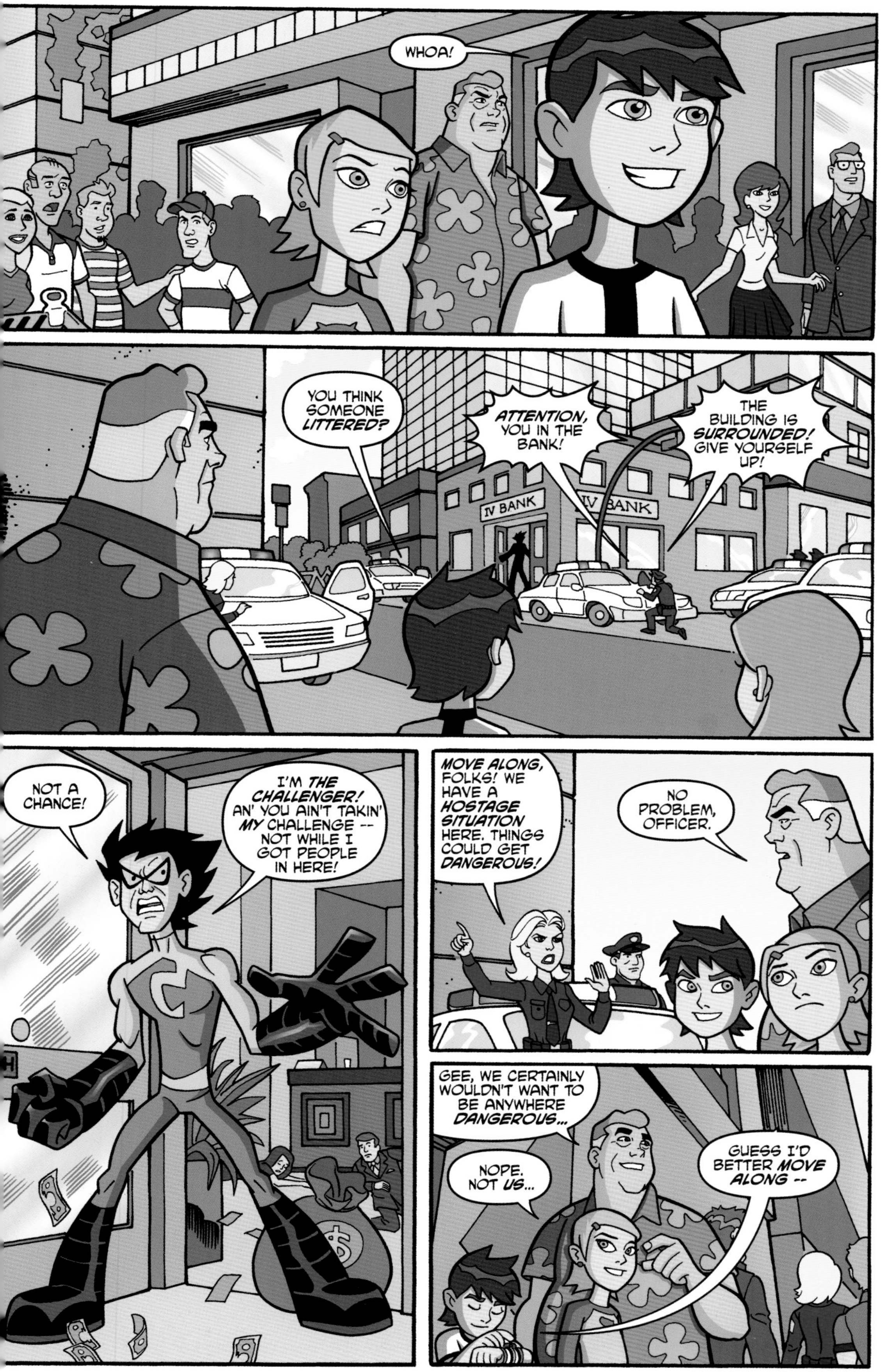
WHOA!
YOU THINK SOMEONE LITTERED?
ATTENTION, YOU IN THE BANK!
THE BUILDING IS SURROUNDED! GIVE YOURSELF UP!
IV BANK
IV BANK
NOT A CHANCE!
I'M THE CHALLENGER! AN' YOU AIN'T TAKIN' MY CHALLENGE -- NOT WHILE I GOT PEOPLE IN HERE!
MOVE ALONG, FOLKS! WE HAVE A HOSTAGE SITUATION HERE. THINGS COULD GET DANGEROUS!
NO PROBLEM, OFFICER.
GEE, WE CERTAINLY WOULDN'T WANT TO BE ANYWHERE DANGEROUS...
NOPE. NOT US...
GUESS I'D BETTER MOVE ALONG --

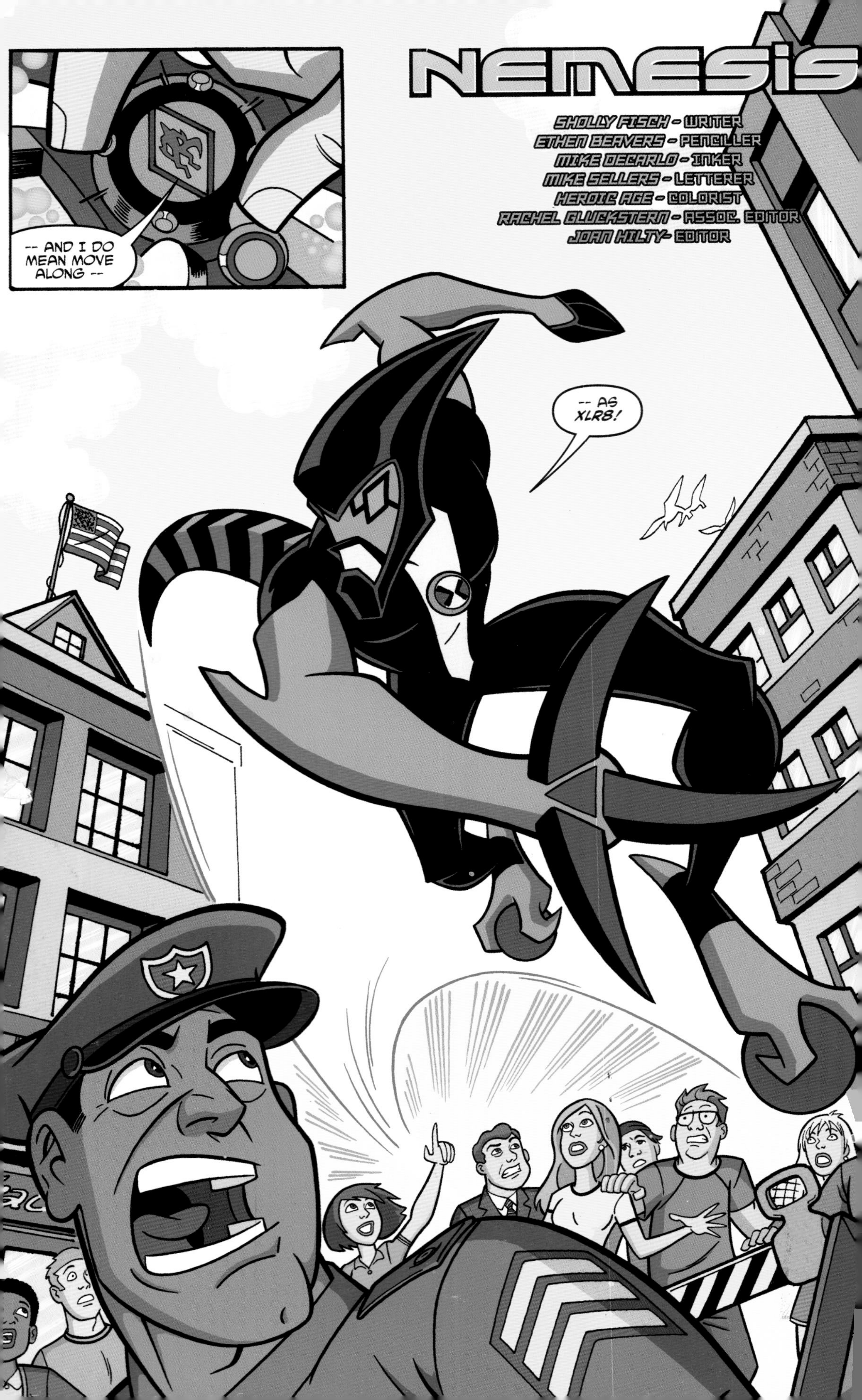
-- AND I DO MEAN MOVE ALONG --
NEMESIS
SHOLLY FISCH - WRITER
ETHEN BEAVERS - PENCILLER
MIKE DECARLO - INKER
MIKE SELLERS - LETTERER
HEROIC AGE - COLORIST
RACHEL GLUCKSTERN - ASSOC. EDITOR
JOAN HILTY- EDITOR
-- AS XLR8!

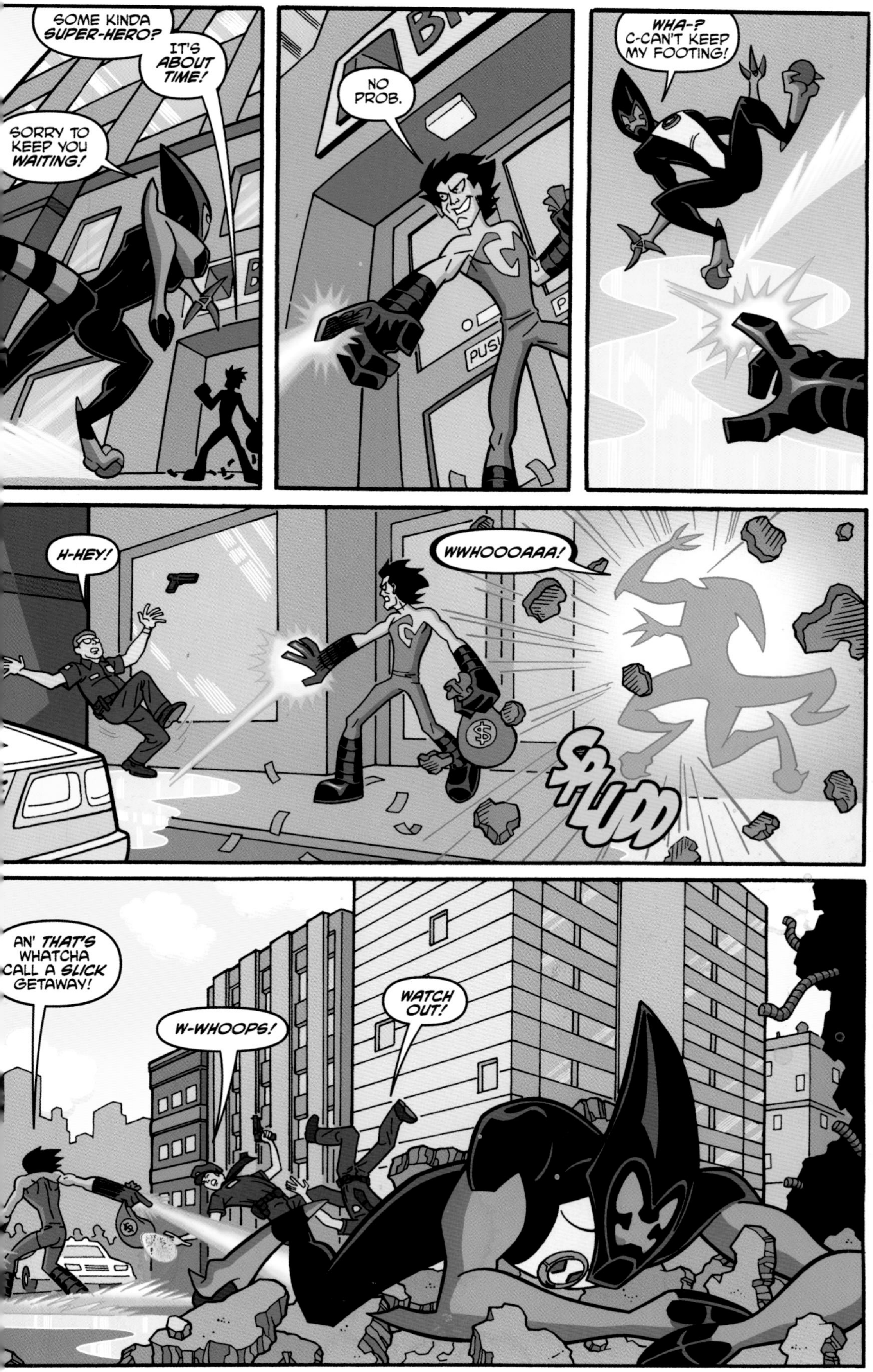
SOME KINDA *SUPER-HERO?*
IT'S *ABOUT TIME!*
SORRY TO KEEP YOU *WAITING!*
NO PROB.
WHA-? C-CAN'T KEEP MY FOOTING!
H-HEY!
WWHOOOAAA!
SPLUDD
AN' *THAT'S* WHATCHA CALL A *SLICK* GETAWAY!
W-WHOOPS!
WATCH OUT!

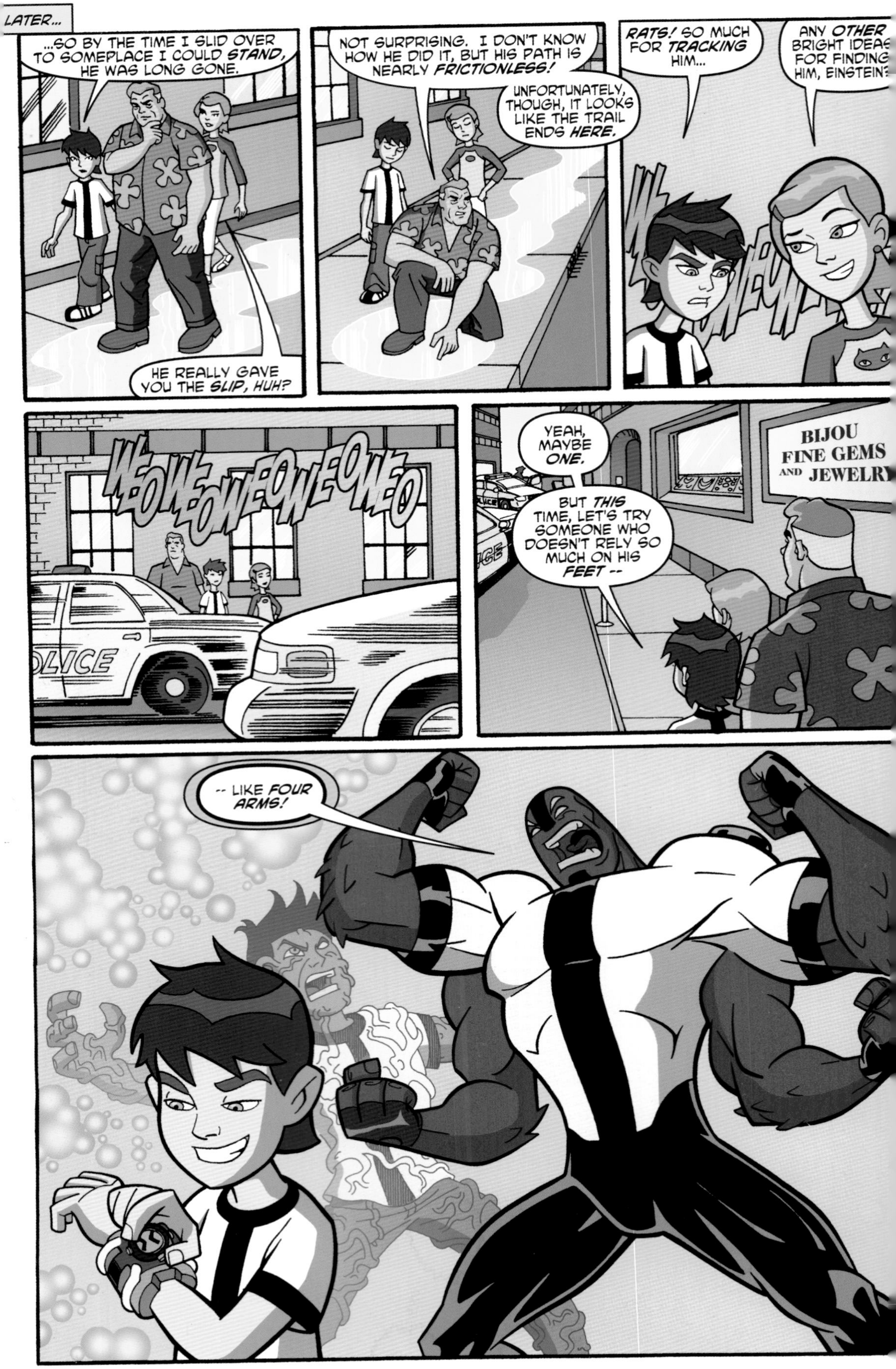
LATER...
...SO BY THE TIME I SLID OVER TO SOMEPLACE I COULD STAND, HE WAS LONG GONE.
HE REALLY GAVE YOU THE SLIP, HUH?
NOT SURPRISING. I DON'T KNOW HOW HE DID IT, BUT HIS PATH IS NEARLY FRICTIONLESS!
UNFORTUNATELY, THOUGH, IT LOOKS LIKE THE TRAIL ENDS HERE.
RATS! SO MUCH FOR TRACKING HIM...
ANY OTHER BRIGHT IDEAS FOR FINDING HIM, EINSTEIN?
WEOWEOWEOWEOWEO
POLICE
YEAH, MAYBE ONE.
BUT THIS TIME, LET'S TRY SOMEONE WHO DOESN'T RELY SO MUCH ON HIS FEET --
BIJOU FINE GEMS AND JEWELRY
-- LIKE FOUR ARMS!

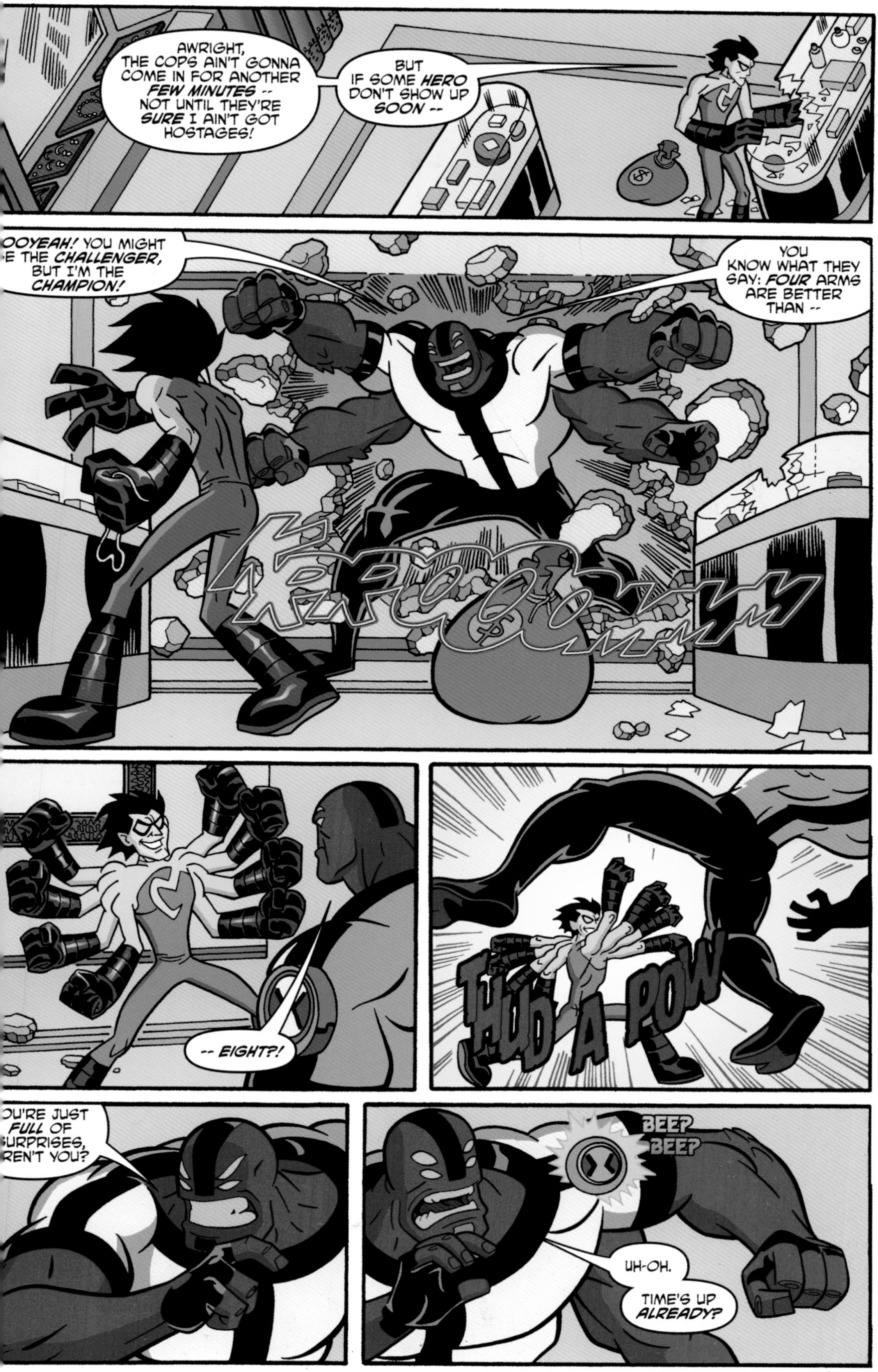
AWRIGHT, THE COPS AIN'T GONNA COME IN FOR ANOTHER *FEW MINUTES* -- NOT UNTIL THEY'RE *SURE* I AIN'T GOT HOSTAGES!
BUT IF SOME *HERO* DON'T SHOW UP *SOON* --
OOYEAH! YOU MIGHT E THE *CHALLENGER,* BUT I'M THE *CHAMPION!*
YOU KNOW WHAT THEY SAY: *FOUR* ARMS ARE BETTER THAN --
-- *EIGHT?!*
THUD A POW
OU'RE JUST *FULL* OF URPRISES, REN'T YOU?
BEEP BEEP
UH-OH.
TIME'S UP *ALREADY?*

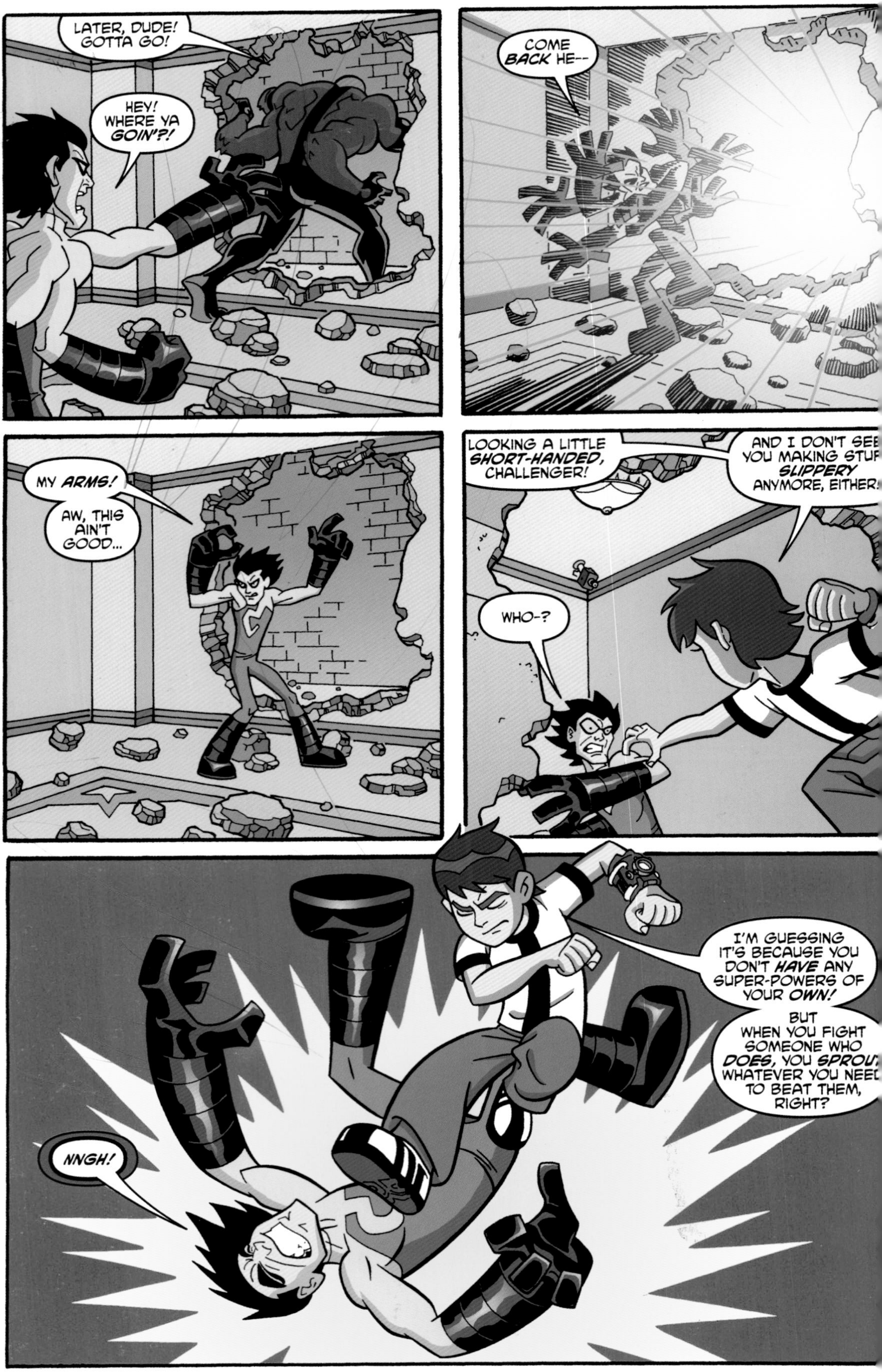
LATER, DUDE! GOTTA GO!
HEY! WHERE YA GOIN'?!
COME BACK HE--
MY ARMS!
AW, THIS AIN'T GOOD...
LOOKING A LITTLE SHORT-HANDED, CHALLENGER!
AND I DON'T SEE YOU MAKING STUF SLIPPERY ANYMORE, EITHER.
WHO-?
I'M GUESSING IT'S BECAUSE YOU DON'T HAVE ANY SUPER-POWERS OF YOUR OWN!
BUT WHEN YOU FIGHT SOMEONE WHO DOES, YOU SPROU WHATEVER YOU NEE TO BEAT THEM, RIGHT?
NNGH!

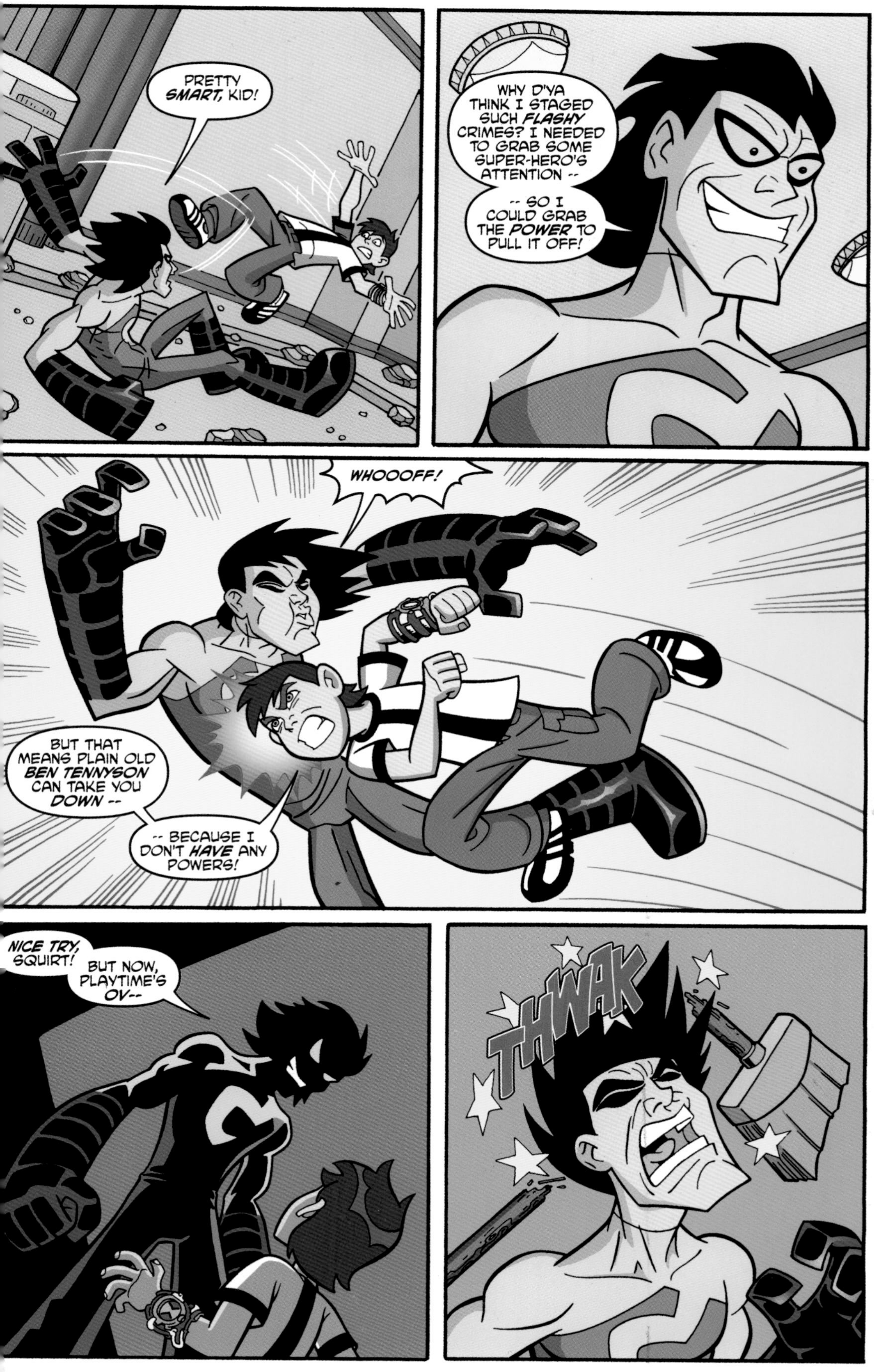
PRETTY SMART, KID!
WHY D'YA THINK I STAGED SUCH FLASHY CRIMES? I NEEDED TO GRAB SOME SUPER-HERO'S ATTENTION --
-- SO I COULD GRAB THE POWER TO PULL IT OFF!
WHOOOFF!
BUT THAT MEANS PLAIN OLD BEN TENNYSON CAN TAKE YOU DOWN --
-- BECAUSE I DON'T HAVE ANY POWERS!
NICE TRY, SQUIRT!
BUT NOW, PLAYTIME'S OV--
THWAK

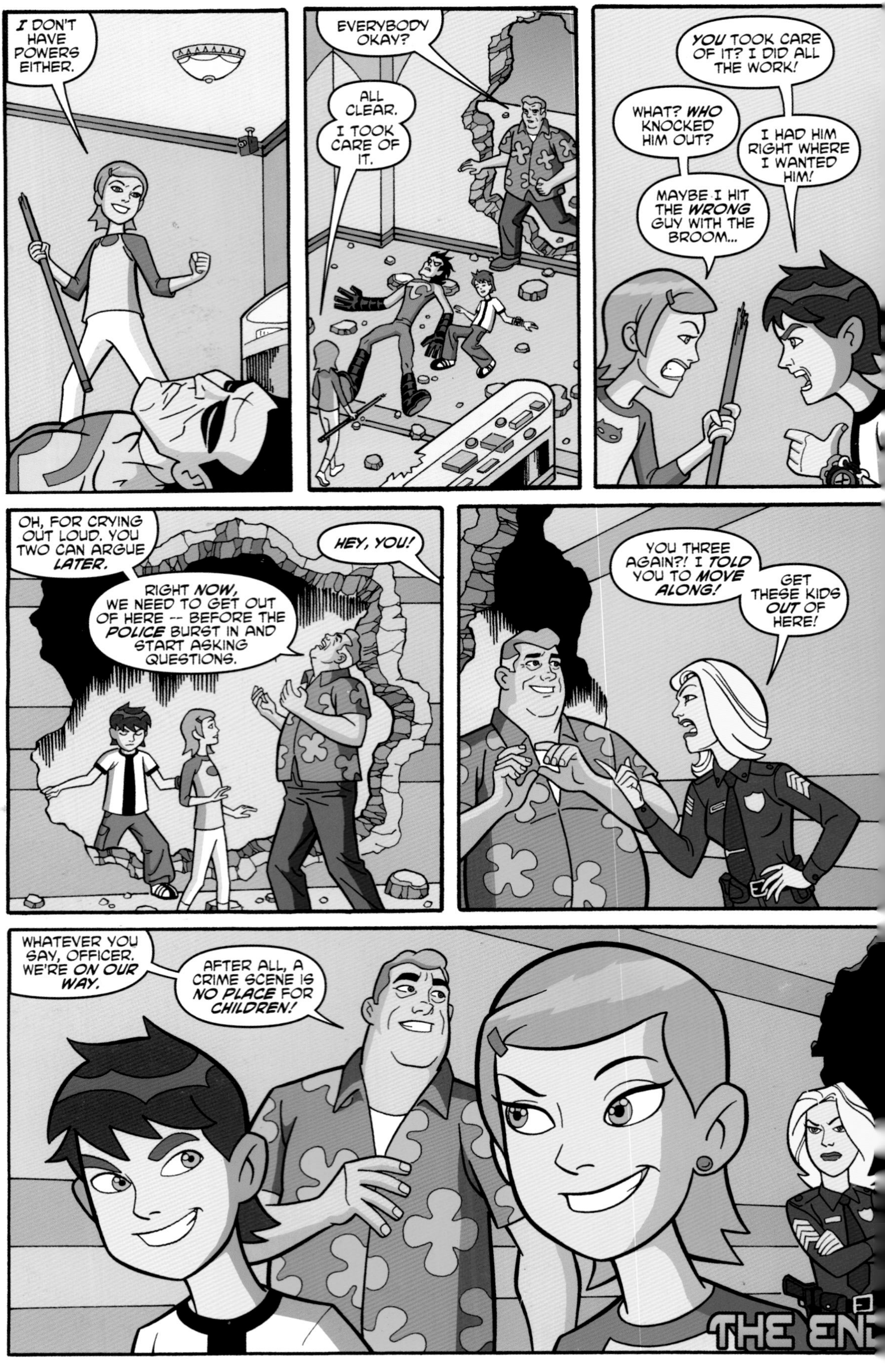
I DON'T HAVE POWERS EITHER.
EVERYBODY OKAY?
ALL CLEAR. I TOOK CARE OF IT.
YOU TOOK CARE OF IT? I DID ALL THE WORK!
WHAT? WHO KNOCKED HIM OUT?
I HAD HIM RIGHT WHERE I WANTED HIM!
MAYBE I HIT THE WRONG GUY WITH THE BROOM...
OH, FOR CRYING OUT LOUD. YOU TWO CAN ARGUE LATER.
RIGHT NOW, WE NEED TO GET OUT OF HERE -- BEFORE THE POLICE BURST IN AND START ASKING QUESTIONS.
HEY, YOU!
YOU THREE AGAIN?! I TOLD YOU TO MOVE ALONG!
GET THESE KIDS OUT OF HERE!
WHATEVER YOU SAY, OFFICER. WE'RE ON OUR WAY.
AFTER ALL, A CRIME SCENE IS NO PLACE FOR CHILDREN!
THE END

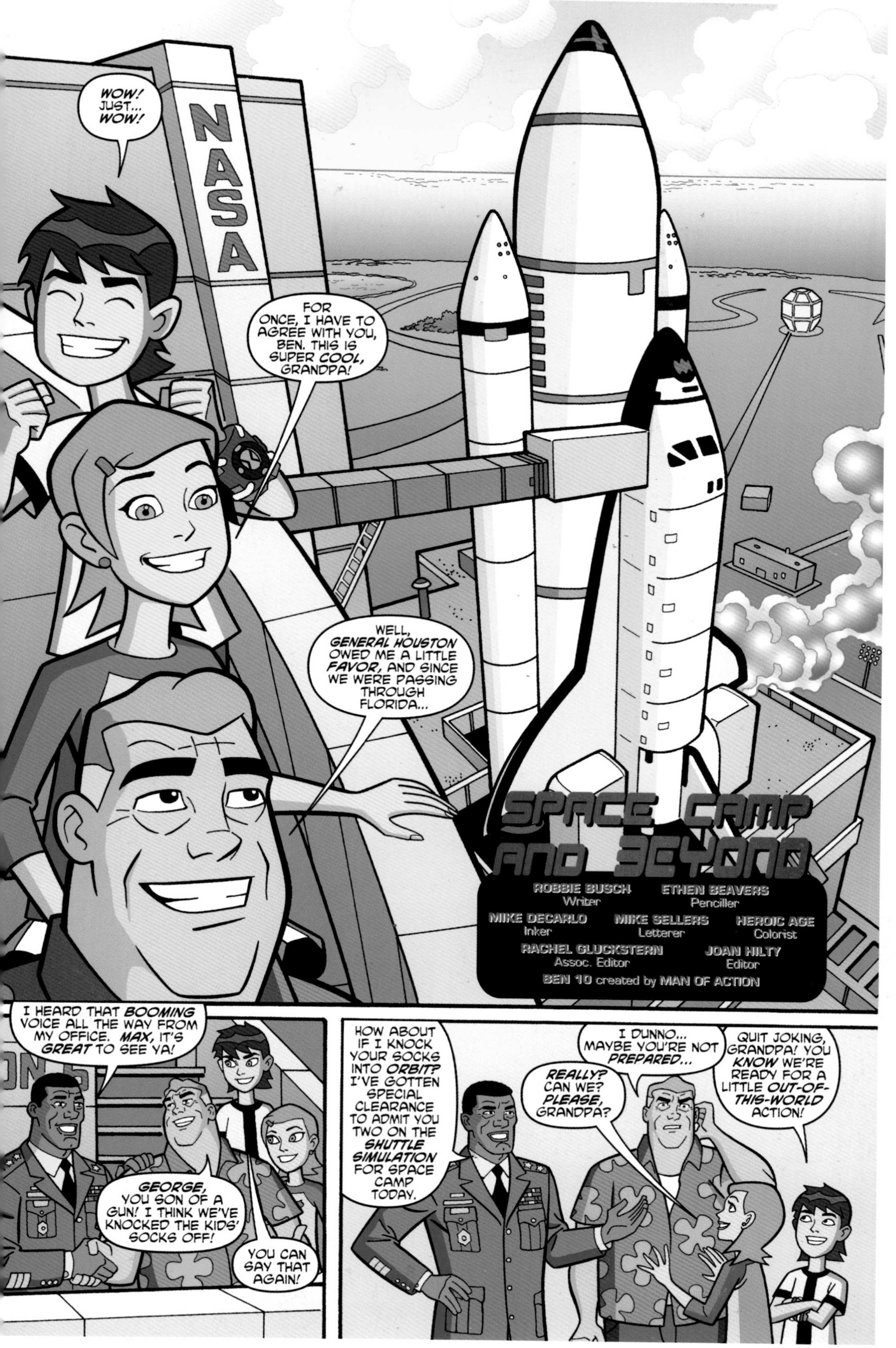
WOW! JUST... WOW!
NASA
FOR ONCE, I HAVE TO AGREE WITH YOU, BEN. THIS IS SUPER COOL, GRANDPA!
WELL, GENERAL HOUSTON OWED ME A LITTLE FAVOR, AND SINCE WE WERE PASSING THROUGH FLORIDA...
SPACE CAMP AND BEYOND
ROBBIE BUSCH Writer
ETHEN BEAVERS Penciller
MIKE DECARLO Inker
MIKE SELLERS Letterer
HEROIC AGE Colorist
RACHEL GLUCKSTERN Assoc. Editor
JOAN HILTY Editor
BEN 10 created by MAN OF ACTION
I HEARD THAT BOOMING VOICE ALL THE WAY FROM MY OFFICE. MAX, IT'S GREAT TO SEE YA!
GEORGE, YOU SON OF A GUN! I THINK WE'VE KNOCKED THE KIDS' SOCKS OFF!
YOU CAN SAY THAT AGAIN!
HOW ABOUT IF I KNOCK YOUR SOCKS INTO ORBIT? I'VE GOTTEN SPECIAL CLEARANCE TO ADMIT YOU TWO ON THE SHUTTLE SIMULATION FOR SPACE CAMP TODAY.
I DUNNO... MAYBE YOU'RE NOT PREPARED...
REALLY? CAN WE? PLEASE, GRANDPA?
QUIT JOKING, GRANDPA! YOU KNOW WE'RE READY FOR A LITTLE OUT-OF-THIS-WORLD ACTION!

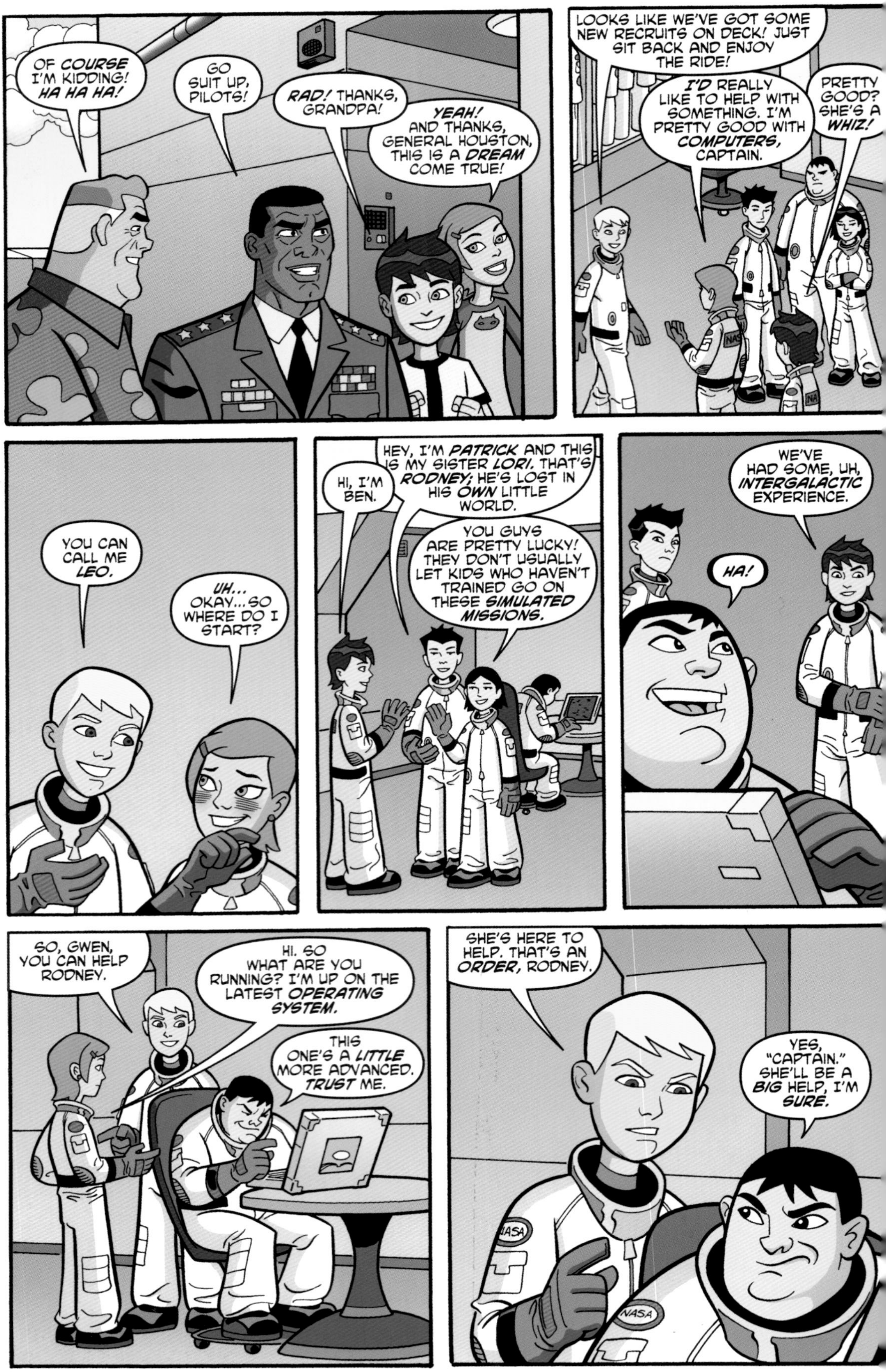
OF COURSE I'M KIDDING! HA HA HA!
GO SUIT UP, PILOTS!
RAD! THANKS, GRANDPA!
YEAH! AND THANKS, GENERAL HOUSTON, THIS IS A DREAM COME TRUE!
LOOKS LIKE WE'VE GOT SOME NEW RECRUITS ON DECK! JUST SIT BACK AND ENJOY THE RIDE!
I'D REALLY LIKE TO HELP WITH SOMETHING. I'M PRETTY GOOD WITH COMPUTERS, CAPTAIN.
PRETTY GOOD? SHE'S A WHIZ!
YOU CAN CALL ME LEO.
UH... OKAY...SO WHERE DO I START?
HI, I'M BEN.
HEY, I'M PATRICK AND THIS IS MY SISTER LORI. THAT'S RODNEY; HE'S LOST IN HIS OWN LITTLE WORLD.
YOU GUYS ARE PRETTY LUCKY! THEY DON'T USUALLY LET KIDS WHO HAVEN'T TRAINED GO ON THESE SIMULATED MISSIONS.
WE'VE HAD SOME, UH, INTERGALACTIC EXPERIENCE.
HA!
SO, GWEN, YOU CAN HELP RODNEY.
HI. SO WHAT ARE YOU RUNNING? I'M UP ON THE LATEST OPERATING SYSTEM.
THIS ONE'S A LITTLE MORE ADVANCED. TRUST ME.
SHE'S HERE TO HELP. THAT'S AN ORDER, RODNEY.
YES, "CAPTAIN." SHE'LL BE A BIG HELP, I'M SURE.

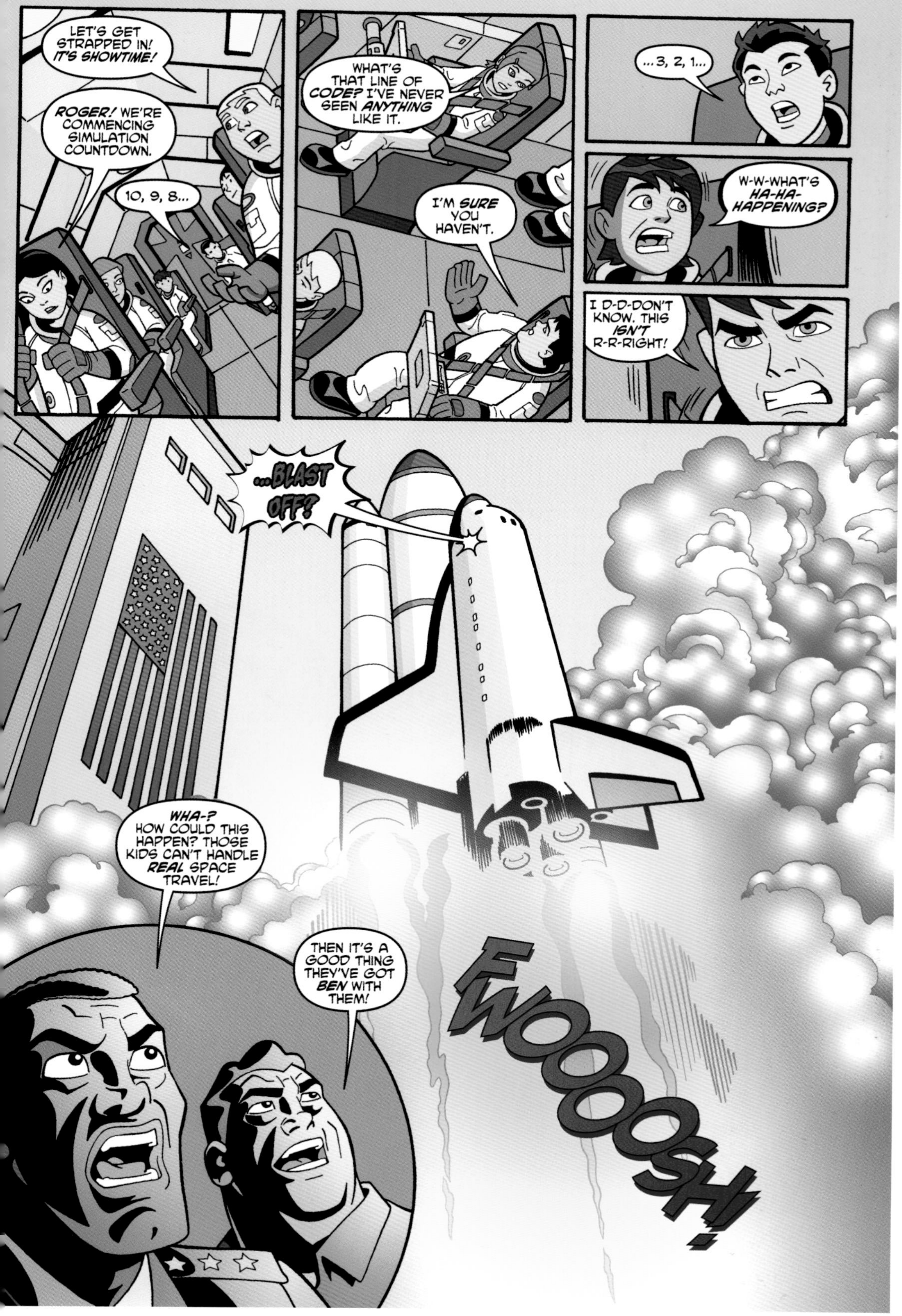

LET'S GET STRAPPED IN! IT'S SHOWTIME!
ROGER! WE'RE COMMENCING SIMULATION COUNTDOWN.
10, 9, 8...
WHAT'S THAT LINE OF CODE? I'VE NEVER SEEN ANYTHING LIKE IT.
I'M SURE YOU HAVEN'T.
...3, 2, 1...
W-W-WHAT'S HA-HA-HAPPENING?
I D-D-DON'T KNOW. THIS ISN'T R-R-RIGHT!
...BLAST OFF?
WHA-? HOW COULD THIS HAPPEN? THOSE KIDS CAN'T HANDLE REAL SPACE TRAVEL!
THEN IT'S A GOOD THING THEY'VE GOT BEN WITH THEM!
FWOOOOSH!

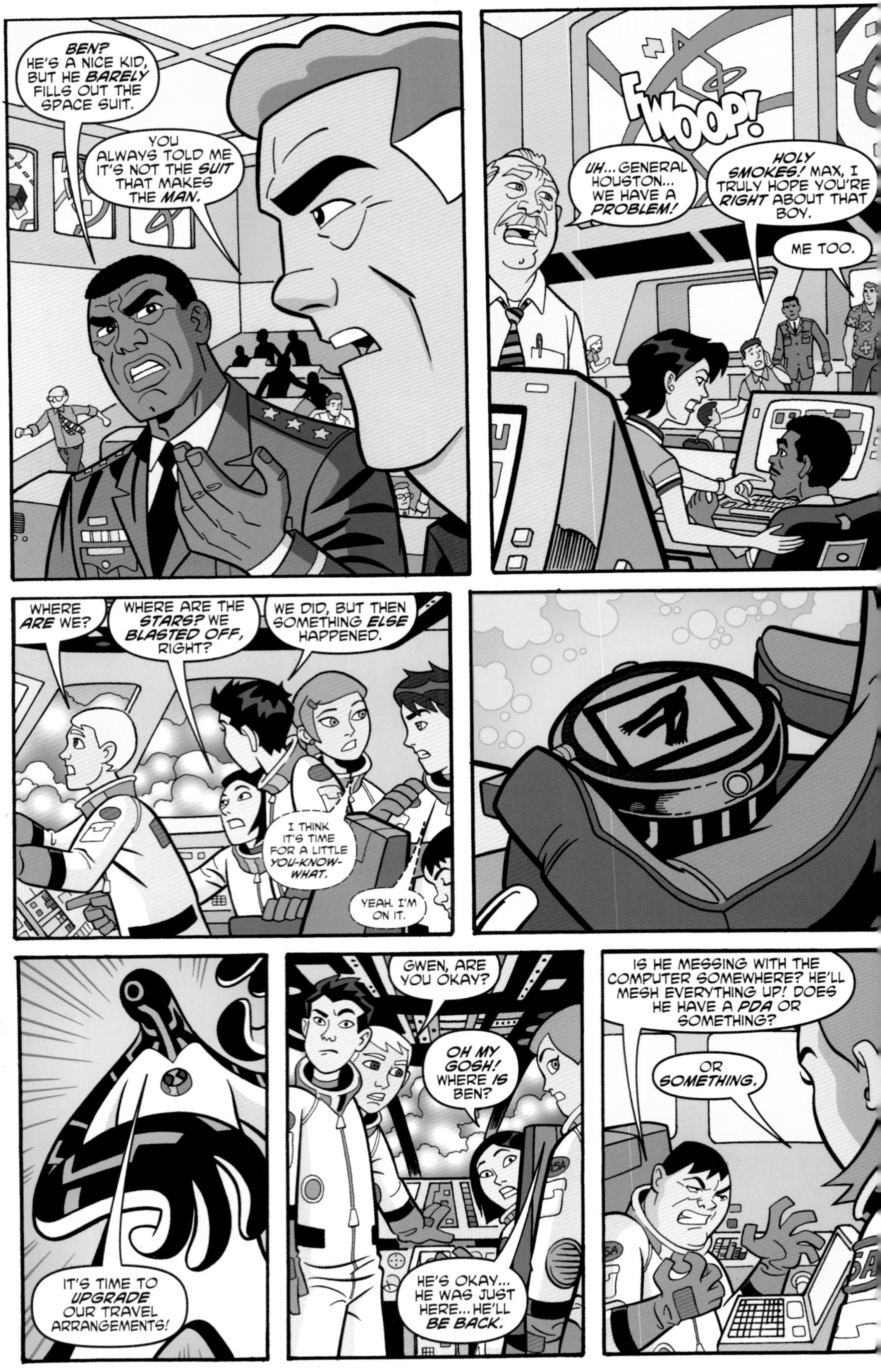
BEN? HE'S A NICE KID, BUT HE BARELY FILLS OUT THE SPACE SUIT.
YOU ALWAYS TOLD ME IT'S NOT THE SUIT THAT MAKES THE MAN.
FWOOP!
UH... GENERAL HOUSTON... WE HAVE A PROBLEM!
HOLY SMOKES! MAX, I TRULY HOPE YOU'RE RIGHT ABOUT THAT BOY.
ME TOO.
WHERE ARE WE?
WHERE ARE THE STARS? WE BLASTED OFF, RIGHT?
WE DID, BUT THEN SOMETHING ELSE HAPPENED.
I THINK IT'S TIME FOR A LITTLE YOU-KNOW-WHAT.
YEAH. I'M ON IT.
IT'S TIME TO UPGRADE OUR TRAVEL ARRANGEMENTS!
GWEN, ARE YOU OKAY?
OH MY GOSH! WHERE IS BEN?
HE'S OKAY... HE WAS JUST HERE... HE'LL BE BACK.
IS HE MESSING WITH THE COMPUTER SOMEWHERE? HE'LL MESH EVERYTHING UP! DOES HE HAVE A PDA OR SOMETHING?
OR SOMETHING.

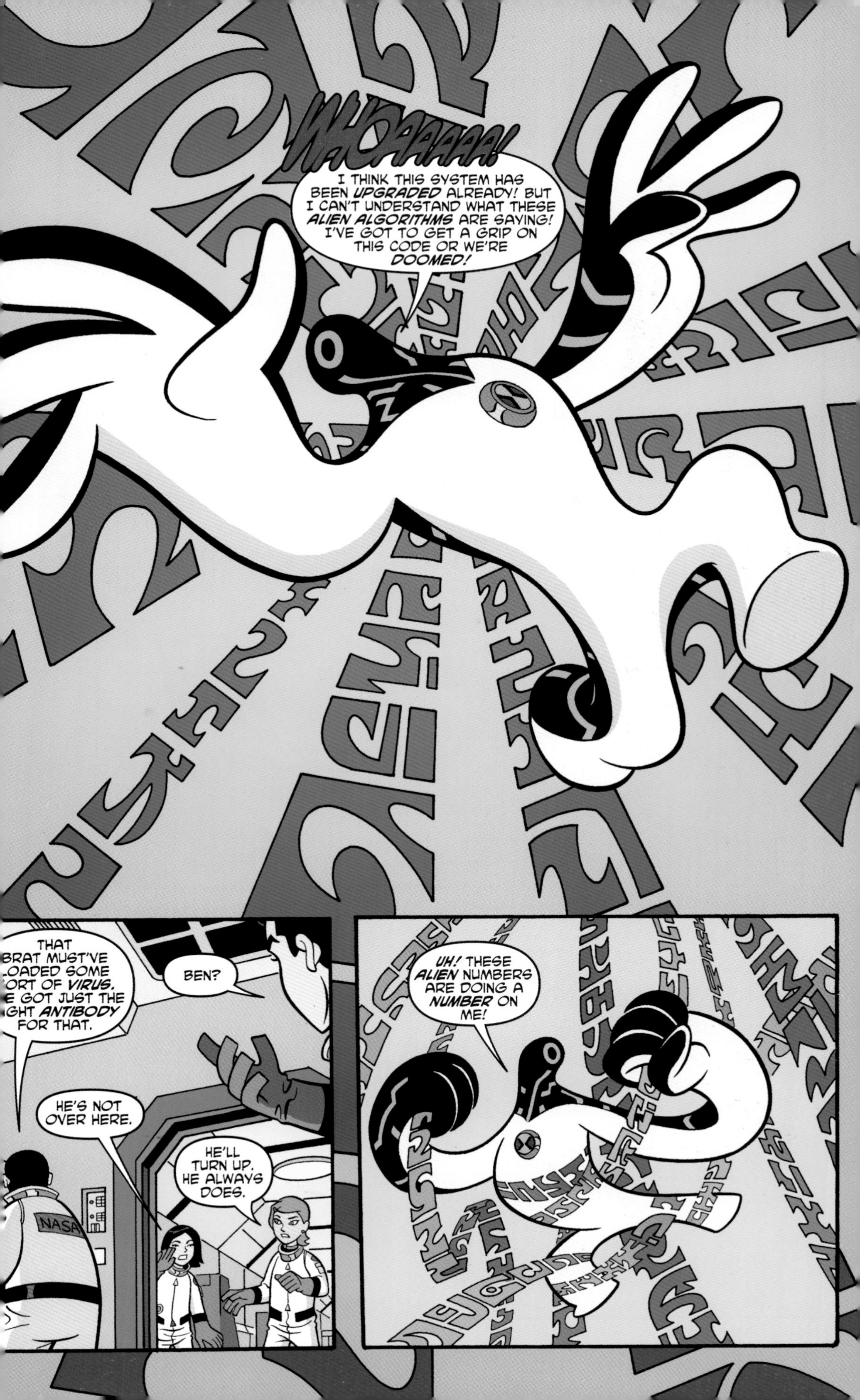
WHOAAAAAA!
I THINK THIS SYSTEM HAS BEEN UPGRADED ALREADY! BUT I CAN'T UNDERSTAND WHAT THESE ALIEN ALGORITHMS ARE SAYING! I'VE GOT TO GET A GRIP ON THIS CODE OR WE'RE DOOMED!
THAT BRAT MUST'VE LOADED SOME ORT OF VIRUS. E GOT JUST THE GHT ANTIBODY FOR THAT.
BEN?
HE'S NOT OVER HERE.
HE'LL TURN UP. HE ALWAYS DOES.
NASA
UH! THESE ALIEN NUMBERS ARE DOING A NUMBER ON ME!

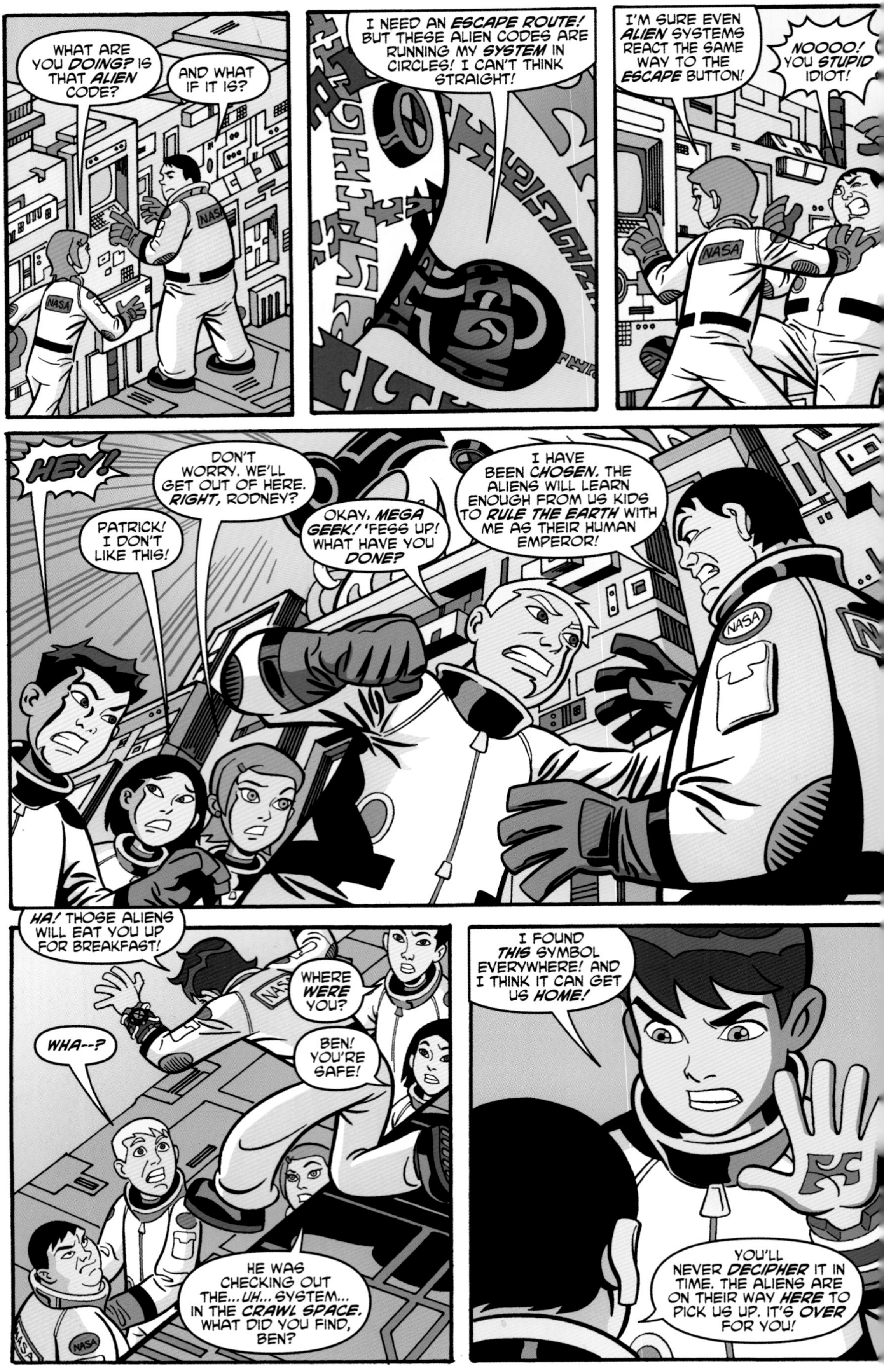

WHAT ARE YOU DOING? IS THAT ALIEN CODE?
AND WHAT IF IT IS?
I NEED AN ESCAPE ROUTE! BUT THESE ALIEN CODES ARE RUNNING MY SYSTEM IN CIRCLES! I CAN'T THINK STRAIGHT!
I'M SURE EVEN ALIEN SYSTEMS REACT THE SAME WAY TO THE ESCAPE BUTTON!
NOOOO! YOU STUPID IDIOT!
HEY!
PATRICK! I DON'T LIKE THIS!
DON'T WORRY. WE'LL GET OUT OF HERE. RIGHT, RODNEY?
OKAY, MEGA GEEK! 'FESS UP! WHAT HAVE YOU DONE?
I HAVE BEEN CHOSEN. THE ALIENS WILL LEARN ENOUGH FROM US KIDS TO RULE THE EARTH WITH ME AS THEIR HUMAN EMPEROR!
HA! THOSE ALIENS WILL EAT YOU UP FOR BREAKFAST!
WHA--?
WHERE WERE YOU?
BEN! YOU'RE SAFE!
HE WAS CHECKING OUT THE...UH... SYSTEM... IN THE CRAWL SPACE. WHAT DID YOU FIND, BEN?
I FOUND THIS SYMBOL EVERYWHERE! AND I THINK IT CAN GET US HOME!
YOU'LL NEVER DECIPHER IT IN TIME. THE ALIENS ARE ON THEIR WAY HERE TO PICK US UP. IT'S OVER FOR YOU!

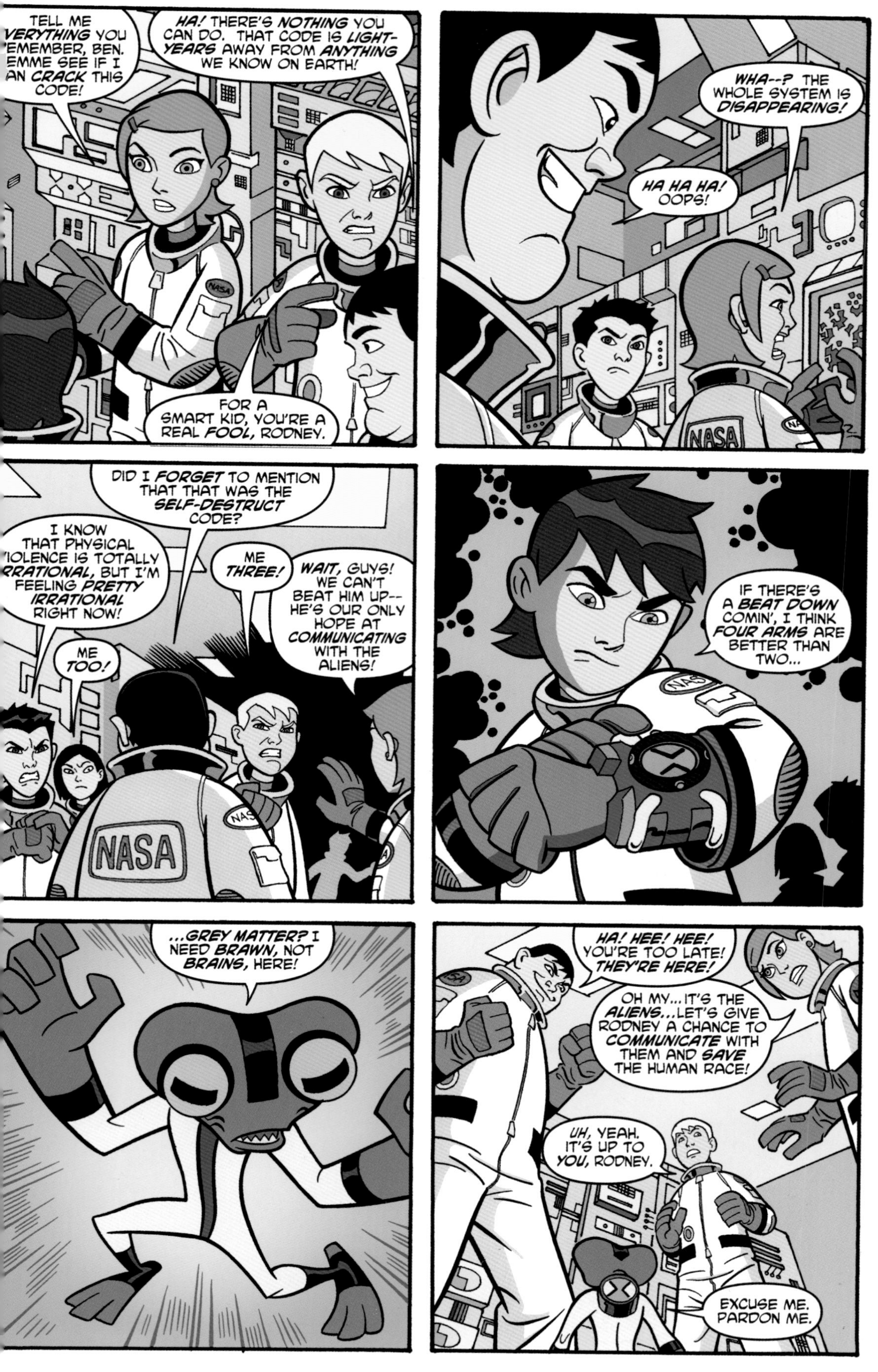
TELL ME VERYTHING YOU EMEMBER, BEN. EMME SEE IF I AN CRACK THIS CODE!
HA! THERE'S NOTHING YOU CAN DO. THAT CODE IS LIGHT-YEARS AWAY FROM ANYTHING WE KNOW ON EARTH!
FOR A SMART KID, YOU'RE A REAL FOOL, RODNEY.
WHA--? THE WHOLE SYSTEM IS DISAPPEARING!
HA HA HA! OOPS!
DID I FORGET TO MENTION THAT THAT WAS THE SELF-DESTRUCT CODE?
I KNOW THAT PHYSICAL IOLENCE IS TOTALLY RRATIONAL, BUT I'M FEELING PRETTY IRRATIONAL RIGHT NOW!
ME TOO!
ME THREE!
WAIT, GUYS! WE CAN'T BEAT HIM UP-- HE'S OUR ONLY HOPE AT COMMUNICATING WITH THE ALIENS!
IF THERE'S A BEAT DOWN COMIN', I THINK FOUR ARMS ARE BETTER THAN TWO...
...GREY MATTER? I NEED BRAWN, NOT BRAINS, HERE!
HA! HEE! HEE! YOU'RE TOO LATE! THEY'RE HERE!
OH MY... IT'S THE ALIENS... LET'S GIVE RODNEY A CHANCE TO COMMUNICATE WITH THEM AND SAVE THE HUMAN RACE!
UH, YEAH. IT'S UP TO YOU, RODNEY.
EXCUSE ME. PARDON ME.

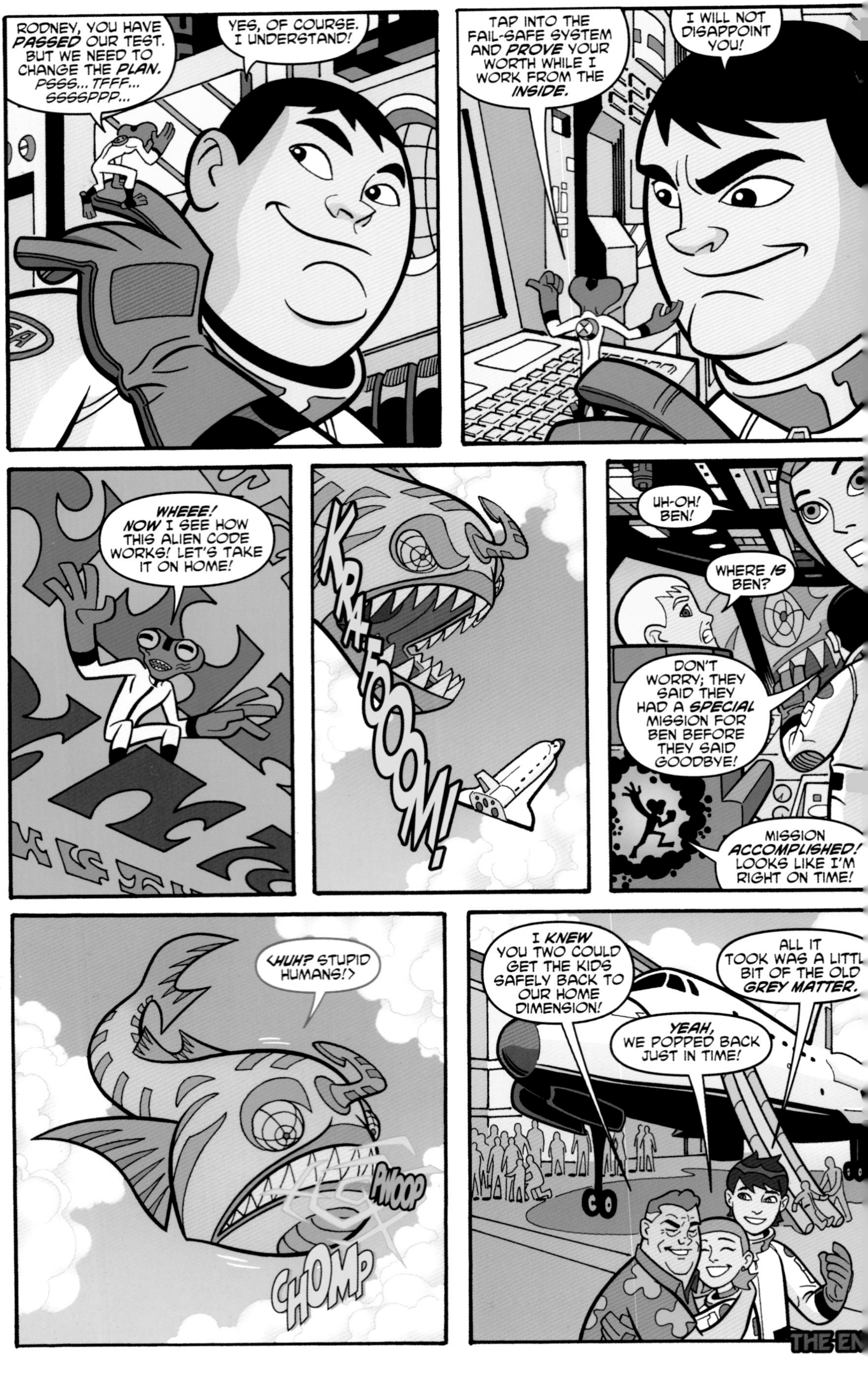

RODNEY, YOU HAVE PASSED OUR TEST. BUT WE NEED TO CHANGE THE PLAN. PSSS... TFFF... SSSSPPP...
YES, OF COURSE. I UNDERSTAND!
TAP INTO THE FAIL-SAFE SYSTEM AND PROVE YOUR WORTH WHILE I WORK FROM THE INSIDE.
I WILL NOT DISAPPOINT YOU!
WHEEE! NOW I SEE HOW THIS ALIEN CODE WORKS! LET'S TAKE IT ON HOME!
KRA-FOOOOM!
UH-OH! BEN!
WHERE IS BEN?
DON'T WORRY; THEY SAID THEY HAD A SPECIAL MISSION FOR BEN BEFORE THEY SAID GOODBYE!
MISSION ACCOMPLISHED! LOOKS LIKE I'M RIGHT ON TIME!
<HUH? STUPID HUMANS!>
PWOOP
CHOMP
I KNEW YOU TWO COULD GET THE KIDS SAFELY BACK TO OUR HOME DIMENSION!
ALL IT TOOK WAS A LITTL BIT OF THE OLD GREY MATTER.
YEAH, WE POPPED BACK JUST IN TIME!
THE EN

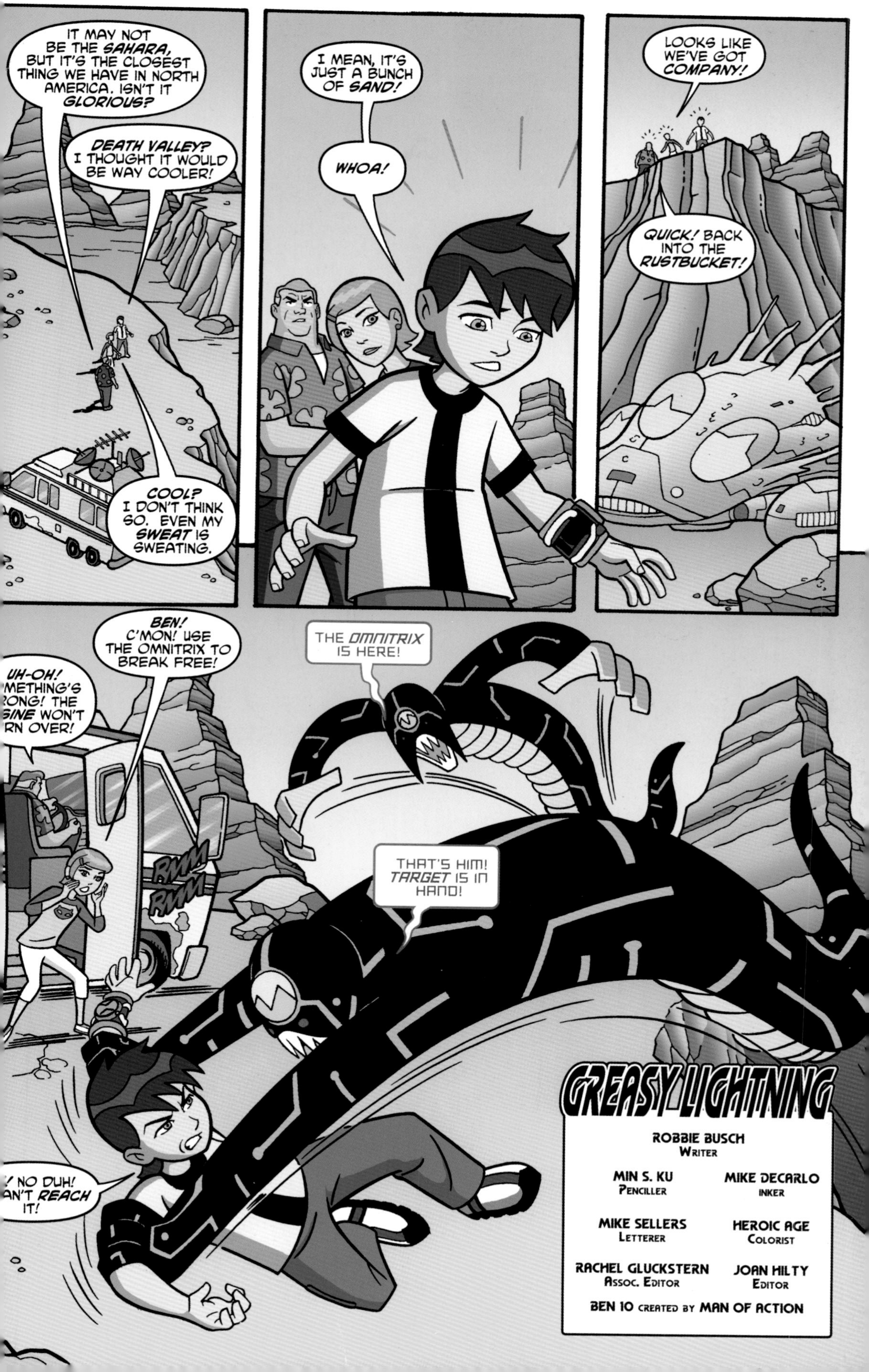

IT MAY NOT BE THE *SAHARA*, BUT IT'S THE CLOSEST THING WE HAVE IN NORTH AMERICA. ISN'T IT *GLORIOUS?*
DEATH VALLEY? I THOUGHT IT WOULD BE WAY COOLER!
COOL? I DON'T THINK SO. EVEN MY *SWEAT* IS SWEATING.
I MEAN, IT'S JUST A BUNCH OF *SAND!*
WHOA!
LOOKS LIKE WE'VE GOT *COMPANY!*
QUICK! BACK INTO THE *RUSTBUCKET!*
UH-OH! METHING'S RONG! THE GINE WON'T RN OVER!
BEN! C'MON! USE THE OMNITRIX TO BREAK FREE!
THE *OMNITRIX* IS HERE!
RMM RMM
THAT'S HIM! *TARGET* IS IN HAND!
NO DUH! AN'T *REACH* IT!
GREASY LIGHTNING
ROBBIE BUSCH
WRITER
MIN S. KU
PENCILLER
MIKE DECARLO
INKER
MIKE SELLERS
LETTERER
HEROIC AGE
COLORIST
RACHEL GLUCKSTERN
ASSOC. EDITOR
JOAN HILTY
EDITOR
BEN 10 CREATED BY MAN OF ACTION

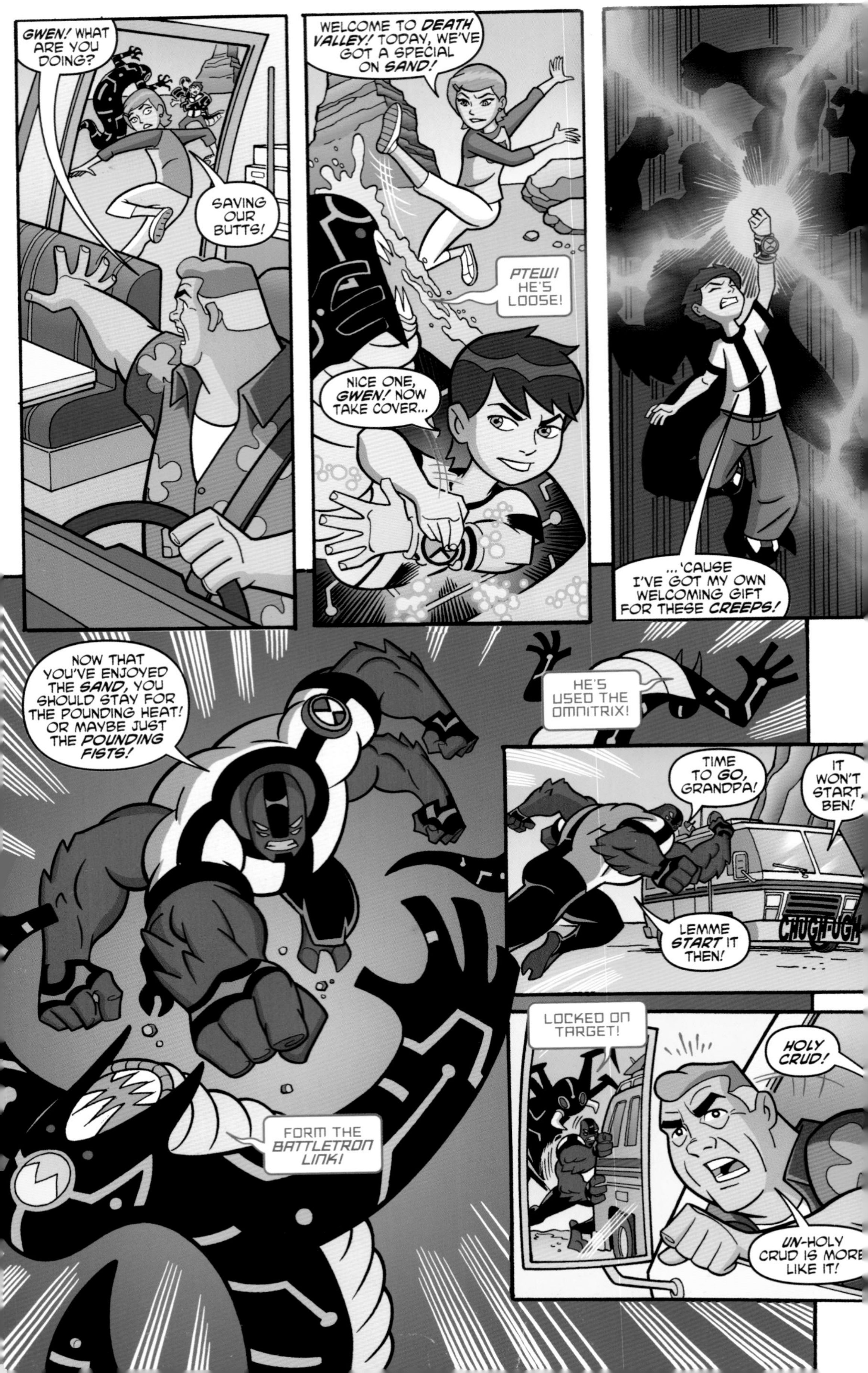
GWEN! WHAT ARE YOU DOING?
SAVING OUR BUTTS!
WELCOME TO DEATH VALLEY! TODAY, WE'VE GOT A SPECIAL ON SAND!
PTEW! HE'S LOOSE!
NICE ONE, GWEN! NOW TAKE COVER...
...'CAUSE I'VE GOT MY OWN WELCOMING GIFT FOR THESE CREEPS!
NOW THAT YOU'VE ENJOYED THE SAND, YOU SHOULD STAY FOR THE POUNDING HEAT! OR MAYBE JUST THE POUNDING FISTS!
HE'S USED THE OMNITRIX!
FORM THE BATTLETRON LINK!
TIME TO GO, GRANDPA!
IT WON'T START, BEN!
LEMME START IT THEN!
CHUGH-UGH
LOCKED ON TARGET!
HOLY CRUD!
UN-HOLY CRUD IS MORE LIKE IT!

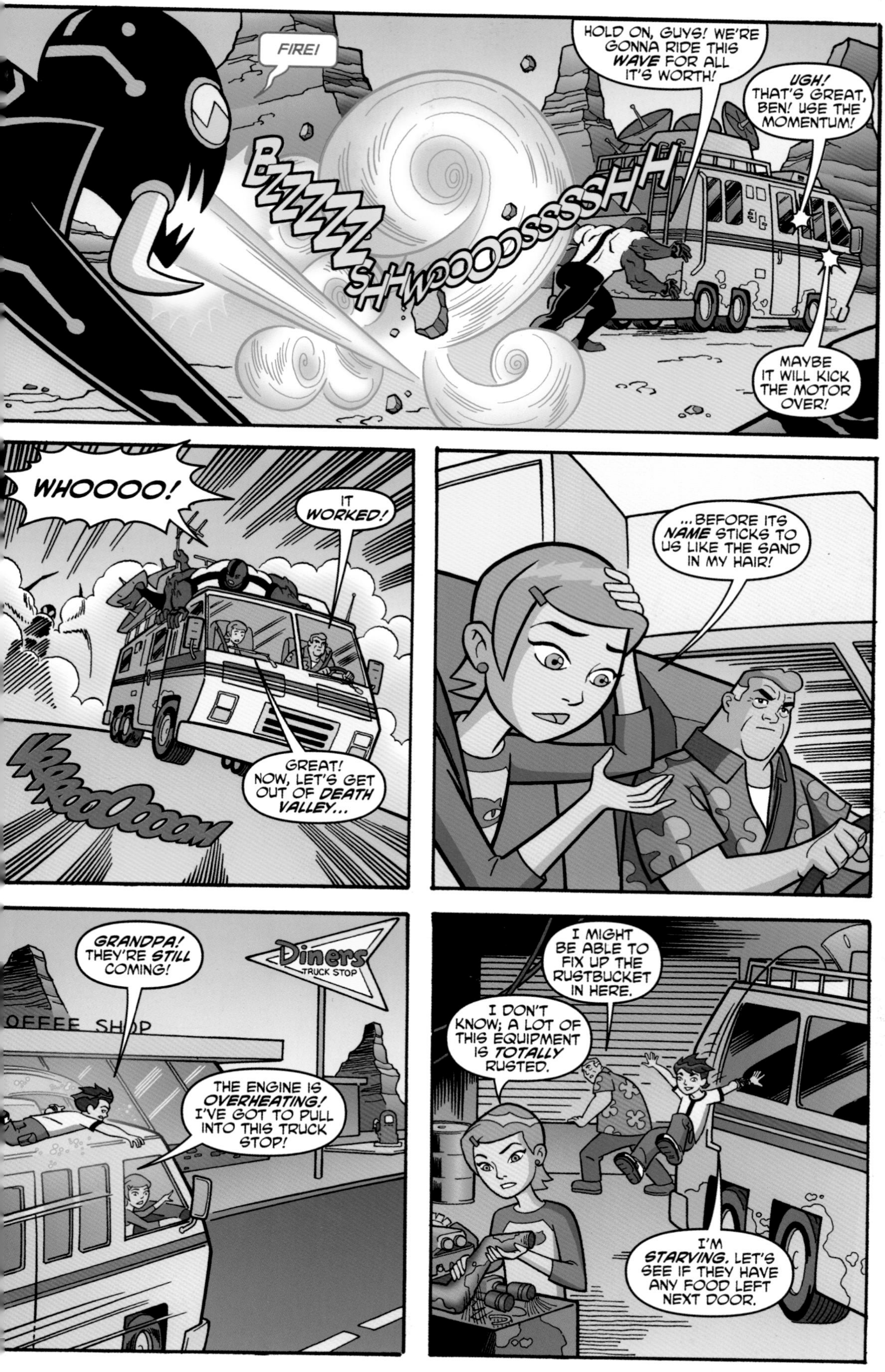
FIRE!
BZZZZZ
SHWOOOSSSSHH
HOLD ON, GUYS! WE'RE GONNA RIDE THIS WAVE FOR ALL IT'S WORTH!
UGH! THAT'S GREAT, BEN! USE THE MOMENTUM!
MAYBE IT WILL KICK THE MOTOR OVER!
WHOOOO!
IT WORKED!
GREAT! NOW, LET'S GET OUT OF DEATH VALLEY...
VROOOOOOOM
...BEFORE ITS NAME STICKS TO US LIKE THE SAND IN MY HAIR!
GRANDPA! THEY'RE STILL COMING!
Diners
TRUCK STOP
OFFEE SHOP
THE ENGINE IS OVERHEATING! I'VE GOT TO PULL INTO THIS TRUCK STOP!
I MIGHT BE ABLE TO FIX UP THE RUSTBUCKET IN HERE.
I DON'T KNOW; A LOT OF THIS EQUIPMENT IS TOTALLY RUSTED.
I'M STARVING. LET'S SEE IF THEY HAVE ANY FOOD LEFT NEXT DOOR.

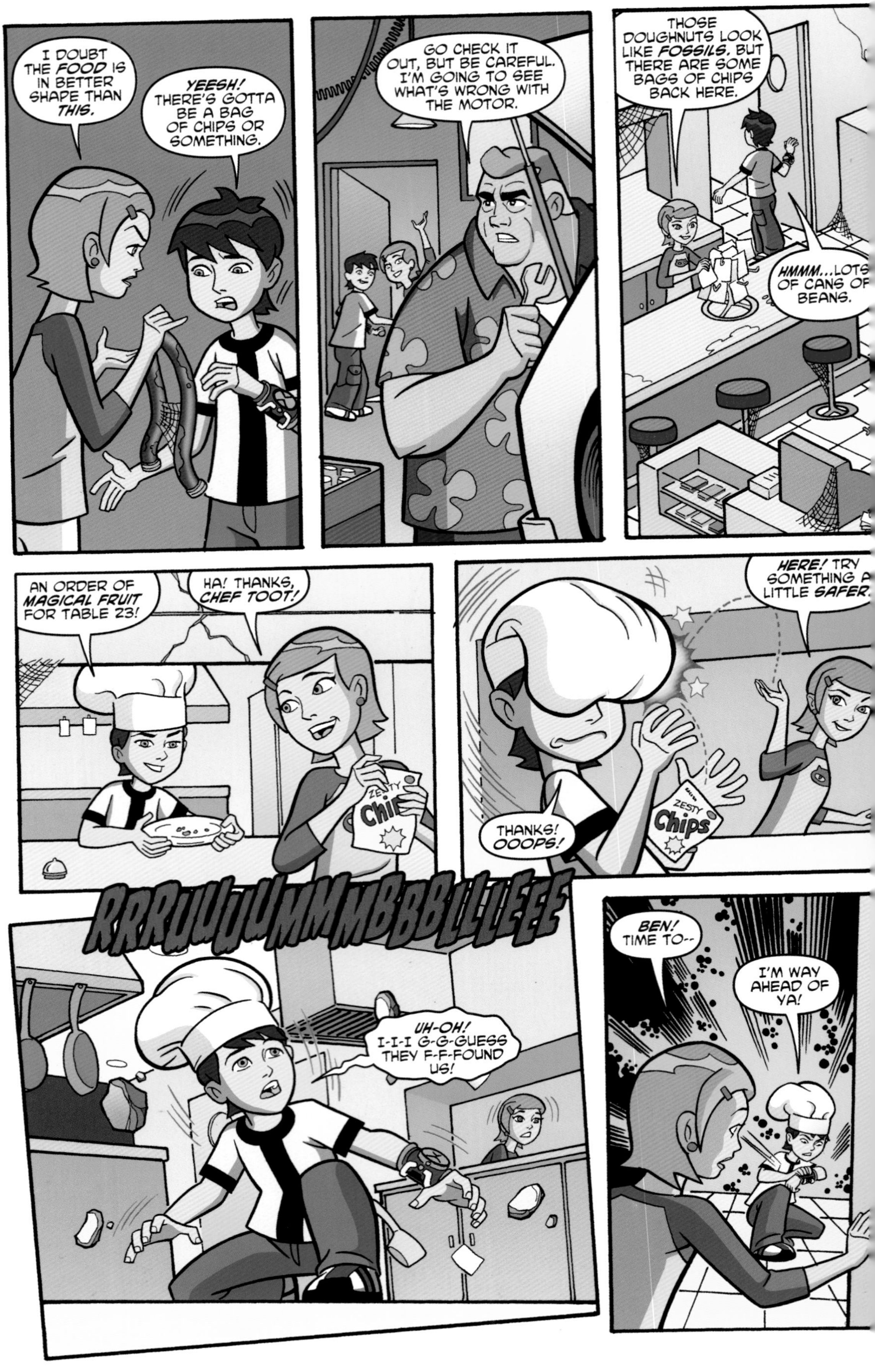
I DOUBT THE FOOD IS IN BETTER SHAPE THAN THIS.
YEESH! THERE'S GOTTA BE A BAG OF CHIPS OR SOMETHING.
GO CHECK IT OUT, BUT BE CAREFUL. I'M GOING TO SEE WHAT'S WRONG WITH THE MOTOR.
THOSE DOUGHNUTS LOOK LIKE FOSSILS. BUT THERE ARE SOME BAGS OF CHIPS BACK HERE.
HMMM...LOTS OF CANS OF BEANS.
AN ORDER OF MAGICAL FRUIT FOR TABLE 23!
HA! THANKS, CHEF TOOT!
ZESTY Chips
HERE! TRY SOMETHING A LITTLE SAFER.
THANKS! OOOPS!
ZESTY Chips
RRRUUUUUMMMBBBLLLEEE
UH-OH! I-I-I G-G-GUESS THEY F-F-FOUND US!
BEN! TIME TO--
I'M WAY AHEAD OF YA!

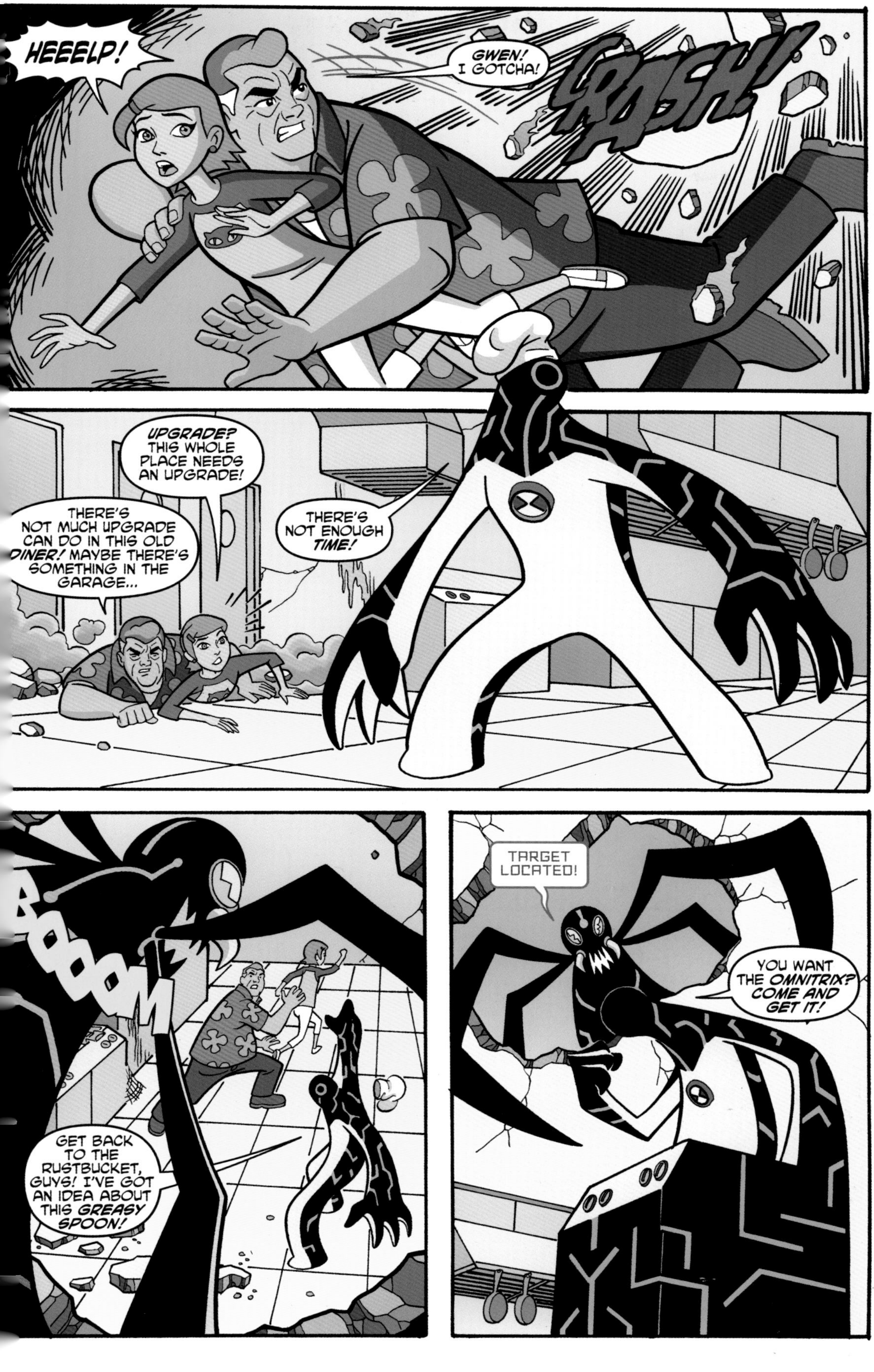
HEEELP!
GWEN! I GOTCHA!
CRASH!
UPGRADE? THIS WHOLE PLACE NEEDS AN UPGRADE!
THERE'S NOT MUCH UPGRADE CAN DO IN THIS OLD DINER! MAYBE THERE'S SOMETHING IN THE GARAGE...
THERE'S NOT ENOUGH TIME!
BOOOM
GET BACK TO THE RUSTBUCKET, GUYS! I'VE GOT AN IDEA ABOUT THIS GREASY SPOON!
TARGET LOCATED!
YOU WANT THE OMNITRIX? COME AND GET IT!

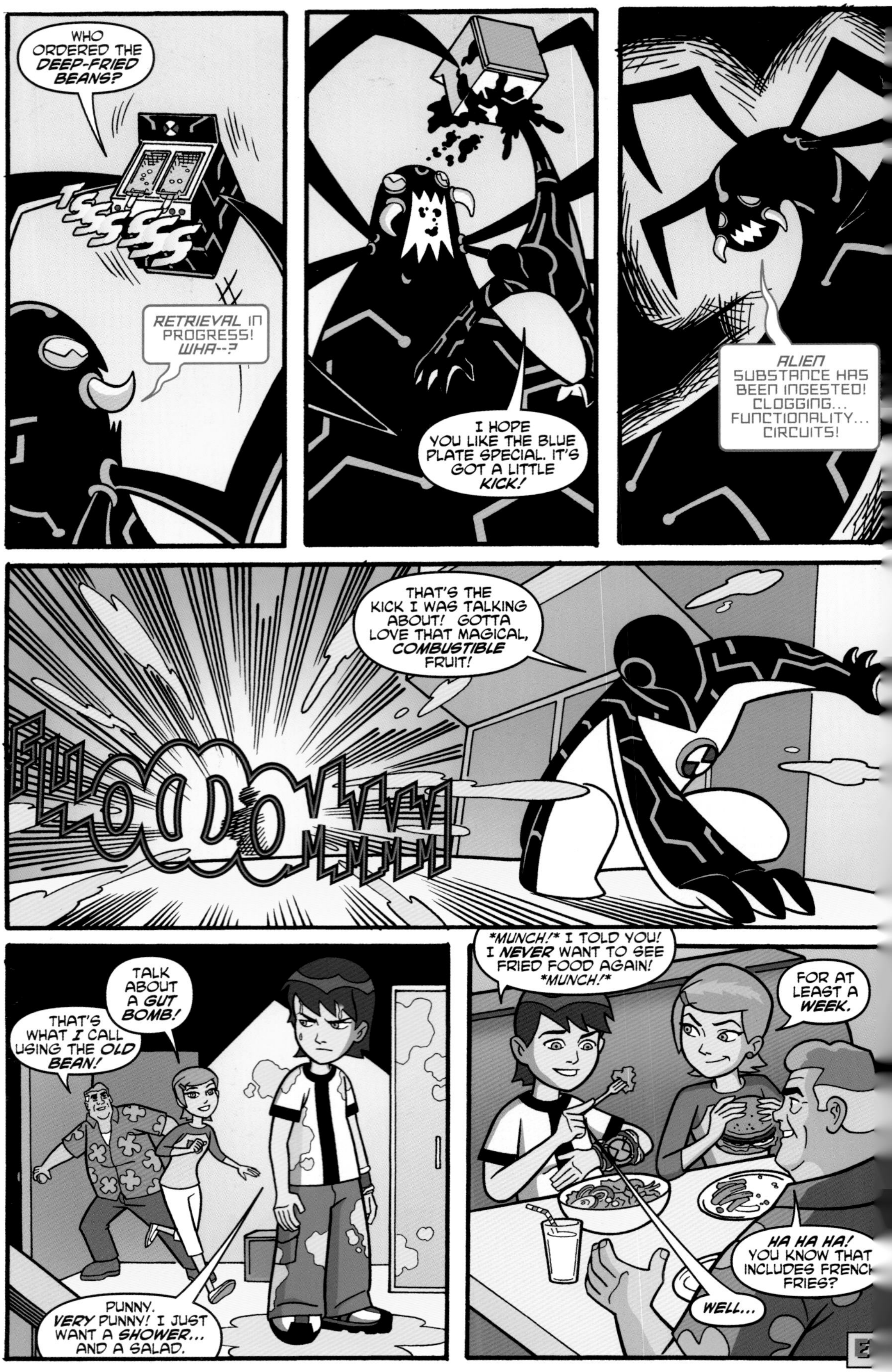
WHO ORDERED THE DEEP-FRIED BEANS?
TSSSSS
RETRIEVAL IN PROGRESS! WHA--?
I HOPE YOU LIKE THE BLUE PLATE SPECIAL. IT'S GOT A LITTLE KICK!
ALIEN SUBSTANCE HAS BEEN INGESTED! CLOGGING... FUNCTIONALITY... CIRCUITS!
THAT'S THE KICK I WAS TALKING ABOUT! GOTTA LOVE THAT MAGICAL, COMBUSTIBLE FRUIT!
FLLOOOOOWWWWMMMMMM
TALK ABOUT A GUT BOMB!
THAT'S WHAT I CALL USING THE OLD BEAN!
PUNNY. VERY PUNNY! I JUST WANT A SHOWER... AND A SALAD.
MUNCH! I TOLD YOU! I NEVER WANT TO SEE FRIED FOOD AGAIN! *MUNCH!*
FOR AT LEAST A WEEK.
HA HA HA! YOU KNOW THAT INCLUDES FRENCH FRIES?
WELL...

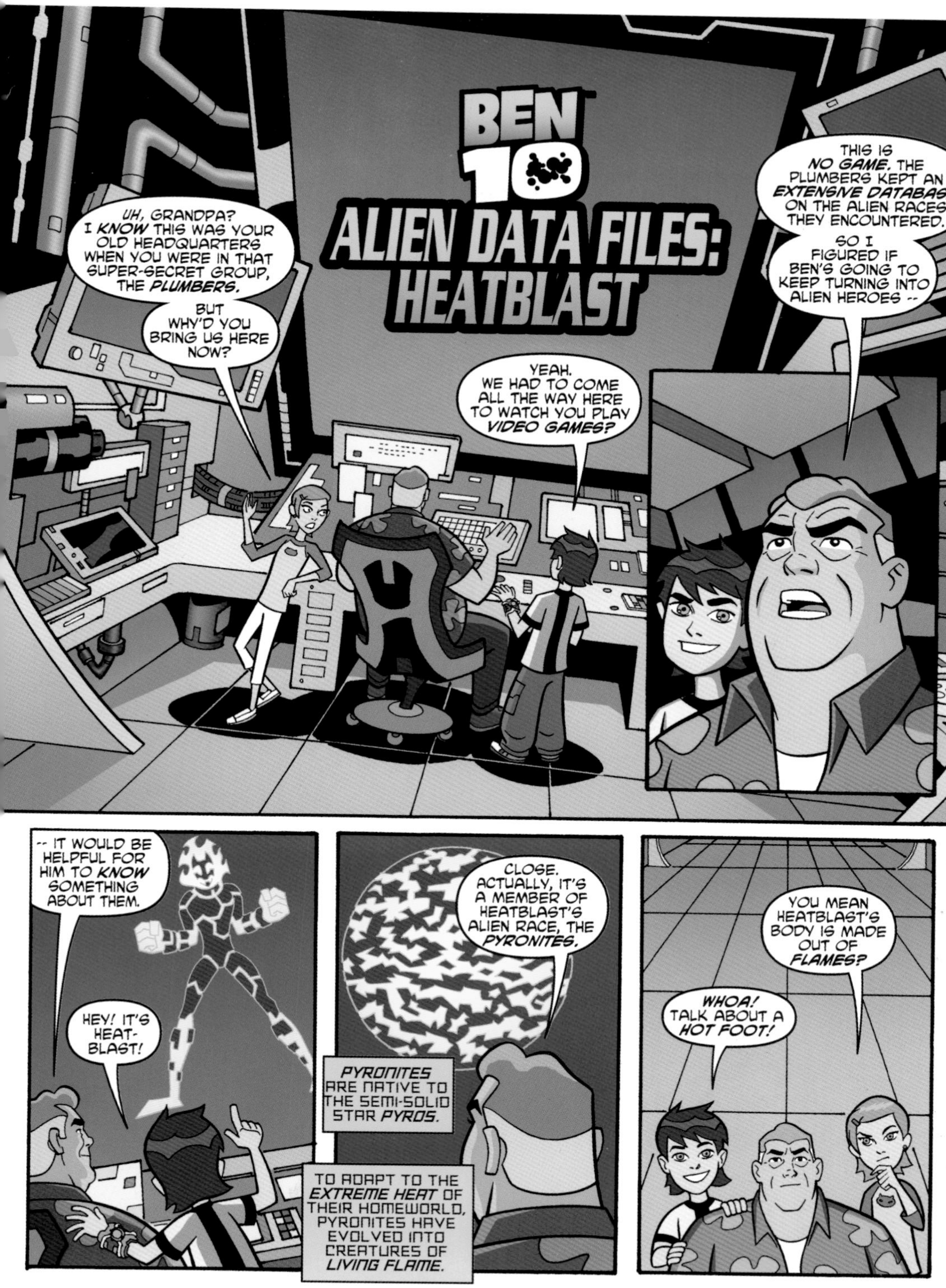
BEN 10
ALIEN DATA FILES: HEATBLAST
UH, GRANDPA? I *KNOW* THIS WAS YOUR OLD HEADQUARTERS WHEN YOU WERE IN THAT SUPER-SECRET GROUP, THE *PLUMBERS.*
BUT WHY'D YOU BRING US HERE NOW?
YEAH. WE HAD TO COME ALL THE WAY HERE TO WATCH YOU PLAY *VIDEO GAMES?*
THIS IS *NO GAME.* THE PLUMBERS KEPT AN *EXTENSIVE DATABASE* ON THE ALIEN RACES THEY ENCOUNTERED.
SO I FIGURED IF BEN'S GOING TO KEEP TURNING INTO ALIEN HEROES --
-- IT WOULD BE HELPFUL FOR HIM TO *KNOW* SOMETHING ABOUT THEM.
HEY! IT'S HEAT-BLAST!
CLOSE. ACTUALLY, IT'S A MEMBER OF HEATBLAST'S ALIEN RACE, THE *PYRONITES.*
PYRONITES ARE NATIVE TO THE SEMI-SOLID STAR *PYROS.*
TO ADAPT TO THE *EXTREME HEAT* OF THEIR HOMEWORLD, PYRONITES HAVE EVOLVED INTO CREATURES OF *LIVING FLAME.*
YOU MEAN HEATBLAST'S BODY IS MADE OUT OF *FLAMES?*
WHOA! TALK ABOUT A *HOT FOOT!*

SHOLLY FISCH Writer
ETHEN BEAVERS Penciller
MIKE DECARLO Inker
MIKE SELLERS Letterer
HEROIC AGE Colorist
RACHEL GLUCKSTERN Assoc. Editor
JOAN HILTY Editor

BEN 10 created by MAN OF ACTION

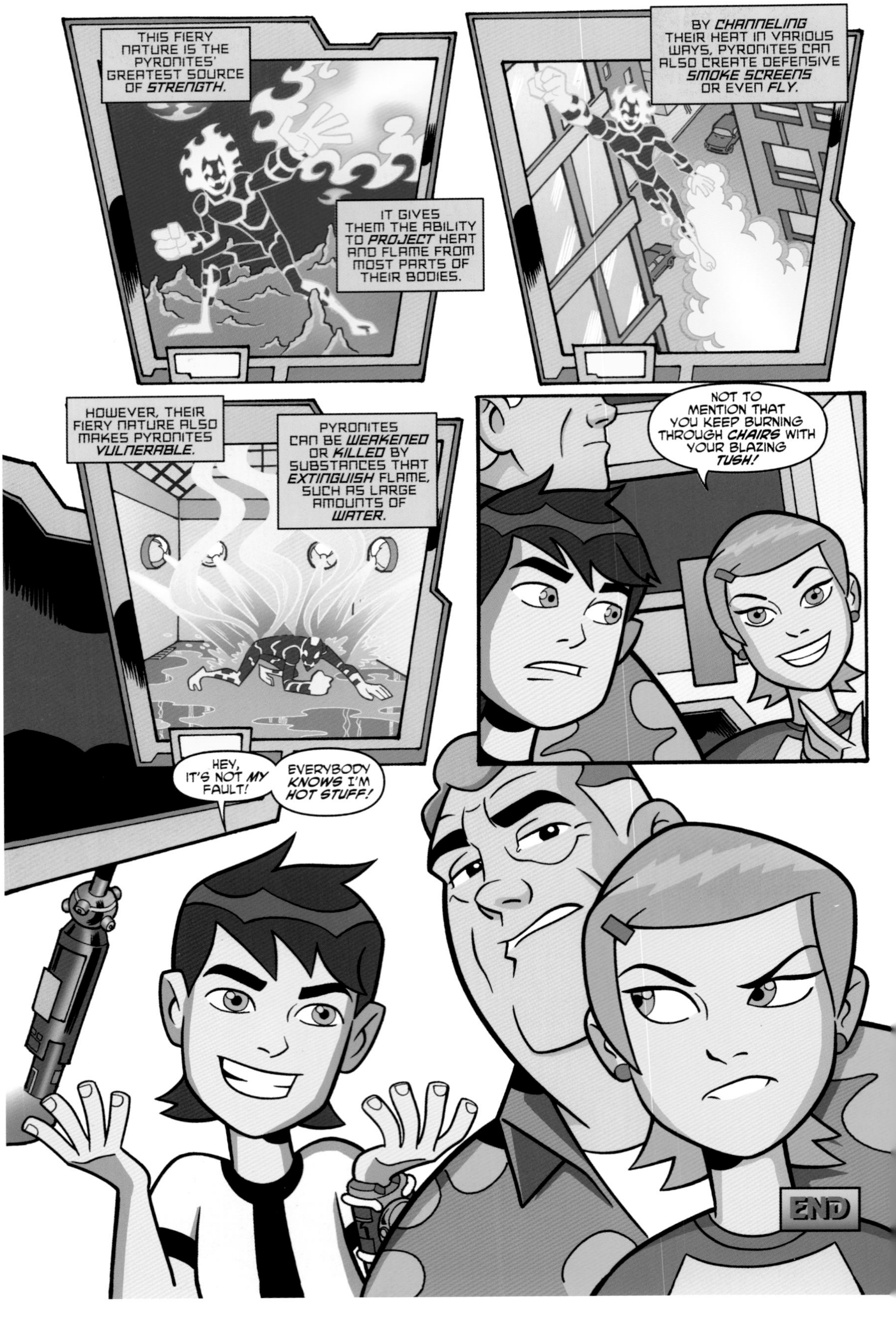
THIS FIERY NATURE IS THE PYRONITES' GREATEST SOURCE OF STRENGTH.
IT GIVES THEM THE ABILITY TO PROJECT HEAT AND FLAME FROM MOST PARTS OF THEIR BODIES.
BY CHANNELING THEIR HEAT IN VARIOUS WAYS, PYRONITES CAN ALSO CREATE DEFENSIVE SMOKE SCREENS OR EVEN FLY.
HOWEVER, THEIR FIERY NATURE ALSO MAKES PYRONITES VULNERABLE.
PYRONITES CAN BE WEAKENED OR KILLED BY SUBSTANCES THAT EXTINGUISH FLAME, SUCH AS LARGE AMOUNTS OF WATER.
NOT TO MENTION THAT YOU KEEP BURNING THROUGH CHAIRS WITH YOUR BLAZING TUSH!
HEY, IT'S NOT MY FAULT!
EVERYBODY KNOWS I'M HOT STUFF!
END

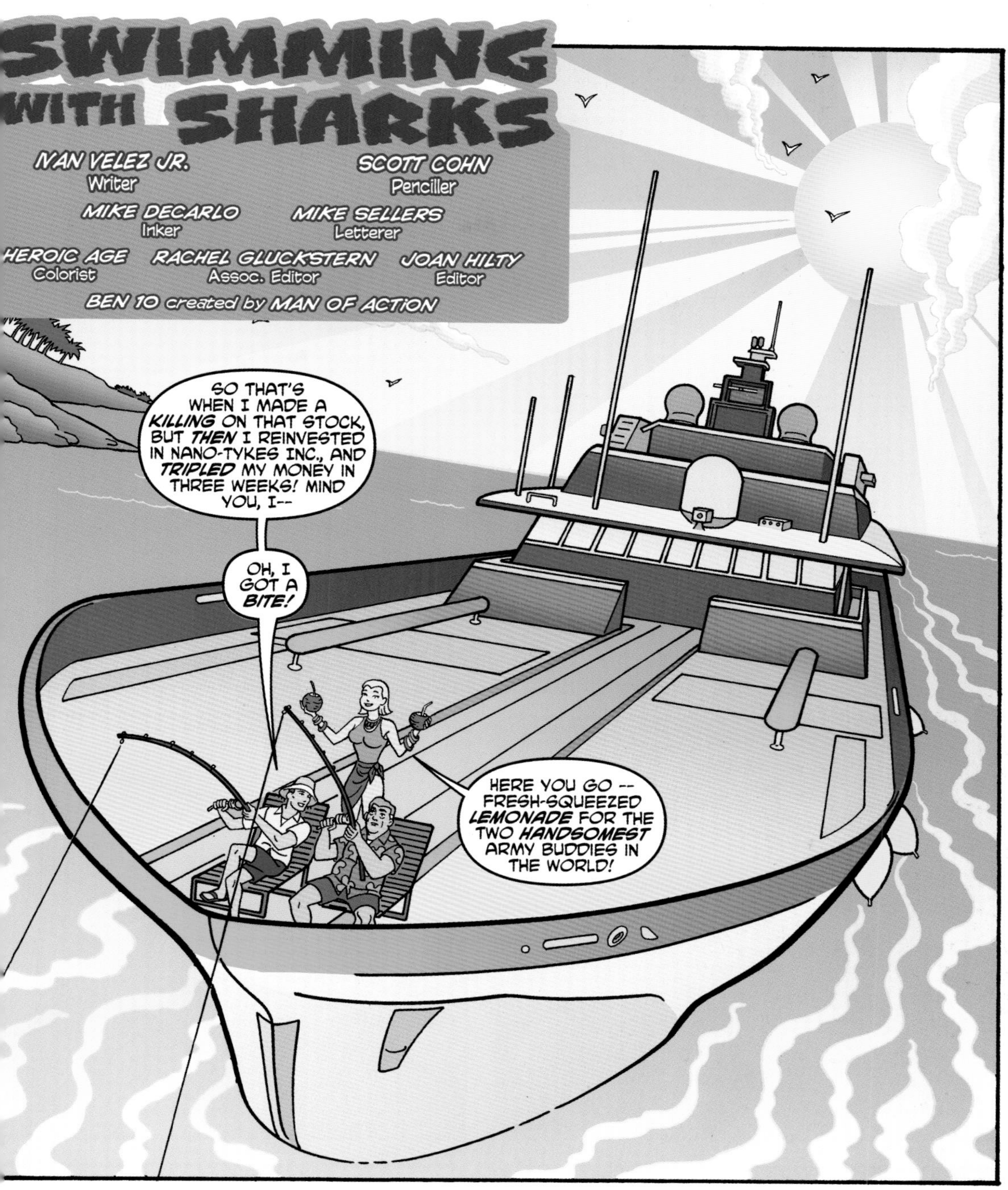
SWIMMING WITH SHARKS
IVAN VELEZ JR. Writer
SCOTT COHN Penciller
MIKE DECARLO Inker
MIKE SELLERS Letterer
HEROIC AGE Colorist
RACHEL GLUCKSTERN Assoc. Editor
JOAN HILTY Editor
BEN 10 created by MAN OF ACTION
SO THAT'S WHEN I MADE A KILLING ON THAT STOCK, BUT THEN I REINVESTED IN NANO-TYKES INC., AND TRIPLED MY MONEY IN THREE WEEKS! MIND YOU, I--
OH, I GOT A BITE!
HERE YOU GO -- FRESH-SQUEEZED LEMONADE FOR THE TWO HANDSOMEST ARMY BUDDIES IN THE WORLD!

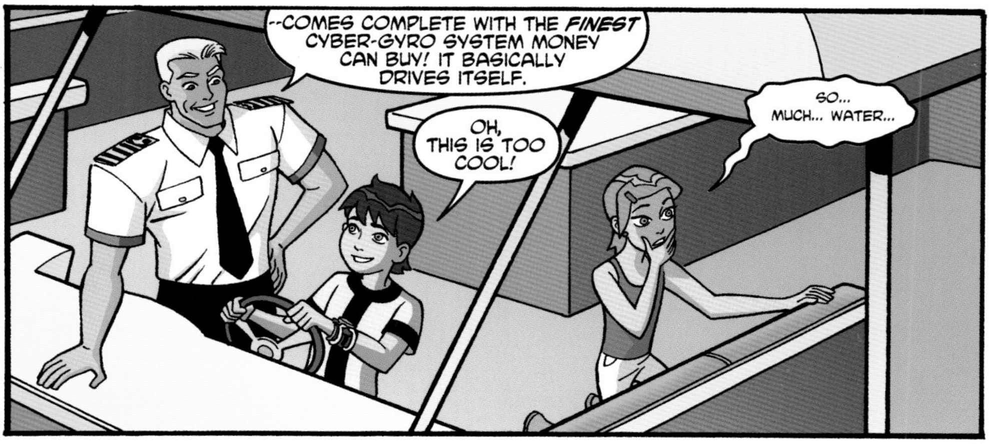
--COMES COMPLETE WITH THE FINEST CYBER-GYRO SYSTEM MONEY CAN BUY! IT BASICALLY DRIVES ITSELF.
OH, THIS IS TOO COOL!
SO... MUCH... WATER...

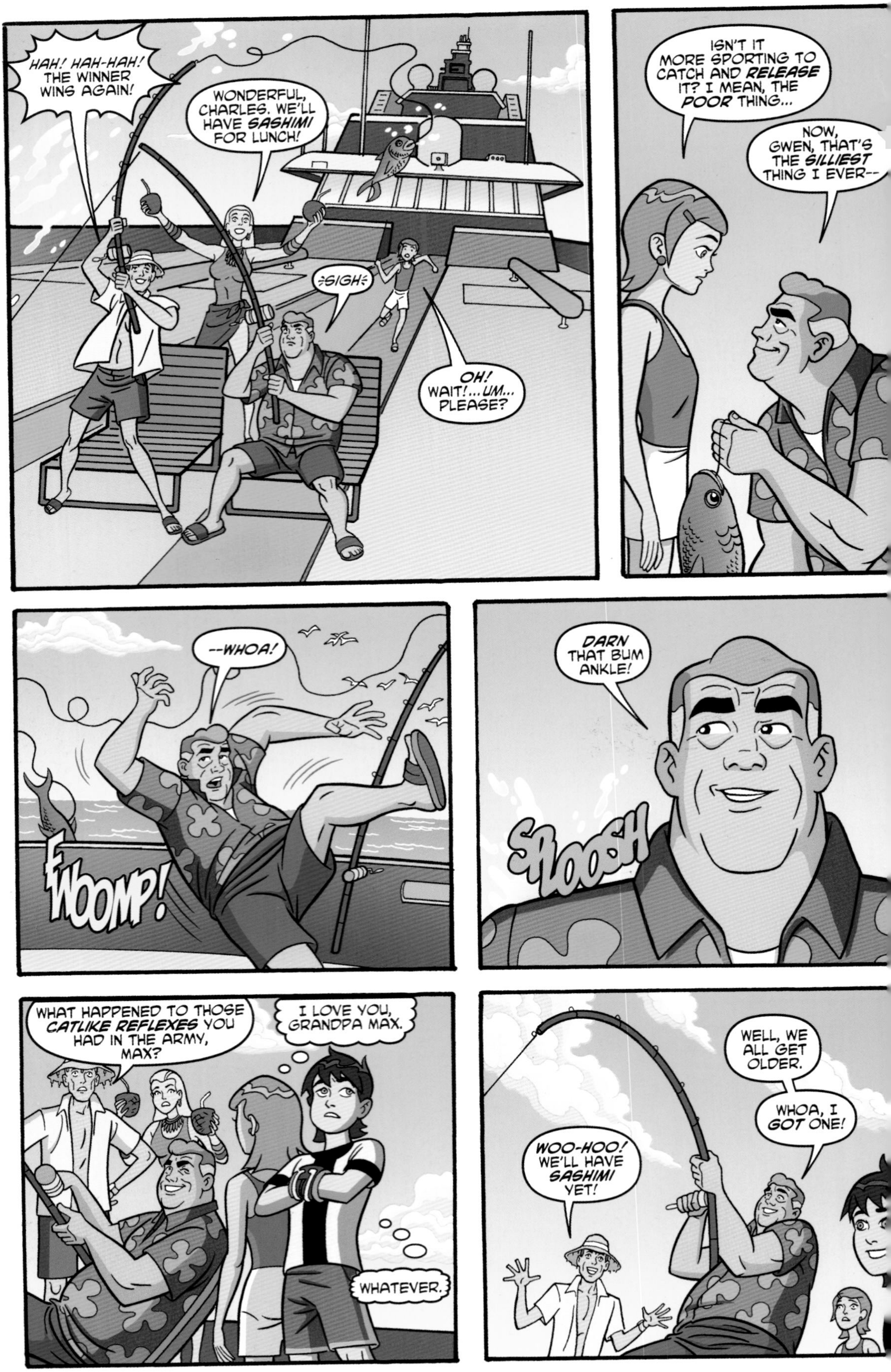
HAH! HAH-HAH! THE WINNER WINS AGAIN!
WONDERFUL, CHARLES. WE'LL HAVE SASHIMI FOR LUNCH!
SIGH
OH! WAIT!...UM... PLEASE?
ISN'T IT MORE SPORTING TO CATCH AND RELEASE IT? I MEAN, THE POOR THING...
NOW, GWEN, THAT'S THE SILLIEST THING I EVER--
--WHOA!
FWOOMP!
DARN THAT BUM ANKLE!
SPLOOSH
WHAT HAPPENED TO THOSE CATLIKE REFLEXES YOU HAD IN THE ARMY, MAX?
I LOVE YOU, GRANDPA MAX.
WHATEVER.
WELL, WE ALL GET OLDER.
WHOA, I GOT ONE!
WOO-HOO! WE'LL HAVE SASHIMI YET!

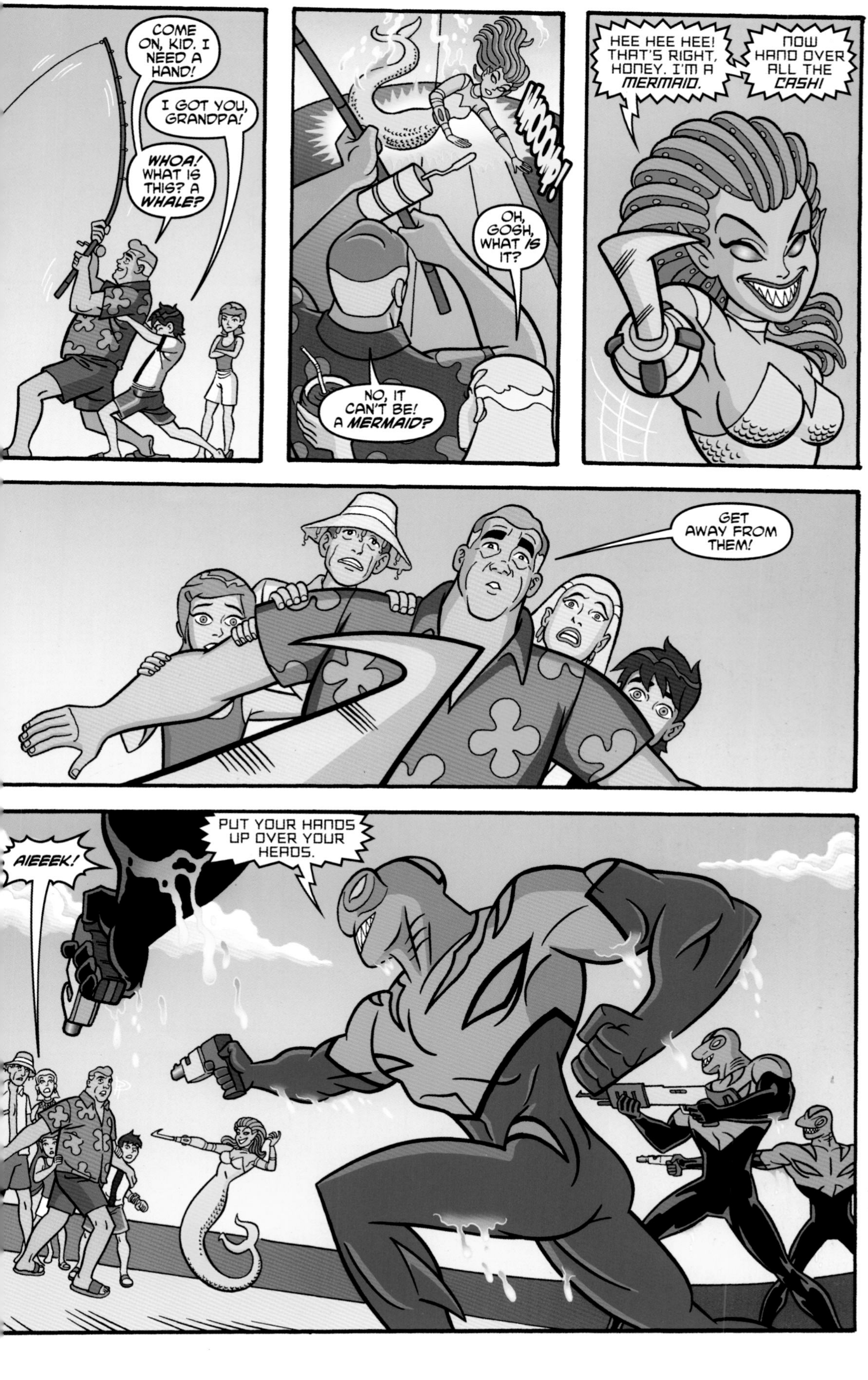
COME ON, KID. I NEED A HAND!
I GOT YOU, GRANDPA!
WHOA! WHAT IS THIS? A WHALE?
WHOOP!
OH, GOSH, WHAT IS IT?
NO, IT CAN'T BE! A MERMAID?
HEE HEE HEE! THAT'S RIGHT, HONEY. I'M A MERMAID.
NOW HAND OVER ALL THE CASH!
GET AWAY FROM THEM!
AIEEEK!
PUT YOUR HANDS UP OVER YOUR HEADS.

DROP ALL YOUR WALLETS AND JEWELRY AND PUT IT INTO THE BAG.

BUT THIS WAS MY BIRTHDAY GIFT.

WELL, HAPPY B-DAY TO ME!

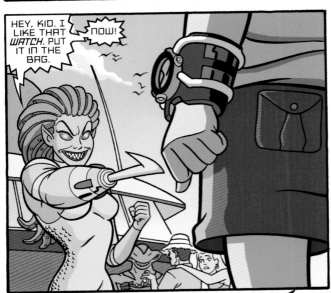

HEY, KID. I LIKE THAT *WATCH*. PUT IT IN THE BAG.

NOW!

OKAY. OKAY. LET ME JUST SET IT RIGHT FOR YOU.

YEAH. IT'S ON, UH, TOKYO TIME.

RIPJAW!

RAWR!

THWAK!

HUH!

AHH!

GWEN! GET THE OTHERS TO THE BACK OF THE BOAT!

WHAT THE—UNGH!

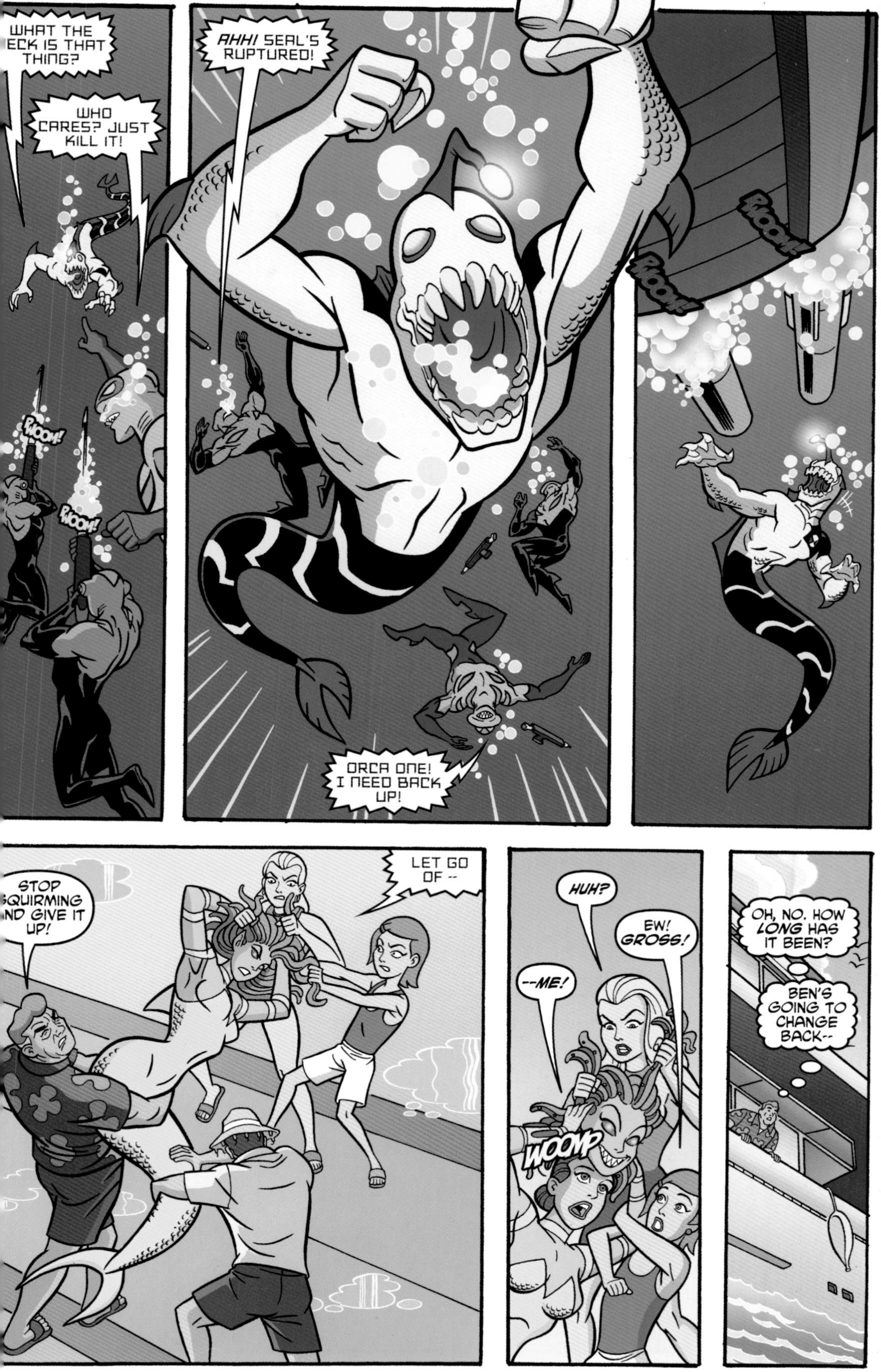
WHAT THE ECK IS THAT THING?
WHO CARES? JUST KILL IT!
PWOOM!
PWOOM!
AHH! SEAL'S RUPTURED!
ORCA ONE! I NEED BACK UP!
PWOOM!
PWOOM!
STOP SQUIRMING ND GIVE IT UP!
LET GO OF --
HUH?
EW! GROSS!
--ME!
WOOMP
OH, NO. HOW LONG HAS IT BEEN?
BEN'S GOING TO CHANGE BACK--

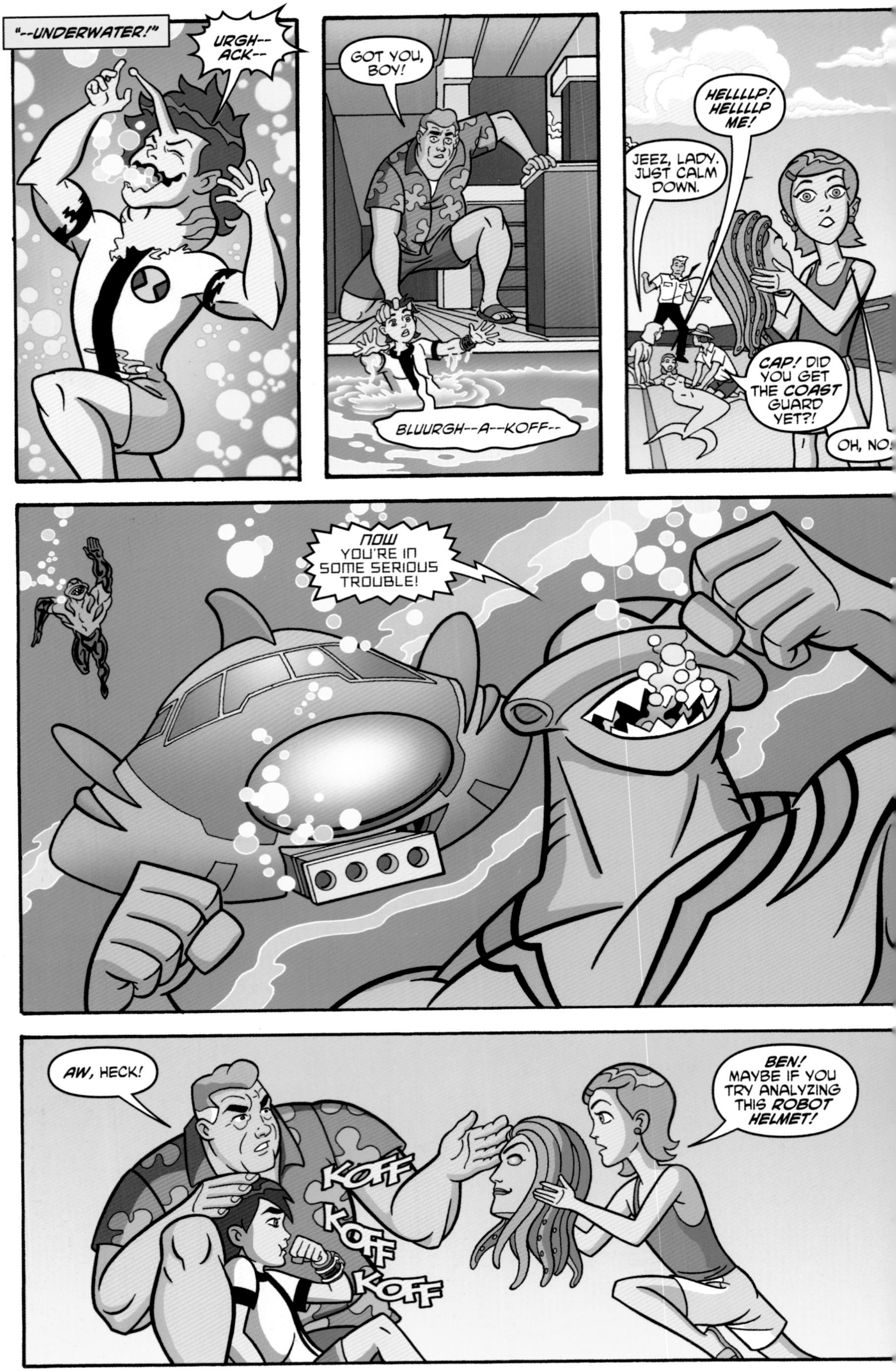
"--UNDERWATER!"
URGH--ACK--
GOT YOU, BOY!
BLUURGH--A--KOFF--
HELLLLP! HELLLLP ME!
JEEZ, LADY. JUST CALM DOWN.
CAP! DID YOU GET THE COAST GUARD YET?!
OH, NO!
NOW YOU'RE IN SOME SERIOUS TROUBLE!
AW, HECK!
KOFF
KOFF
KOFF
BEN! MAYBE IF YOU TRY ANALYZING THIS ROBOT HELMET!

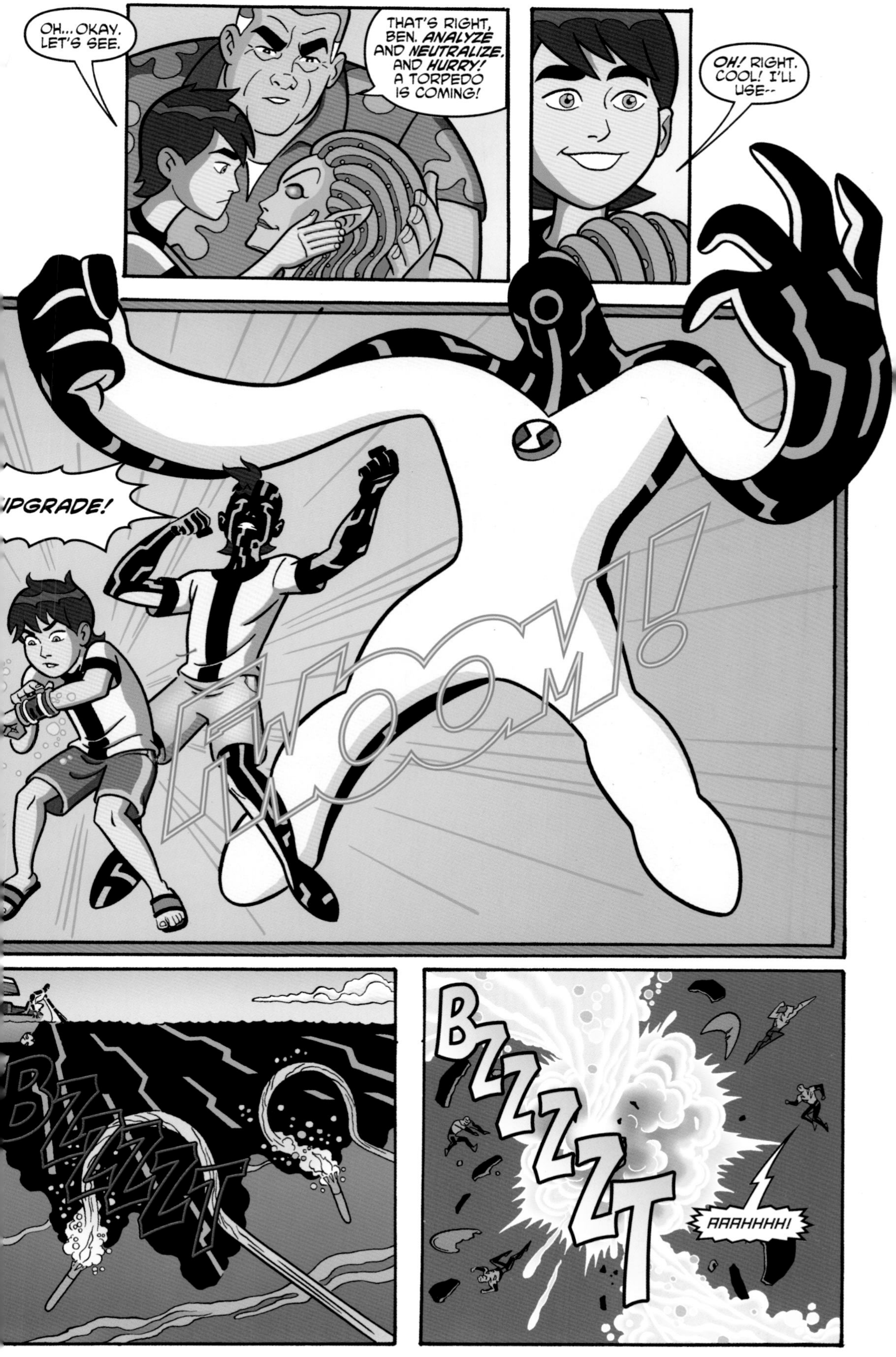
OH... OKAY. LET'S SEE.
THAT'S RIGHT, BEN. ***ANALYZE*** AND ***NEUTRALIZE.*** AND ***HURRY!*** A TORPEDO IS COMING!
OH! RIGHT. COOL! I'LL USE--
UPGRADE!
FWOOOM!
BZZZZZT
BZZZZZT
AAAHHHHH!

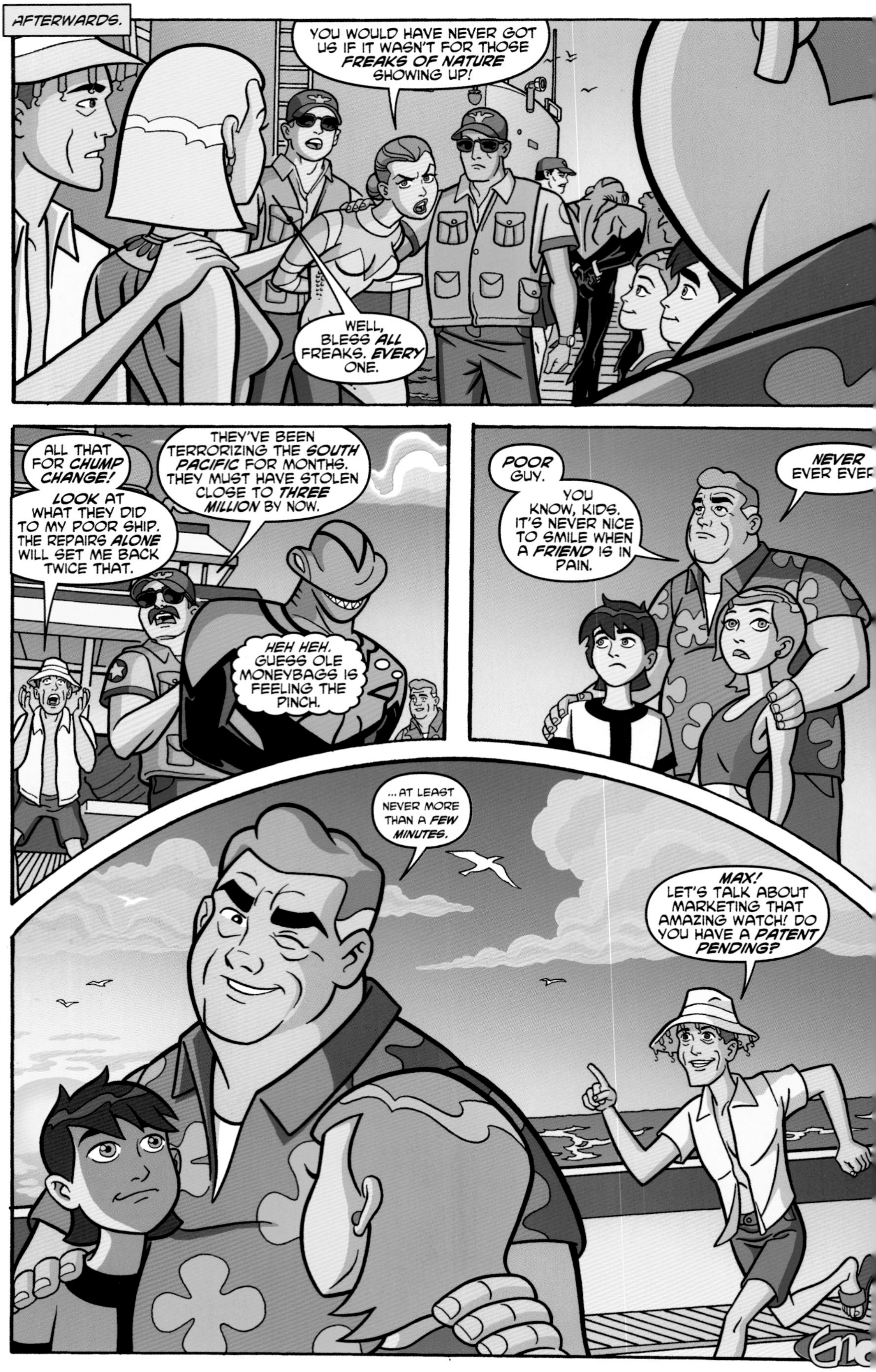
AFTERWARDS.
YOU WOULD HAVE NEVER GOT US IF IT WASN'T FOR THOSE FREAKS OF NATURE SHOWING UP!
WELL, BLESS ALL FREAKS. EVERY ONE.
ALL THAT FOR CHUMP CHANGE!
LOOK AT WHAT THEY DID TO MY POOR SHIP. THE REPAIRS ALONE WILL SET ME BACK TWICE THAT.
THEY'VE BEEN TERRORIZING THE SOUTH PACIFIC FOR MONTHS. THEY MUST HAVE STOLEN CLOSE TO THREE MILLION BY NOW.
HEH HEH. GUESS OLE MONEYBAGS IS FEELING THE PINCH.
POOR GUY.
YOU KNOW, KIDS. IT'S NEVER NICE TO SMILE WHEN A FRIEND IS IN PAIN.
NEVER EVER EVER
...AT LEAST NEVER MORE THAN A FEW MINUTES.
MAX! LET'S TALK ABOUT MARKETING THAT AMAZING WATCH! DO YOU HAVE A PATENT PENDING?

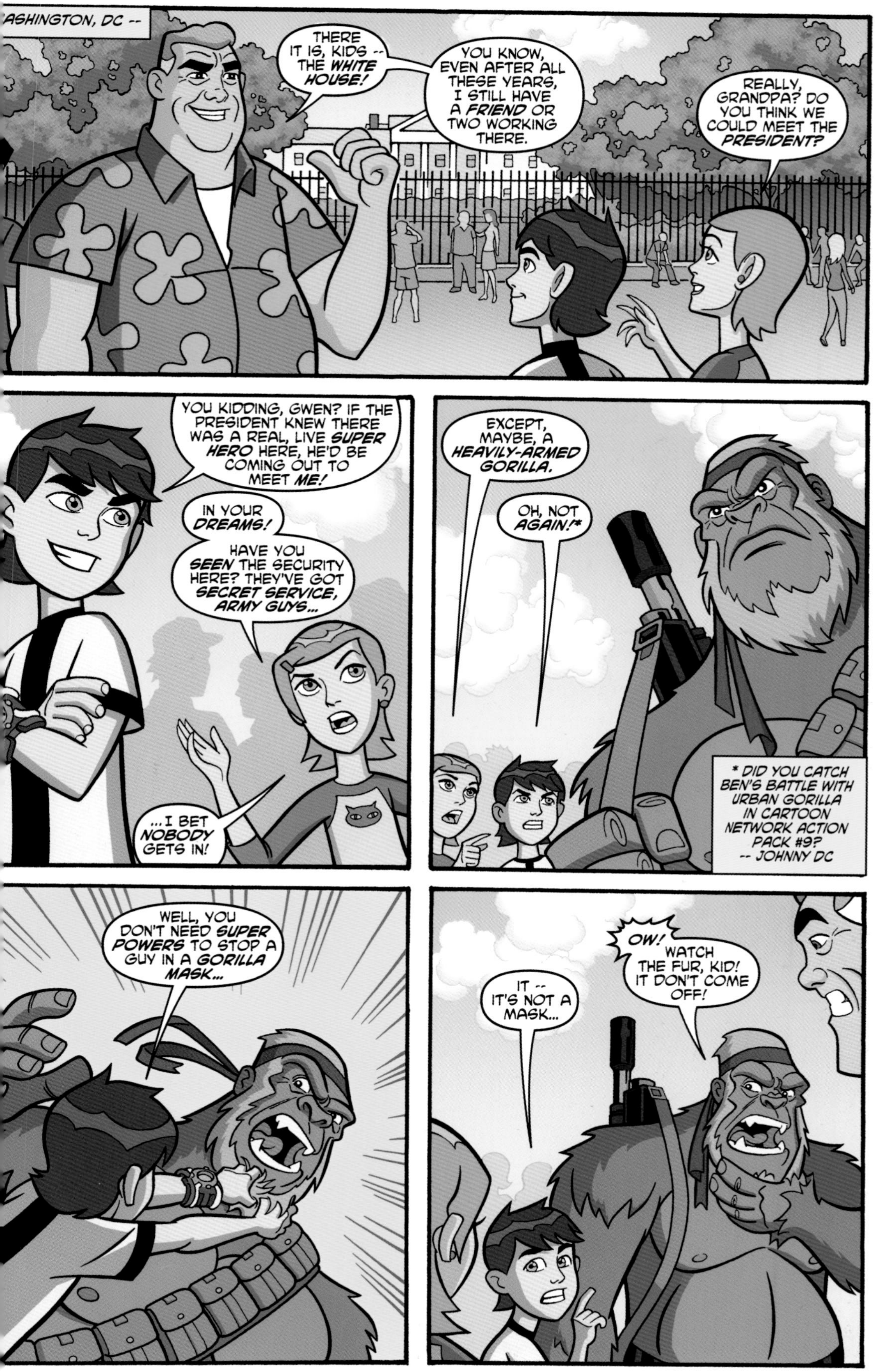
WASHINGTON, DC --
THERE IT IS, KIDS -- THE WHITE HOUSE!
YOU KNOW, EVEN AFTER ALL THESE YEARS, I STILL HAVE A FRIEND OR TWO WORKING THERE.
REALLY, GRANDPA? DO YOU THINK WE COULD MEET THE PRESIDENT?
YOU KIDDING, GWEN? IF THE PRESIDENT KNEW THERE WAS A REAL, LIVE SUPER HERO HERE, HE'D BE COMING OUT TO MEET ME!
IN YOUR DREAMS!
HAVE YOU SEEN THE SECURITY HERE? THEY'VE GOT SECRET SERVICE, ARMY GUYS...
...I BET NOBODY GETS IN!
EXCEPT, MAYBE, A HEAVILY-ARMED GORILLA.
OH, NOT AGAIN!*
* DID YOU CATCH BEN'S BATTLE WITH URBAN GORILLA IN CARTOON NETWORK ACTION PACK #9? -- JOHNNY DC
WELL, YOU DON'T NEED SUPER POWERS TO STOP A GUY IN A GORILLA MASK...
IT -- IT'S NOT A MASK...
OW! WATCH THE FUR, KID! IT DON'T COME OFF!

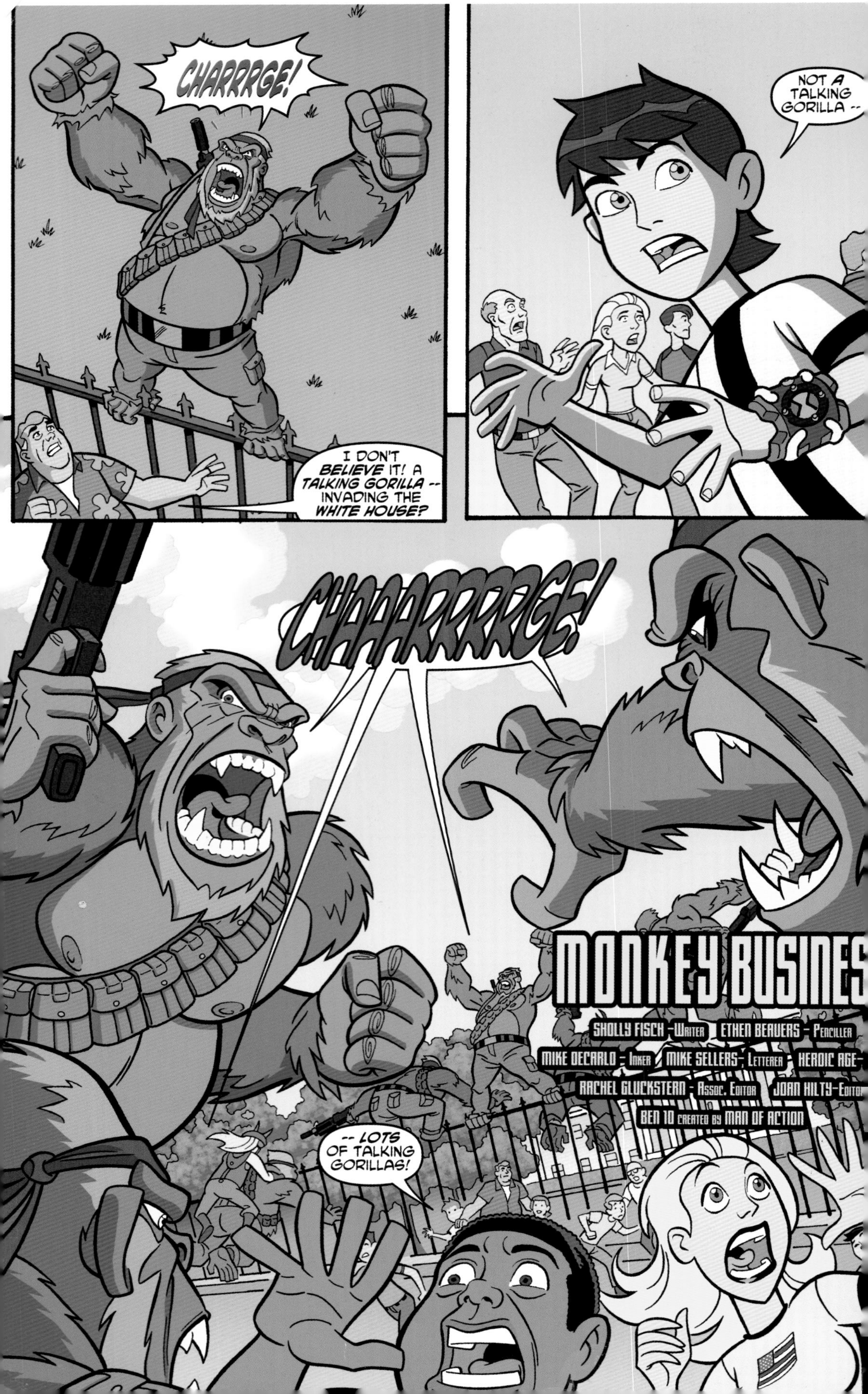
CHARRRGE!
I DON'T BELIEVE IT! A TALKING GORILLA -- INVADING THE WHITE HOUSE?
NOT A TALKING GORILLA --
CHAAARRRRRGE!
-- LOTS OF TALKING GORILLAS!
MONKEY BUSINES
SHOLLY FISCH - WRITER
ETHEN BEAVERS - PENCILLER
MIKE DECARLO - INKER
MIKE SELLERS - LETTERER
HEROIC AGE -
RACHEL GLUCKSTERN - ASSOC. EDITOR
JOAN HILTY - EDITOR
BEN 10 CREATED BY MAN OF ACTION

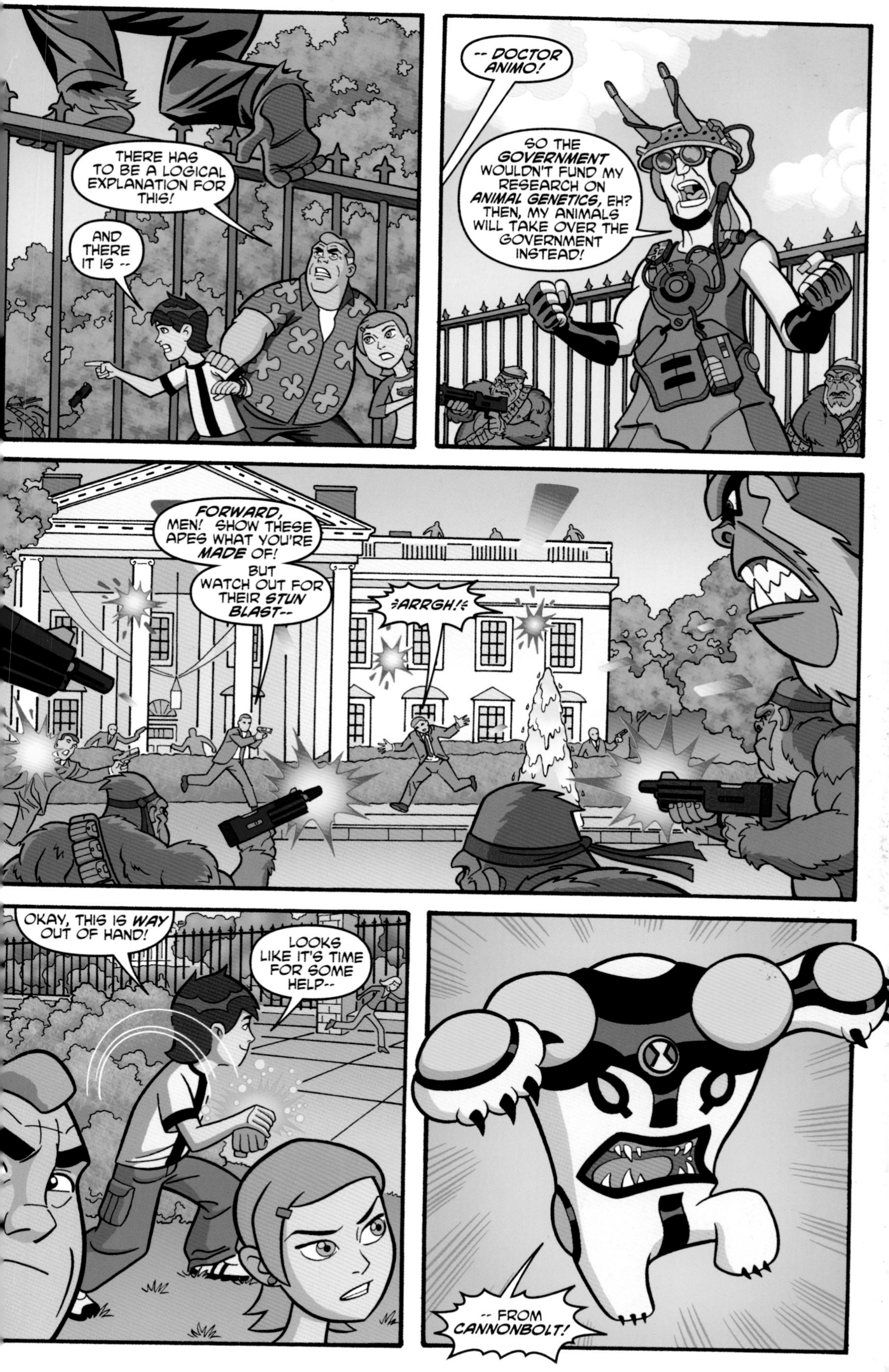
THERE HAS TO BE A LOGICAL EXPLANATION FOR THIS!
AND THERE IT IS --
-- DOCTOR ANIMO!
SO THE GOVERNMENT WOULDN'T FUND MY RESEARCH ON ANIMAL GENETICS, EH? THEN, MY ANIMALS WILL TAKE OVER THE GOVERNMENT INSTEAD!
FORWARD, MEN! SHOW THESE APES WHAT YOU'RE MADE OF!
BUT WATCH OUT FOR THEIR STUN BLAST--
ARRGH!
OKAY, THIS IS WAY OUT OF HAND!
LOOKS LIKE IT'S TIME FOR SOME HELP--
-- FROM CANNONBOLT!

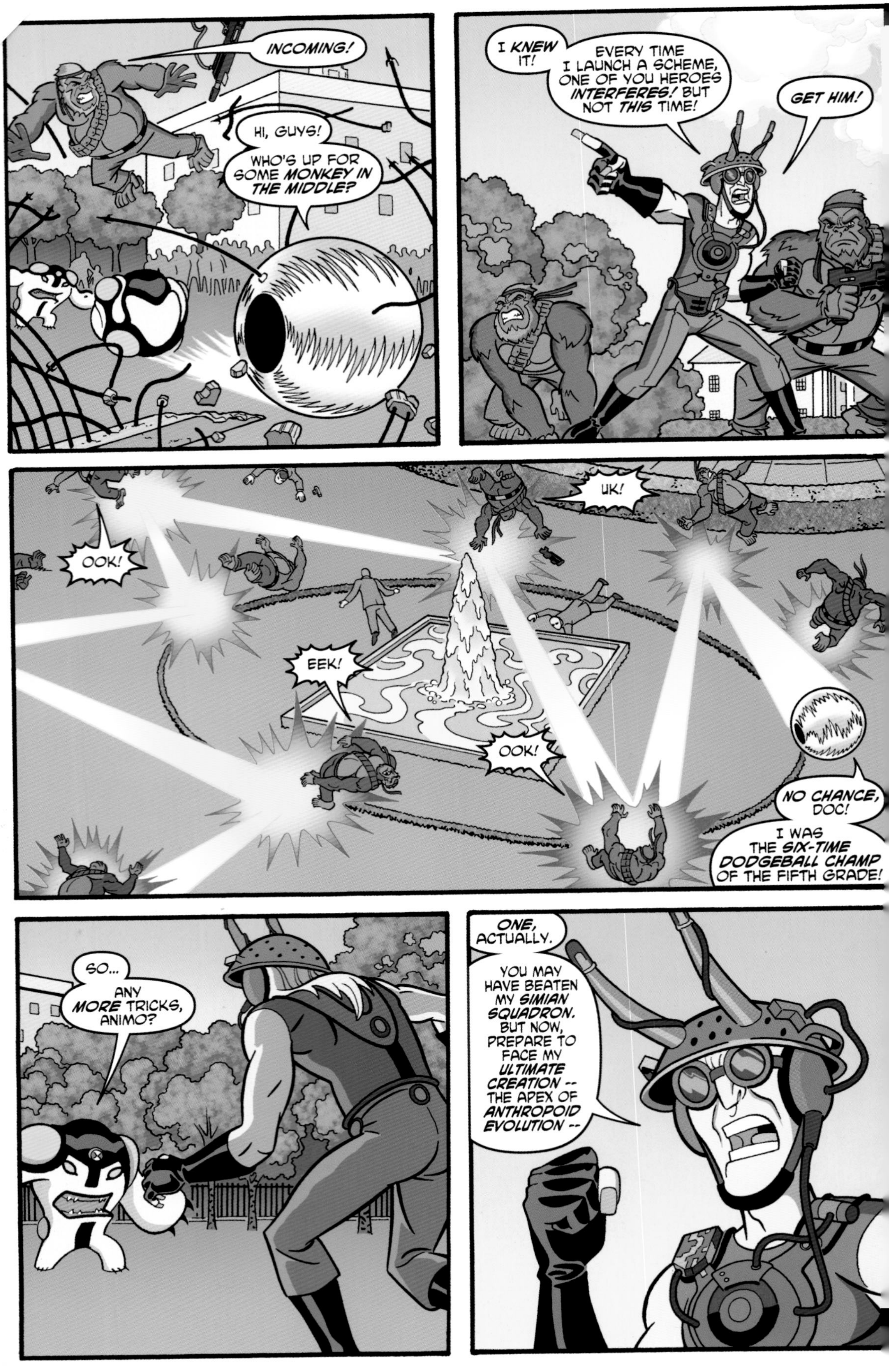
INCOMING!
HI, GUYS!
WHO'S UP FOR SOME MONKEY IN THE MIDDLE?
I KNEW IT!
EVERY TIME I LAUNCH A SCHEME, ONE OF YOU HEROES INTERFERES! BUT NOT THIS TIME!
GET HIM!
OOK!
UK!
EEK!
OOK!
NO CHANCE, DOC!
I WAS THE SIX-TIME DODGEBALL CHAMP OF THE FIFTH GRADE!
SO... ANY MORE TRICKS, ANIMO?
ONE, ACTUALLY.
YOU MAY HAVE BEATEN MY SIMIAN SQUADRON. BUT NOW, PREPARE TO FACE MY ULTIMATE CREATION -- THE APEX OF ANTHROPOID EVOLUTION --

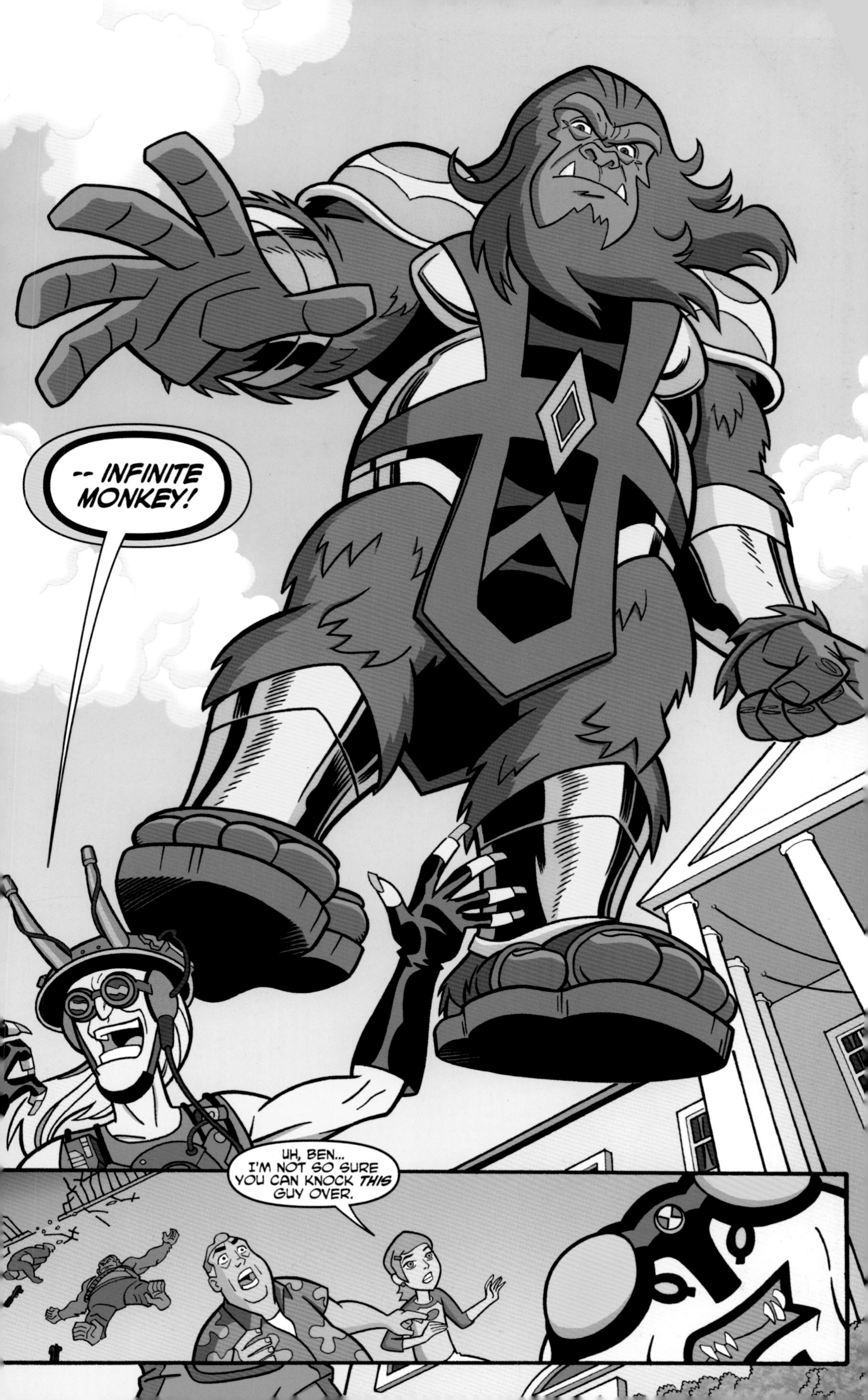
-- INFINITE MONKEY!
UH, BEN... I'M NOT SO SURE YOU CAN KNOCK *THIS* GUY OVER.

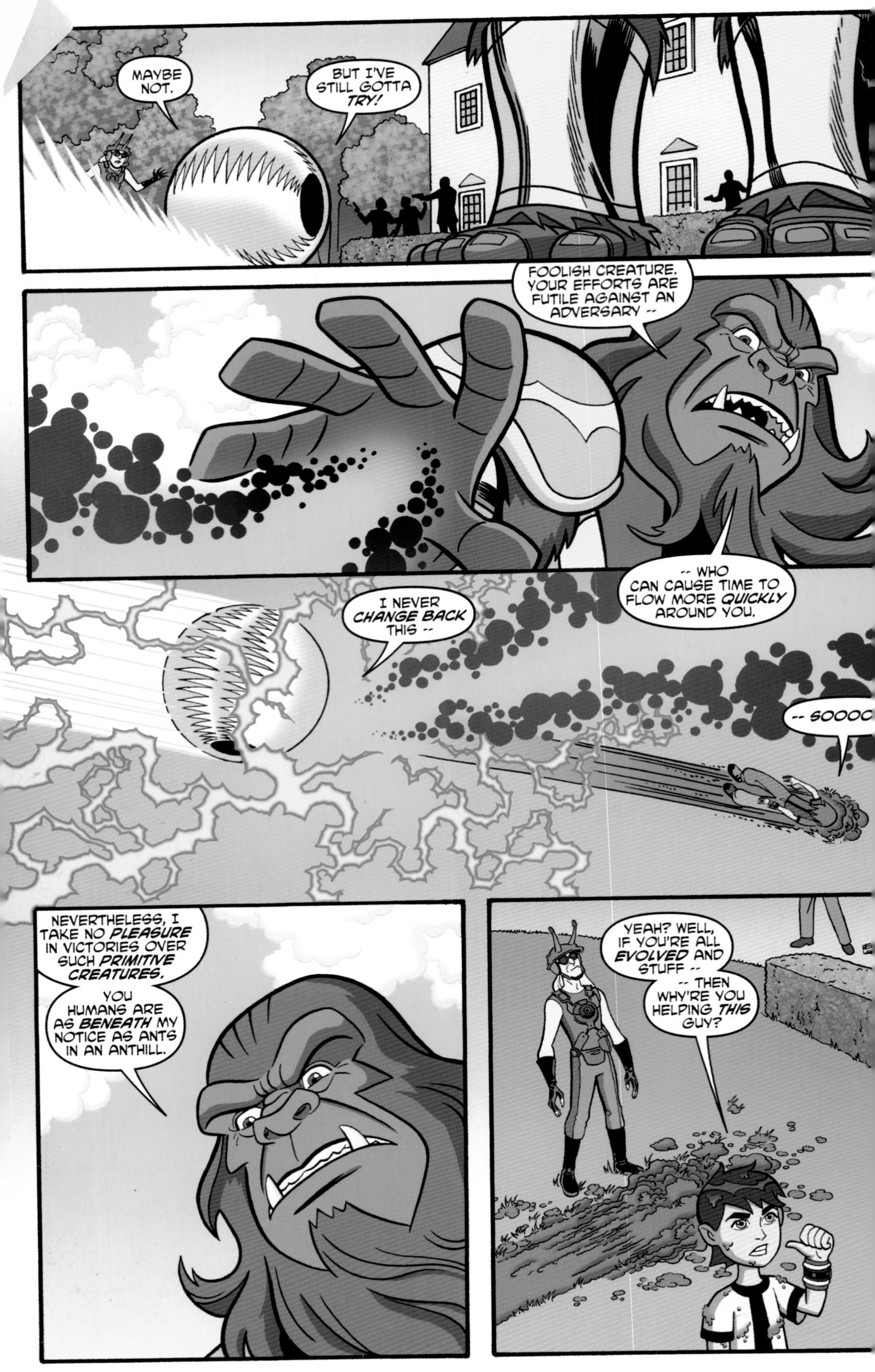
MAYBE NOT.
BUT I'VE STILL GOTTA TRY!
FOOLISH CREATURE. YOUR EFFORTS ARE FUTILE AGAINST AN ADVERSARY --
-- WHO CAN CAUSE TIME TO FLOW MORE QUICKLY AROUND YOU.
I NEVER CHANGE BACK THIS --
-- SOOOO
NEVERTHELESS, I TAKE NO PLEASURE IN VICTORIES OVER SUCH PRIMITIVE CREATURES.
YOU HUMANS ARE AS BENEATH MY NOTICE AS ANTS IN AN ANTHILL.
YEAH? WELL, IF YOU'RE ALL EVOLVED AND STUFF --
-- THEN WHY'RE YOU HELPING THIS GUY?

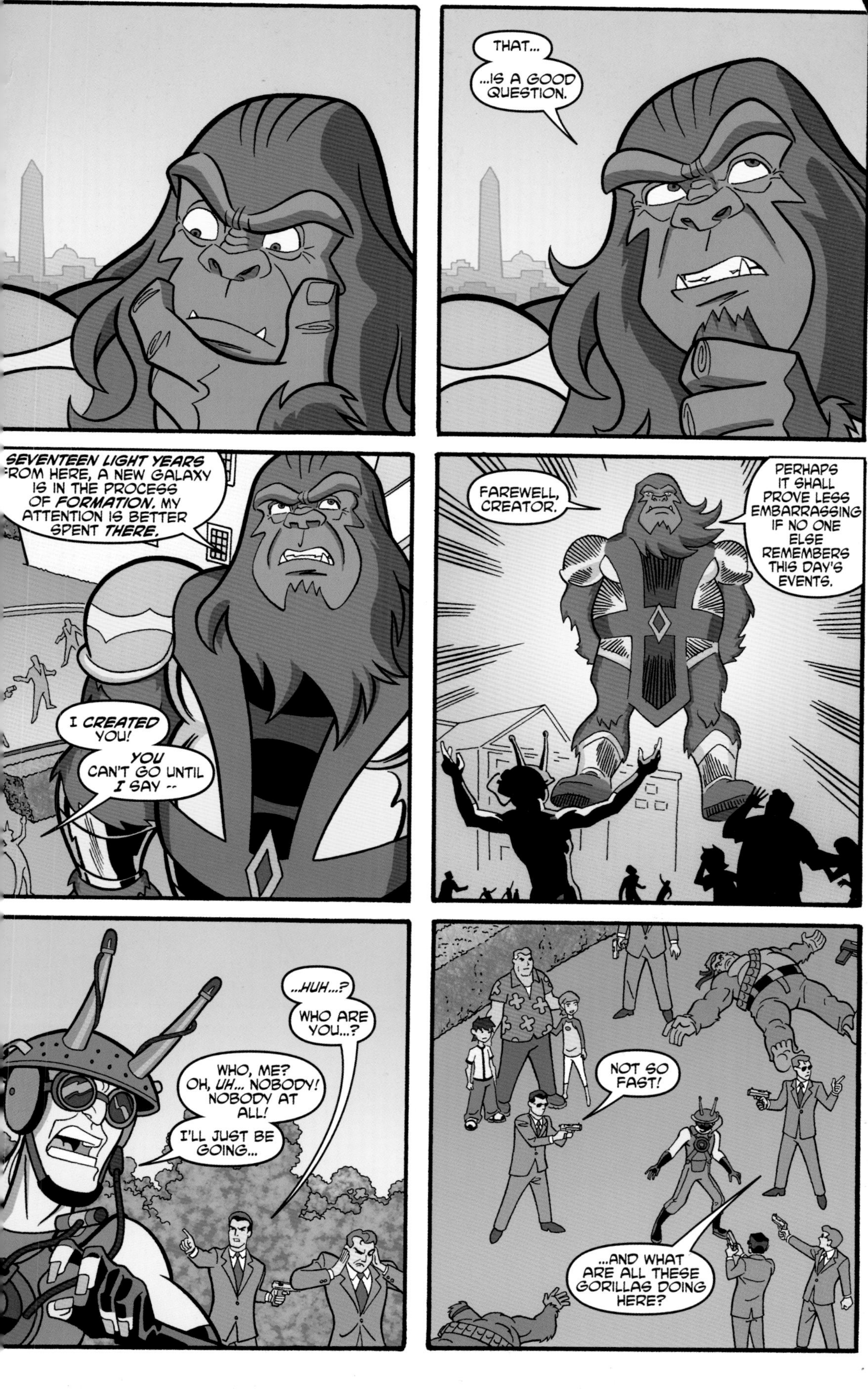
THAT...
...IS A GOOD QUESTION.
SEVENTEEN LIGHT YEARS FROM HERE, A NEW GALAXY IS IN THE PROCESS OF FORMATION. MY ATTENTION IS BETTER SPENT THERE.
I CREATED YOU!
YOU CAN'T GO UNTIL I SAY --
FAREWELL, CREATOR.
PERHAPS IT SHALL PROVE LESS EMBARRASSING IF NO ONE ELSE REMEMBERS THIS DAY'S EVENTS.
...HUH...?
WHO ARE YOU...?
WHO, ME? OH, UH... NOBODY! NOBODY AT ALL!
I'LL JUST BE GOING...
NOT SO FAST!
...AND WHAT ARE ALL THESE GORILLAS DOING HERE?

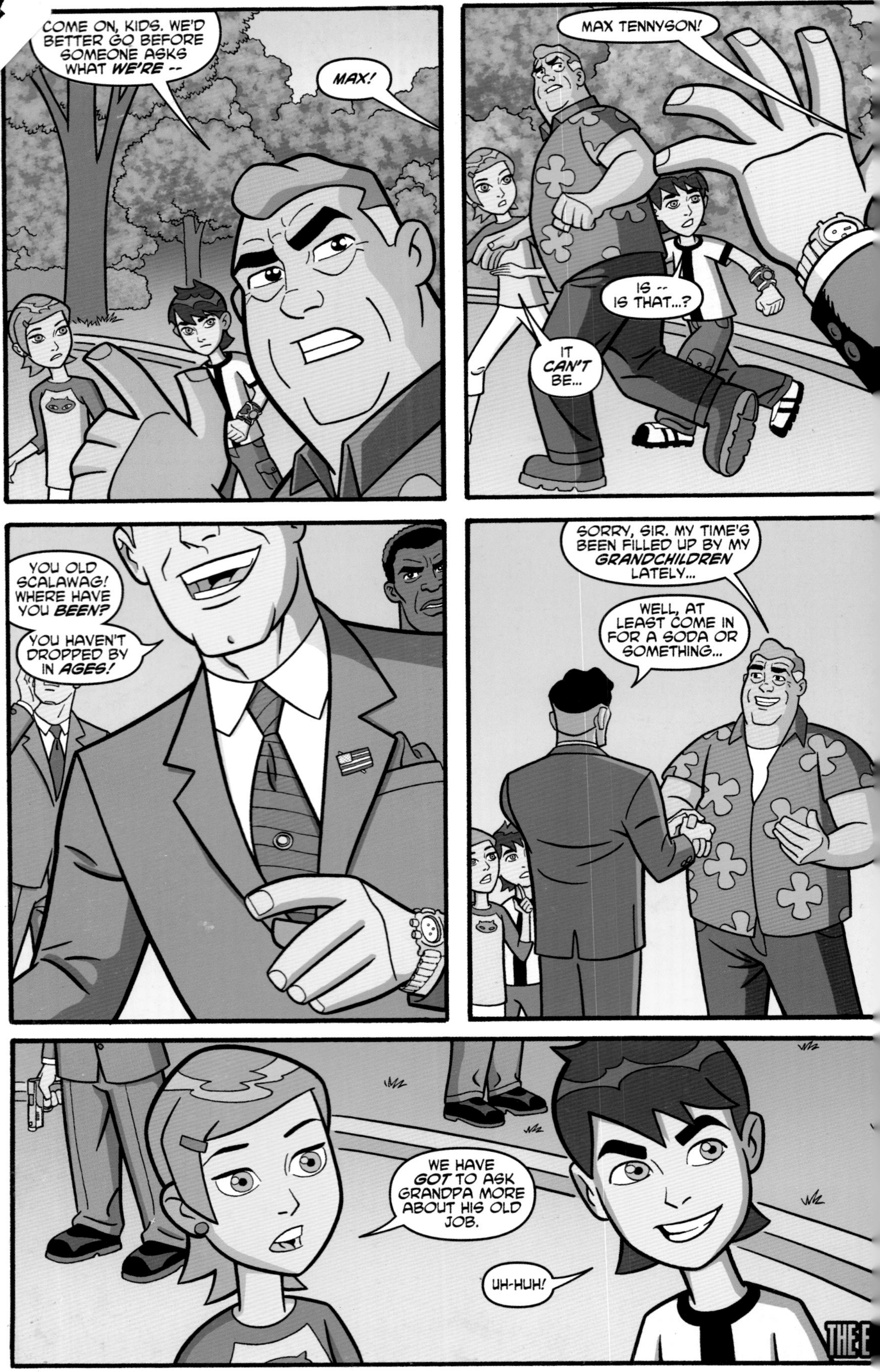
COME ON, KIDS. WE'D BETTER GO BEFORE SOMEONE ASKS WHAT WE'RE --
MAX!
MAX TENNYSON!
IS -- IS THAT...?
IT CAN'T BE...
YOU OLD SCALAWAG! WHERE HAVE YOU BEEN?
YOU HAVEN'T DROPPED BY IN AGES!
SORRY, SIR. MY TIME'S BEEN FILLED UP BY MY GRANDCHILDREN LATELY...
WELL, AT LEAST COME IN FOR A SODA OR SOMETHING...
WE HAVE GOT TO ASK GRANDPA MORE ABOUT HIS OLD JOB.
UH-HUH!